Deciding factors in British politics

Deciding Factors in British Politics looks at questions of how decisions are made in British government and which explanations best fit the decision-making process.

The book provides students with a wide variety of case-studies from the mid-1950s to the present illustrating different facets of political life. Among them are the nuclear power programme, the handling of the Falklands crisis, Trident missiles and government AIDS policy. This detailed material on the practical results of institutional behaviour is combined with a comprehensive and approachable review of the key theoretical perspectives on decision-making, encouraging readers to think analytically about the processes of policy-making and to test their analyses against the known details of actual decisions. In the final chapter the theoretical and practical elements of the book are synthesized to provide a deep and multi-faceted understanding of how politics works.

Deciding factors in British politics

A case-studies approach

John Greenaway
Steve Smith
John Street

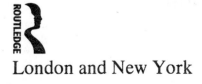

London and New York

First published 1992
by Routledge
11 New Fetter Lane, London EC4P 4EE

Simultaneously published in the USA and Canada
by Routledge
a division of Routledge, Chapman and Hall, Inc.
29 West 35th Street, New York, NY 10001

Typeset in Times by
Selectmove Ltd, London
Printed in Great Britain by
Biddles Ltd, Guildford and King's Lynn

British Library Cataloguing in Publication Data
Greenaway, John *1947–*
    Deciding factors in British politics: a case-studies approach.
    1. Great Britain. Politics
    I. Title II. Smith, Steve *1952–* III. Street, John *1952–* 320.941
    ISBN 0–415–02015–8
    ISBN 0–415–03728–X pbk

Library of Congress Cataloging in Publication Data
Greenaway, J.R.
    Deciding factors in British politics : a case-studies approach /
John Greenaway, Steve Smith, and John Street.
        p.   cm.
    Includes bibliographical references and index.
    ISBN 0–415–02015–8 (hard). – ISBN 0–415–03728–X (pbk.)
    1. Great Britain – Politics and government – 1945- – Decision
making – Case-studies. I. Smith, Steve, 1952–   . II. Street,
John, 1952–   . III. Title.
JN231.G74   1992
354.417'25--dc20
                                                        91–13718R
                                                        CIP

941080

To: Denise Carlo
Marysia Zalewski
Marian Brandon

Contents

Preface   ix

1   **Introduction**   1
2   **Theories of decision-making**   15
3   **Models of British politics**   47
4   **The response to AIDS**   69
5   **The Falklands War**   92
6   **Nuclear power decisions**   116
7   **The rise and fall of the Civil Service Department**   139
8   **Legislating for trade unions**   164
9   **Trident**   183
10 **Conclusion**   211

Notes   241
Index   256

Preface

Like many books, this one has its origins in a course. Throughout the last decade the three of us have taught on the course, 'Theory and Practice of British Politics', at the University of East Anglia. Although we have used a variety of textbooks for this course, we have always felt that there was a gap in the literature. There has been no lack of general textbooks on British politics, nor of books on the theories of how British politics works. Moreover, there has certainly been no shortage of anecdotal evidence to support these general surveys and these theories, but there has been a real absence of detailed examples of decision-making in British politics. Not surprisingly, this book is an attempt to fill that gap. We hope that, with this book, teachers will no longer have to struggle to find detailed examples to illustrate the main themes and theories of British politics. As will become clear, our focus is on decision-making in British politics, and our primary concern is to study how decisions get made in Britain. We feel that there is no book comparable to this one, and therefore we hope that the book will be of use to students of British politics who need some case-studies to illuminate both how decisions get made in British politics and how the British political system operates.

We will discuss the rationale for the book in the next chapter, but at this stage we would like to point out that we have written it for first- and second-year undergraduates taking British politics courses. Critically, we hope that the book will stimulate readers to pursue the case-study approach as a way of analysing British politics. There are many other case-studies that have been and could be written, and we hope that our book will act as a catalyst for readers to undertake their own case-studies. Note, though, that we advocate structured comparisons, within a theoretical framework; we need to stress at the outset that in our view theory and empirical material are inexorably interlinked, and so we are very concerned to deal with theoretical questions explicitly. Indeed this concern has been the most distinctive feature of the British politics course from which this book emerged.

Although we have incurred many debts in writing this book, we would especially like to thank the 750 or so students who have taken the course over the last decade. It is their questioning and interest which has led us to write about British politics in this way. We would also like to thank Francine Hunt and especially Anne Martin for typing the manuscript; even in the age of wordprocessors, someone has to pick up the pieces and make a coherent final copy. We would also like to thank the School of Economic and Social Studies at the University of East Anglia for providing financial assistance to help us produce the typescript.

Finally, we should point out that this is very much a cowritten book. Naturally, each of us wrote the case-studies that fitted into our own areas of expertise, but in every instance the other two revised the manuscript. In particular, the first three chapters and the conclusion have gone through several drafts. This may have the result that none of us can disclaim responsibility for any chapter of the book, but hopefully this also has the result that this is a coherent and genuinely integrated book. We still have our disagreements about some of the issues raised by the case-studies and the theories, but we all agree that the case-study method has much to offer the study of British politics.

1 Introduction

This book is concerned with the question of how decisions get made in British politics. We are not as much interested in contemporary developments in British politics as in trying to use a specific approach to answer this question. Our approach is the case-study method, and our main aim is to try and locate the six case-studies chosen within a theoretical framework. This framework comprises the main theories of decision-making, and the main accounts of how the British political system operates. A second aim is to see what the case-studies tell us about the theories that comprise our framework. That is to say, we want not only to use the theories of decision-making and British politics to illuminate our case-studies, but also to use the findings from our case-studies to say something about the relative utility of the theories.

Accordingly, the book proceeds in the following way: in the next chapter we outline the main theories of political decision-making. In chapter three we summarise the main accounts of how the British political system operates. These two chapters provide a framework for the book, giving us both an overview of the theoretical literature on decision-making, which is general in nature and therefore applicable to any political system, and a summary of theoretical approaches to the British political system. The next six chapters consist of our case-studies. We conclude by summarising our findings both in terms of the theories of decision-making dealt with in chapter two and the accounts of the British political system dealt with in chapter three. We hope that our case-studies demonstrate the relative usefulness of the various decision-making theories and the explanatory power of the accounts of British politics.

Before we turn to the theories of decision-making and the accounts of British politics, we will in this introduction say something about other approaches to British politics. We will then briefly examine the main political developments of the period covered by our case-studies in order to place our detailed and necessarily fragmented examples in their correct context. Finally, we will say why we have chosen the case-studies we have, as well as saying something about the strengths and weaknesses of our approach.

Because Britain claims to be a democracy, it is often assumed that decisions are made by 'the Government' which is, or at any rate should be, responsive to the wishes and aspirations of the citizens. However, in Britain very few of those governed have any idea of what is being done in their name. Most citizens are content with the notion that Parliament governs and confine their political participation to the act of voting. But neither Parliament nor the distribution of votes determines how government behaves. One reason for this is that government is not monolithic. Government is made up of a network of overlapping and sometimes jealously competing authorities including the houses of the legislature, different Whitehall departments, the judiciary, local government bodies, the police, and a host of quasi-independent appointed boards, authorities and advisory bodies. The rudimentary language and practice of democracy is inadequate to understanding the way in which decisions get taken in British government.

If the concept of democracy is not a sufficient guide to how decision-making proceeds, then the formal organisation of the state may provide a more useful starting point. Here the metaphor often used is that of a constitutional structure. Institutions of the state are seen as parts of an interlocking edifice, with some subordinate to others and those at the summit resting upon basic foundations. The constitution provides the institutional framework within which the battles for power and the allocation of resources are carried out. Studying decision-making from within this perspective will mean concentrating on, among other things, the relationship of constitutional provisions to changing political reality. To change the analogy, knowledge of a country's constitutional arrangements provides some kind of a basic map by whose aid travellers may hope to find their way around the labyrinth of confusing and proliferating institutions.

However important it is to know about the formal institutions of the state, this approach has some obvious limitations. A glance around the world scene is sufficient to show how often constitutions are circumvented or ignored. Moreover, formal procedures very often mask the importance of informal arrangements or conventions. Walter Bagehot, who wrote the classic study *The English Constitution* in 1867, recognised this when he made the distinction between the 'dignified' elements of the state and the 'efficient secrets'. The former served to provide a focus of loyalty and to add legitimacy to the polity whereas the latter elements ensured its smooth day-to-day running. In Bagehot's day the citizens concentrated on the dignified: the Monarchy, the Lords and the grandees; whereas those who had the greatest impact upon policy-making remained anonymous. The same is true in our own age. The media covers the parliamentary élites while largely ignoring what is happening in local authorities, in Whitehall departments or even in parliamentary select committees. But even the institutions which could be more closely scrutinised do not include all the key actors in the political process. Secrecy enshrouds many of the key bodies. Cabinet committees, vital components of modern British government, are jealously hidden from public view. And beyond the institutions are the informal links. It is even more difficult to unearth the workings of informal networks – discreet working lunches or telephone calls – which may crucially determine the outcomes of decisions. To return to our analogy of a map, it has been said that to discover how British government works by studying only the formal institutional framework would be like trying to find one's way in the streets of London with the underground map as one's sole guide.[1]

A study of institutions, moreover, can all too easily become descriptive and unduly static, for politics is about conflict and change. Institutions evolve and alter their place in the political scheme of things. In Britain there is a particular difficulty because the absence of a written constitution means that the political system is particularly elastic. Bagehot once again expressed this well when he likened an ancient and ever-altering constitution to 'an old man who still wears with attached fondness clothes in the fashion of his youth: what you see of him is the same; what you do not see is wholly altered'.[2] Unlike France or Germany, Britain has not experienced any revolutionary changes of regime, at least not since the seventeenth century. Yet institutions such as the Monarchy, Parliament or the Cabinet are continually evolving. Developments such as the rise of organised political parties since 1860 have drastically altered the character of British politics.

Another approach to the study of government and politics, therefore, is the historical one. Here the emphasis is upon tracing the course of certain issues, ideas or institutions through time. Historians are fond of the metaphors of organic growth or the evolving body politic. Historians can point to the way in which institutions, like the House of Lords, evolve and are reshaped in response to events or forces. Moreover, institutions, if they are planned as the result of some reform, do not always operate in practice as their founders intend. There are, of course, a variety of historical approaches: some concentrating upon the lives of individuals (biographies); others studying the fortunes of individual ministries; others tracing the evolution of institutions of state or the course of policies in particular areas; yet others relating the political changes to social or economic developments or to those of international relations. The historical approach in all its variety puts flesh upon the bare bones of institutional description. It tests general hypotheses by concentrating upon the particular.

Historical approaches can, though, also suffer from certain limitations. One of these is the tendency to adopt too linear an approach, where hindsight may be at once a useful and a misleading explanatory tool. The knowledge of how things turned out can illuminate the politics of a particular episode; but it can also serve to narrow one's interpretation, since options or outcomes, which may have been possible but which in fact did not take place, can too easily be ruled out of court. Hindsight can also blind us to the concerns, fears and aspirations of contemporaries. Some kinds of historical narrative can also do violence to the complexity of the political process. Biographies, for example, by isolating the actions of an individual can often fail to place the work or political activity of that individual in the proper context. The history of an institution or an area of policy (like pensions or education) can suffer from similar deficiencies, so that the importance of party political or personal manoeuvring may be played down. The historical approach may also tend to ignore general theories which explain how a society operates or where power lies. Finally, historians may not be explicit about (or even aware of) the general theories they are testing, and rarely do they deal with theories that are not country-specific.

Other approaches, which became especially popular in the 1950s and 1960s, were those which sought to explain political activity in terms of political process. Here the favourite metaphor is the 'system'. The political process is likened to some fluid process, like a water or electrical system, which responds to certain forces or inputs; or it may be likened to some living organism where all the constituent parts have a role and balance each other in a harmonious systematic interaction. According to the advocates of this approach, traditional political science had placed too much emphasis upon formal institutional structures and paid insufficient attention to patterns of behaviour. Although the institutions and machinery of the state might have a life of their own, they also reflected patterns of behaviour. The individual state indeed was not necessarily a system on its own. The most fruitful focuses of study were the roles of particular institutions or mechanisms in the system, the type of 'political culture' existing within the system, or the methods of 'political socialisation'. A book on British politics which adopted this approach would have chapters not on particular institutions – like the Cabinet, Parliament, local government; nor on particular policy areas – like foreign affairs, education, economics; but would arrange the material under such headings as recruitment, participation, élites, political socialisation, legitimation, implementation and the like.

The systems approach has provided some useful explanatory tools. Particularly valuable has been the idea of the interaction of the political system with the broader social environment. It has also helped reveal the flexibility of the policy-making process. Some concepts such as inputs and outputs of policy and feedbacks, drawn from computer science, have helped to illuminate the workings of government. The decision-making process is never cut-and-dried: it is continuous. The way in which decisions are implemented can affect the nature of the policy process. General theories of the operation of organisations or bureaucracies add to an understanding of the workings of government in a particular country.

Despite these benefits the systems approach can be faulted on a number of counts. On the one hand the analogy between a polity and a machine or an organism can be questioned. Are social or political systems as coherent as social scientists make out? Although they have some systematic features they are also greatly affected by chance, personality and random factors. Also, is there a scientific or objective way of defining a main system or a sub-system of a political system? The tendency has been for systems theorists to invest ever more time and energy in rather sterile definitions of an abstract kind. Such exercises can become increasingly remote from the real world of politics and verge on the tautologous. In short, systems theorists tend to spend too much time formulating abstract concepts and too little explaining how and why things happen; and their concern with what happens is overwhelmingly to do with how things stayed the way they were, rather than with how they changed. Systems theories are of little use in explaining change. A further criticism is that too little attention is paid by systems theorists to the impact of political ideas or beliefs upon the actors in any political situation.

Another approach to the study of British politics comes from those who focus upon parties and ideologies and the effect of political ideas or beliefs on political behaviour. The assumption here is that these factors play a major part in shaping the outcome of politics. A whole range of books may be found in this broad category. There are straightforward histories or studies of one or more of the political parties themselves. Then there are those works which seek to trace the evolution and development of certain political beliefs: for example, studies of the complexity of socialist ideas in British political history.

Against those who dwell upon the impact of ideas are ranged the arguments of those who ask where those ideas come from and whose interests they serve. These writers focus upon the location of power in the political system. Ideas, for them, are just the way power disguises itself, the way inequalities are legitimated or justified. Sometimes power location is easier to identify than at others. The easy cases are those that involve clear winners and losers. When Mrs Currie, a minister at the Department of Health, resigned over a statement she made about the preponderance of salmonella in eggs, it was evident that she had been forced out by the greater power of the Ministry of Agriculture (and the farming lobby) which denied her claims. But there is another, less transparent form of power, which resides in the structure of society itself. The way people think and act, the goals they make for themselves, these may all be subject to the exercise of power, even if they appear as opinions or common sense. Those concentrating on this approach will wish to pay less attention to parties, elections or legislation and more to the economic organisation of society and the way in which powerful groups, such as large corporate interests or the mass media, manage the conduct of political processes.

As will be clear by now, we do not accept any of the above approaches as the best way of explaining how political decisions get made in Britain. Our preference is to look at specific decisions in order to analyse how the policy-making process actually operated. However, whilst we find the general approaches discussed above to be of limited use in explaining exactly how decisions get made, they may have much more to say about the overall direction of the political system. This is certainly the case with accounts that stress the role of ideology or the interests served by specific policies. Indeed, we will return to this theme in our concluding chapter. For the moment it is sufficient to say that, since our concern is with how to explain decision-making, we believe that none of the general approaches discussed above provides a convincing account.

Before turning to outline our approach it is important to say a little about the main recent developments in British politics. As our focus is on how decisions are made, our object is not to offer a comprehensive account but to provide a context for the case-studies that form the core of our book; our aim here is to set the scene.

Our case-studies are taken from the 1950s to the present. The early part of this period was seen as one when Britain began to experience increasing economic and political difficulties. This was accompanied by a tendency to look back on the politics of the 1945–65 period as those of normal times and to regard any changes as temporary and largely undesirable aberrations from the norm. This period of 'normal times' was in fact comparatively short, applying to only a decade or so of the 1945–65 period; but it has taken on an almost mythical status. Overall it was viewed as a period of considerable complacency in which Britain enjoyed an ordered polity, a stable society and a prospering economy. Underlying everything perhaps was an assumption that the days of economic depression were over. These were the years of the long boom when governments seemed to have learnt the arts of economic management. Keynesian fine-tuning was supposed to have provided the mechanism whereby governments could manipulate economic variables and even engineer economic booms in order to win elections at the appointed time.

Economic prosperity was seen as cementing the inherent stability of British society. In contrast to many Continental countries Britain was seen as enjoying the benefits of a homogeneous society. There were no ethnic or linguistic divisions of note, and religious cleavages were not a force to be reckoned with. (Virtually all observers of this period ignored Northern Ireland.) Although social and geographical divergencies existed, neither class divisions nor regional variations were translated into sharp political cleavages. Class divisions merely served to underpin party politics.

The two main parties, Conservatives and Labour, each enjoyed a national basis of support, although each had pockets of regional strength and weakness. Each drew support from a particular social stratum: the Conservatives from the middle class and the Labour Party from the working class – but not exclusively so. Each party managed to attract a degree of support from outside its core base: in the case of the Conservatives, a third of their support came from the working classes. Thus both parties had distinct roots in the social structure but were broadly based and widened their appeal wherever possible, taking on many of the overall characteristics of Kirchheimer's catch-all political parties. Both parties shared the same consensus values, although each emphasised different facets. Both endorsed the need for a mixed economy, containing both private and public sectors; both accepted the welfare state; and both supported an Atlantic alliance in the shape of NATO. Interest groups, like the trade unions, the representatives of industrial management and of commerce, the farmers and welfare organisations, had access to the political process but did not dominate it.

The workings of a stable and responsible party system were underpinned by what were seen to be tried and proven political institutions. First there was a respected parliamentary system: the British Parliament was described during this period as the mother of parliaments to the newly-emerging states of the British Commonwealth. Then there was the administrative system: a neutral, efficient and uncorrupted civil service; a healthy local government system; an independent judiciary; and a network of public agencies which were independent of government, such as the British Broadcasting Corporation.

Such was the picture of Britain as it was portrayed by liberal political scientists in the two decades or so after the war. The picture was always a somewhat selective one and ignored the existence of strong counter-cultures in such areas as the Welsh valleys and industrial areas of Scotland. It tended also to glide over the divisions between business and the trade unions, and to portray the workings of the political system, especially Parliament and local government, as being unduly smooth. Nevertheless it was a credible picture.

During the 1960s a good deal of disquiet crept into the picture. These were years of culture shock and the outright rejection by many young people of the values of their elders. Satire directed against the political establishment became popular, and even in more sedate academic circles it became fashionable to criticise British institutions and to call for wholesale modernisation of the various processes of administration and government. The effects of economic decline also came to be felt. The following decade saw continual efforts to modernise institutions, although these were seldom very sustained and certainly lacked cohesion.

Whereas in the late 1960s problems were portrayed as departures from the so-called normal times of the 1950s and early 1960s, by the 1980s an increasing number of commentators saw the British polity as entering a truly critical or transformative phase. Increasingly doubts were expressed as to whether the political system could retain or regain equilibrium. Significantly, many of the same American political scientists who had in the earlier period praised the British system now portrayed it as having led to social and political stagnation: a notable example being Samuel Beer.[3] There were many facets of this perceived crisis. In the first place there were the mounting economic problems of rising inflation together with economic recession: the so-called 'stagflation' effect. To many, the British economy seemed to be on the verge of absolute rather than relative decline. Industrial action and trade union militancy severely shook successive governments in the 1970s. Social unrest was also mounting in the large cities. Many doubted the capacity of government to cope.

Such developments were by no means unique to Britain and are the background against which new political ideas sought to challenge the broad intellectual consensus of the post-war period. On the one hand there was a revitalisation and rejuvenation of Marxist and neo-Marxist thinking. There was talk of a legitimation crisis in the state whereby the political and social structures could no longer provide sufficient compensation for the citizens of the state to alleviate the inequalities and injustices of capitalism. Such ideas had an appeal in socialist circles outside the ambit of Marxist influence. Between 1975 and 1985 the Labour Party moved sharply left. Labour activists were disillusioned with the performance of past Labour governments under Wilson and Callaghan. From 1976–82 a sustained effort was made by left-wing activists to shift party policy to the left on such issues as the economy, industry and defence and, even more far-reaching, to insist upon a series of constitutional changes which had the result of giving more say to the rank and file as opposed to MPs and the party leaders. This culminated in the Wembley Conference of 1981 which further had the effect of driving moderates out of the Party into the Social Democratic Party then in the process of formation.

Even more striking was the rise of ideas on the so-called New Right which also challenged both the practice and the theoretical justification of the post-war polity. Drawing its inspiration from thinkers such as Hayek, Milton Friedman and American critics of bureaucracy, such as Niskanen, the New Right advocated a substantial rolling back of the powers and the scope of the state. Keynesian management of the economy was rejected in favour of monetarist mechanisms. Excess state intervention in the economy, driven by corporatist pressure, was seen to harm economic performance. By the 1970s British government was claimed to be dangerously overloaded and in danger of suffering paralysis. Many of the state services, such as the provision of health care or education, needed to become more responsive to consumer demands and to have more elements of private enterprise injected into them. Bureaucracy itself needed to become more responsive to the enterprise culture.

In more directly political terms the replacement of Mr Heath by Mrs Thatcher in 1976 marked a desire within the Conservative Party for a fresh direction. Not only did many Conservatives feel disappointed at the lack-lustre performance of the Conservative administration of 1970–4, they also felt that somehow conservatism in Britain had gone down the wrong track in the Churchill-Macmillan era between 1951 and 1964. The party, they maintained, had been seduced into supporting quasi-socialist planning and had given insufficient attention to the need for economic incentives. Mrs Thatcher entered office with a messianic determination to roll back the frontiers of the state and to turn her back upon the fudging compromises of the consensus years. During the subsequent decade of office, although not as radically as some New Right theorists such as Sir John Hoskyns or Alfred Sherman would have wished, the Thatcher Governments embarked upon a series of striking upheavals affecting whole areas of life. Trade unions, local government, education, health, the social services, universities, the Civil Service, broadcasting and transport, as well as the economy, were all substantially changed during the 1980s.

During the past decade, Britain has experienced something unusual: a government of the right which has sought to bring about radical change. The Thatcher Governments possessed an exceptionally strong strategic sense. But they also were adept at pragmatically adjusting to the changing world around them and to the pressure of events, as any study of the details of their economic policy will indicate. Unusually in Britain, there was a high degree of continuity in the 1980s, with a single Prime Minister enjoying a consistently firm degree of support in electoral terms and within her own party. Yet the 1980s were not a period of any marked or radical institutional change. The changes which occurred were inserted into existing practices. The advent of Mrs Thatcher to power in 1979 marked a significant change, but in no sense a radical revolution in the state along the lines of Germany in 1945–8 or France in 1958.

In this book we draw upon both the theoretical and the historical elements of the study of British politics. We concentrate on the details of decision-making, examining a limited number of case studies taken from the politics of the last two decades and drawn from a range of contrasting policy areas. Our concern is to learn how British politics works by looking in detail at how decisions are made. We do not claim that this approach supplants any of the others or is inherently superior to them. It does, though, have certain advantages. It is in one sense an historical approach which allows us to examine the dynamism of the political process. It does not, however, abstract from the complexities of the political system an unduly unilinear account. The study of decision-making allows us to study the exercise of power: both to look at the behaviour of individuals under pressure and to examine the effect of the structural constraints upon the outcomes of policy decisions. We can take some account of both the personal and political motives of individual actors and the influence of ideologies and economic and social constraints. It is hoped that this book will therefore supplement both textbooks which introduce students to the workings of politics and general accounts of the nature of the policy process or of the political sociology of modern Britain.

Of course case-studies are nothing new, British political scientists have fruitfully adopted this approach for decades. But our approach involves more than merely a set of historical examples; it is based on the view that the case-studies must be understood within a theoretical context. Historical accounts may be interesting and informative, but they are, in our view, no substitute for an explicit theoretical framework. Specifically, we think that since any case-study has to rely on some theoretical perspective simply to be able to decide on what counts as relevant information, then we should be explicit about the theories that we are using. Moreover, we believe that the theoretical literature on decision-making offers some powerful explanations of political decisions. We outline these theories in chapter two. In linking our case-studies to this body of literature, two questions arise. First, what do the theories of decision-making tell us about the cases we examine? Second, do our case-studies tell us anything about the utilities of the various theories? We deal with these questions in our concluding chapter. Finally, there are many accounts of how the British political system operates, and we summarise these in chapter three. Again, we return to these in our conclusion with the thought that our case-studies might tell us something about the utility of these approaches. But before we outline these two sets of theoretical literature we need to say something about the strengths and weaknesses of our approach.

Case-studies make politics come to life. They show the complexity of the process of government. They reveal the uniqueness of any situation. The contingencies of chance, uncertainty and personality can be set against the power of structures and the constraints of systemic forces. They may be used to illuminate and evaluate a whole variety of theoretical approaches. Case-studies, however, do present certain problems. One is the relationship of the specific to the general.

Sir Geoffrey Vickers has powerfully criticised the approach on these grounds. He writes:

> Case histories are a laborious approach to understanding. For situations are so varied that even a large number of cases may be a misleading sample, whilst each is so complex that even a detailed description may be too summary; and none is comprehensible outside the historical sequence in which it grew.[4]

Vickers was writing from the standpoint of a theorist of decisions. He was interested in the processes and the arrangements whereby individual managers or administrators come to take decisions. He is right to highlight the difficulty of steering between the Scylla of excessive detail, derived from a limited range of examples, and the Charybdis of too many examples, resulting in very abstract generalisations about the political system which are divorced from political reality.

Certainly, there is a danger that recounting a series of case-studies can turn out to be too descriptive an exercise. Analysis of the significance of what is happening can be lost sight of amid a plethora of detail. Case-studies may be interesting in their own right, but they are only really useful if they tell us more about the workings of the political system. The same empirical case-study can be read in a variety of ways. It will rarely fit any particular model or theory of how politics works; instead elements will be found which endorse, qualify or sometimes contradict particular theoretical approaches. Case-studies will not prove anything; considered in conjunction with theories of politics they will, however, provide the evidence with which any theory must deal.

We need also to be wary of another feature of studying decision-making. This approach by its very nature concentrates on what is done rather than what is not done; upon the successes rather than the failures. Yet the failure of dogs to bark in the night may be of the utmost significance. The absence of items from the political agenda can tell us a lot about the distribution of power in society. A truly adequate account of decision-making should take into consideration 'non decision-making'. Continuity is as important as shifts of policy.

Another problem when adopting the case-study approach is knowing how many to choose and which to select. Quantity can only be purchased at the expense of depth; but depth can cause a loss of breadth. In this book we present six case-studies. In an ideal world twice that number might be preferable, but it would be impractical to include so many in a single volume whilst leaving space for the general material. The six case-studies we have chosen are: the Government's response to AIDS (Acquired Immune Deficiency Syndrome); the decisions leading up to the Falklands crisis; the story of nuclear power; the rise and fall of the Civil Service Department; industrial relations legislation; and the development of Trident. These are chosen partly, of course, because they reflect the interests and expertise of the authors. But they are also representative of different facets of the governmental process and illustrate different fields of policy. The Falklands crisis represents an example of the handling of a classic diplomatic or foreign affairs problem, scarcely different in essence from those in the days of Palmerston or Disraeli. It makes a particularly valuable study because of the way the Franks Report, the official inquiry into the Falklands venture, takes the lid off the workings of the Cabinet system. Trident and nuclear power, by contrast, involve long-term policy in areas which are technologically complex and which also happen to be the subject of quite intense public interest and controversy. The response to AIDS shows government reacting to a new problem where uncertainties are high and on which public concern, while considerable, is both malleable and potentially volatile. Industrial relations legislation, on the other hand, represents the latest stage in the old issue of high political salience at the heart of party political conflict where attitudes of participants tend to be entrenched. The abolition of the Civil Service Department is different again. This case-study relates to the arcane area of the machinery of government, of major concern to those within government but of little interest to those outside it. Obviously six case-studies cannot be fully representative of all facets of British government. Our hope is that once readers have worked their way through the examples in this volume they can move on to others which they can then read in the light of the theoretical frameworks we offer.

There is one final caveat which should be mentioned. That is the difficulty of writing authoritatively about the decision-making of the relatively recent past. British government is not particularly open or easy for the outsider to penetrate. Some of the issues, like AIDS or Trident, are highly sensitive and in any case have not run their course. The organisation of the Civil Service is not an area of popular concern and the decision-making process is bound to be remote. The Falklands crisis involved high drama but also intense secrecy. A fuller account of all our case-studies would be possible in a generation's time, after more inside documents are released at the Public Record Office under the terms of the Thirty Year Rule. There is indeed a sense in which we might learn more about the nature of British government by studying the decisions of the Attlee or Macmillan era; but that of course would not be exactly the same political system. In this connection it is striking how much and how rapidly British politics have changed since the mid-1970s. Since the case-studies in this book all relate to the Thatcher era they can be expected to illustrate the workings of this new and evolving pattern of politics. Conversely, it may be interesting to see if, in the world of policy and decision-making, as much has changed as we might expect. Are the power structures so very different? Maybe less has changed than we might imagine.

On balance, therefore, we believe that the case-study approach, when combined with an explicit set of theories, is a very promising way for us to answer our initial question. To reiterate, we are fundamentally concerned to use the theories to see if they can help us understand the case-studies better, and we also want to see what the case-studies tell us about the applicability of the (mainly American) theories. We do not think that this type of approach has been done before in quite this way; usually, case-studies are either not explicitly theory dependent (although, as we have said, they must of necessity rely on theory) or are tests of only one particular theory. Our book is unique, therefore, in trying to look both at the impact of the theories on our understanding of the case-studies and at what the case-studies tell us about the usefulness of the various theories.

Finally, our case-studies are related to accounts of the more general developments in British politics, as our discussion in chapter three makes clear. We want to reflect on the issue of what our case-studies tell us about these broader accounts of British politics, and, again, we will return to this question in the conclusion. This is, however, our secondary aim, because we are aware that our case-studies are much more likely to provide insights about decision-making theories than the broader picture of British political life. The broader sweep of political change is part of the story which our case-studies tell. They reveal the details of the larger picture. At the same time they point us to questions which the historical perspective does not reveal: how were the changes made? Who decided what and why? For us the history of the post-war era is, therefore, the backdrop to our analysis. In the foreground are the decisions that form part of the general changes; also in the spotlight are the theories and assumptions which help to explain those decisions.

2 Theories of decision-making

INTRODUCTION

In this chapter we wish to introduce some general theories about how decisions are taken in political systems. Why is it useful to spend time on this before immersing ourselves in the case-studies? One answer to this is that any student of politics or contemporary history needs some kind of a conceptual lens through which to make sense of the mass of empirical material available to him or her. Another is that by being aware of a variety of different theoretical approaches we may add to our understanding of what happened. The same story may fruitfully be read from different perspectives. A theory of how things work or where power lies is designed to offer explanations. It is the explanatory power of a theory rather than the richness of description that is of value. At the same time all theories and general analyses must be in some degree unsatisfactory when set against the complexity of events in the real world. They are abstractions and oversimplifications and will rarely, if ever, fit snugly the awkward contours of history. In return empirical examples, let alone a single case-study, cannot serve as the basis for a theory; they may only suggest ways in which it falls short or may be modified. In our final chapter we review the theories in the light of the six case-studies. Here we set out the various competing models.

THE RATIONAL ACTOR MODEL

Central to this theory of decision-making is the vision of the policy-maker determining an objective and assessing and weighing up the means available to him or her to achieve this objective. By rational in this context is meant not necessarily that the policy is best in any historical sense but that rational policy-makers will make their policy according to the link between ends and means, and will choose the policy which they judge after exhaustive analysis best achieves their goal. This view of rationality is well expressed in Anthony Downs' adaptation of Kenneth Arrow's pioneering work on social choice. Downs states that a rational person is one who:

1 can always make a decision when confronted with a range of alternatives;
2 ranks all the alternatives facing him or her in order of his or her preference in such a way that each is either preferred to, indifferent to, or inferior to each other;
3 his or her preference ranking is always transitive (i.e. if alternative x is preferred to alternative y, and y is preferred to z, then x will always be preferred to z);
4 he or she always chooses from among the possible alternatives that which ranks highest in his or her preference ordering; and
5 he or she always makes the same decision each time he or she is confronted with the same alternatives.

It is essential to note Downs' rider to this definition: 'Rationality thus refers to processes of action, not to their ends or even to their success at reaching desired ends'.[1]

The rational actor theory of decision-making assumes that there are clear-cut stages in the policy process. First, the decision-maker identifies the nature of the problem; he or she then determines the overriding policy objectives; next he or she identifies all the possible means of achieving his or her objective and assesses the consequences of adopting each, finally selecting the means – policy – which seems best able to secure the overriding objective.

Before discussing the imperfections of this theory it is important to note its appeal. The rational actor model with its stress on the individual decision-taker has a common-sense attraction to us as individuals in the way we like to visualise our lives. Whether we are planning a career, deciding on a holiday or choosing which film to see, we like to think we are in command, weighing up the choices and competing factors which will best satisfy our overall requirements. Perhaps a moment's reflection will suggest that in practice we rarely run our lives along such straightforward principles, but the vision of such rational decision-making is one which few individuals would easily part with.

Similarly, the rational actor model is one which strikes an instinctive chord with politicians. The hierarchical implications of the model are appealing. Politicians like to feel that they are in command of a hierarchy of administration, that they have clear-cut objectives and that they are responsible for achieving those objectives. They will claim that their policy is the best one to arrive at a specified end. Thus if the major goal is identified as the reduction of inflation, politicians will discuss various policies in terms of the extent to which they lead to that goal and will justify their choices of policy in those terms. More limited policy objectives, such as the reduction in road deaths, will be presented in the same terms.

Journalists are also happiest with this view of the decision-making process. It allows for clear-cut responsibilities and judgement in terms of success and failure. Accordingly much of the rhetoric of British politics – the electoral process and the accounts of Parliamentary or Cabinet battles – tends to be presented in terms of the rational model of decision-making.

The rational actor model in its crudest form clearly fits most easily into a world where the individual leader sits at the apex of a hierarchy. In reality most formal decision-making falls to collective bodies of one kind or another, committees or boards of directors. This raises immediate problems since not all members of such bodies may necessarily share identical objectives; personal and corporate objectives may coexist and come into conflict and the members of the corporate governing body may represent competing sub-divisions of the whole enterprise (a point to which we shall return). Nevertheless the rational actor model has had a strong appeal for commercial enterprises where relatively simple distinctions may be made between overall goals and the means to achieve them. Thus the directors of a retailing chain will generally aim to increase profits or market share as a goal and then examine such matters as advertising strategy, product range and siting of stores in the light of what they judge to be prevailing market trends. Naturally the larger and more diverse the business becomes, the more complex will this exercise grow.

There has been a strong presupposition to see the work of government in analogous terms. In the British context it was Bagehot in the 1860s, for example, who first described the Cabinet as a 'board of control'.[2] Clearly the work of running a country is infinitely more complex than any commercial undertaking, but the role of the Cabinet is commonly interpreted as providing some kind of strategic guidance. It is a common observation or complaint by politicians who rise to Cabinet rank that the experience of the actual Cabinet falls far short of their expectations in this respect. The point we should bear in mind is that the rational actor model of decision-making, like the others to be considered, is normative as much as explanatory: it is not only descriptive but prescriptive. There is a strong assumption on the part of its adherents that this is how the decision-making process should be ordered.

According to the rational actor view of the decision process policy-making is concerned with maximising utility, with utility treated as a homogeneous good. Thus in any policy-making situation decision-makers will aim to produce the maximum amount of utility and will do so by selecting from the available options that which offers the maximum of their single good. This assumes, of course, that utility is a good, in that all outcomes can be measured in terms of the amount of it produced; it also assumes that decision-makers have a set of well-defined and mutually exclusive alternatives from which to choose; finally, it assumes that decision-makers are able to calculate the amount of utility to be derived from pursuing each of the alternatives. Cost Benefit Analysis (CBA) is the best example of how these general concepts have been applied in practice. CBA is the analysis of a social or economic policy in terms of predicted costs and benefits, where these are cast as widely as possible, in order that all issues which the policy involves may be assessed and weighed. CBA has commonly been used in areas such as transport planning, for example when deciding whether to build a new road or to invest in an urban light railway system. A CBA study would seek to take into account the cost of constructing the road or railway and set this against projected economic benefits that are expected to ensue. In addition an attempt would be made to bring into the equation such factors as environmental destruction of buildings or habitat, pollution caused or saved, aesthetic factors, the impact upon settled communities, the effect upon traffic safety and accident rates and so on. CBA attempts to weigh both long- and short-term effects of a decision and to assess some overall mechanism, usually a financial one, to evaluate the impact of a decision upon a varied range of factors. The whole exercise may be seen as a latter-day version of Bentham's celebrated 'felicific calculus'.

The most grandiose example of CBA in Britain was the Roskill Commission which spent over £3 million in an attempt to assess the relative costs and benefits in monetary terms of the four proposed sites for the third London airport. The experience of this Commission clearly illustrates the limitations of the CBA approach. As Peter Self has concluded:

> There was heated and inconclusive argument about the figures to be attached to those items which were quantified, while the

Commission accepted that some important items could not be quantified at all. The main effect of the exercise was to translate policy issues into complicated technical analysis without thereby elucidating or resolving those issues.[3]

CBA assumes firstly that all costs and benefits are quantifiable. This is highly questionable: can one really put a quantifiable value upon an eighteenth century listed building which may be threatened by a road scheme? Secondly, it assumes that the various costs and benefits are in some way commensurate with each other. Moreover, the values which will be placed upon particular items are bound to reflect the broader values and beliefs of the individuals who assess them. This gives them an arbitrary character and can, therefore, be suddenly changed for no apparent reason, except to suit the interests of those in control of the process. A particularly stark instance of this occurred on day 134 of the first East London River Crossing Public Inquiry. The Department of Transport has a standard financial value which is placed upon the time motorists spend in traffic jams. On this occasion the Department's officials, desperate because their pet scheme showed a negative economic value, arbitarily changed this figure because in their view the motorists in this particular area were judged to be engaged in especially important work. At a stroke this had the effect of increasing the notional benefit of the proposed river crossing by £14.5 million.[4]

CBA has been most commonly employed in planning exercises, but over the last twenty years strenuous efforts have been made to apply similar techniques to assessing the performance of government itself. The art of programme budgeting in government, for example, is to cost the outputs, services or programmes provided by government departments and assess their effectiveness, rather than to concentrate on the traditional input costs of staff, buildings and equipment and the like. The objective is to know exactly what different sorts of services or facilities cost and to allow government to tailor its provision according to political or other demands. More radical still are attempts, favoured among the New Right, to evaluate the services provided by government, such as education, welfare, health, defence and environmental protection in quantifiable terms. All the various techniques of management efficiency – which we need not analyse here – stem from the rational approach to decision-making. Rational approaches to political behaviour also form the core of many of the public-choice theories of the New Right. These explain areas such as voting behaviour and policy-making primarily in terms of the individual citizen acting as a rational consumer. New Right theorists adapt theories of economic behaviour to the world of politics. They have been extremely influential in the 1980s in both Britain and America.

The rational actor approach makes certain implicit assumptions about the political process which it is important to spell out. The rational model assumes that hierarchies are the natural order of political organisation. There are clear chains of command and information flows freely throughout the government machine. It is possible to evaluate information and choices in a coherent and scientific manner. For this reason the adherent of the rational view of decision-making will tend to hold the expert in high esteem; the professional will be at a premium over the layperson. The unpredictability of democratic politics may represent an unwelcome intrusion into the ordered world of planning and programme analysis. Furthermore, the adherent of the model will find it hard to cope with sudden ideological shifts in opinion or values. It would be difficult for the rational decision-maker to take on board sea-changes in public opinion, such as the rise of Green values and opinions in recent years.

The rational actor model of decision-making is open to criticism on several grounds. In the first place, the model has little room for changing ideological values; all too often the politics can be squeezed out. For the identification of a problem itself is no simple matter. Not only will different individuals see it differently, but it may undergo dramatic changes in the course of a generation. We now interpret the problems of inner city decay, Third World development, the environment and health-care very differently from the way they were assessed in the 1950s, for example. Problems themselves are fluid or elastic and the appreciation of them will be affected by the impact of policies designed to overcome them. The rational actor model of policy-making tends in this respect rather artificially to separate stages of policy-making when it is, in fact, often a continuous process.

Secondly, the rational actor model, however credible an account of decision-making in an organisation of limited scope, such as a small firm or a charitable organisation, clearly simplifies the work of government to the point of absurdity. Any governing body has a myriad of objectives which must be juggled with and pursued simultaneously. One only has to think of the competing objectives of government economic policy. An economic ministry will be concerned to promote economic growth, control inflation, hold down unemployment, safeguard the balance of payments, ensure investment in industry and so on. The broader and more representative a body, the more it will be composed of distinct sections or departments each having its own peculiar *raison d'être* or objective. In Britain the Cabinet can be represented as essentially a collection of departmental interests, but the same might equally be said of individual departments of state themselves. Moreover, apart from strategic policy goals the actors in politics will also be influenced by more narrowly political or personal ambitions, such as winning the next election or securing personal career advancement. The rational actor model, in short, has been criticised for underrating the pluralist and fragmented nature of the policy process.

Thirdly, the rational actor model can be criticised for underrating the difficulties of compiling and assessing information. The costs of tabulating and making sense of information can be vast and in any case not all necessary information can be assessed readily in a quantifiable manner. The rational actor model assumes the decision-maker examines all possible means available to achieve his or her objective. In practice however, many possible solutions or means may be filtered out simply because they are original and novel and there may not be the necessary information available for the solution to spring to mind. In other words decision-making may be more routine than the rational actor model suggests. Courses of action are chosen because they have been chosen before and a pattern is established; whereas other procedures, potentially equally effective, may not occur to the decision-maker simply because they are novel. Creative brainstorming is costly in terms of effort and mental energy; processing the in-tray is altogether a more comfortable occupation.

BOUNDED RATIONALITY

These last considerations of limitations to the decision-maker's capacities led some theorists to refine and modify the rational actor model of decision-making. Foremost here was Herbert Simon in his work *Administrative Behavior* published in 1957. Simon points out that it is impossible for the decision-maker to analyse and select all the possible choices. Some feasible ones will never occur to him or her or be ruled out because they conflict with deeply entrenched values: they will be ruled out from the word go.[5] Writing in another context, Michael Oakeshott, in criticising rationalist approaches to politics, gives a piquant example of this. After the invention of the safety bicycle when ladies took to riding the machines, much thought was given to designing the 'rational' dress for ladies to wear.

The Victorians came up with bloomers. In point of fact shorts are a far more satisfactory solution, but the very idea of such a garment was ruled out because of the prevailing ideas of etiquette and decorum.[6]

Similarly, it is asking too much of the decision-maker to come up with a carefully-weighed analysis of the consequences of various competing policies. Prediction of consequences takes us into the realm of the 'guesstimate' rather than of scientific analysis. Even in routine decisions like the building of a road, predictions of consequential change, for example in traffic flows, can prove to be wildly inaccurate, as the experience of the M25 has shown. This difficulty will be all the greater when tackling novel or unique problems where past precedent is of little guidance. Assessing the impact of government-sponsored advertising upon sexual behaviour and the incidence of AIDS, for example, may amount to little more than imaginative guesswork. Similarly the foreign policy analyst will have the task of predicting the reaction of unpredictable foreign leaders in far-away countries whose cultural values may be quite alien to him or her. This is a problem which has bedevilled successive American administrations in their relations with both Iran and Iraq over the past decade or so.

The values and conceptions of purpose of the decision-maker are also likely to be at odds in some respect from those of the organisation. Individuals do not have a free hand in exercising their pure rationality in analysing ends and means. The organisation within which they work will shape their options and their behaviour by virtue of its structure. It will also tend to internalise its dominant values within the psychology or mind-set of the individuals who work within it.

According to Simon therefore, decision-makers in the real world are bounded by various constraints. Their own unconscious habits and reflexes, the values they hold apart from the organisation in which they work, and the extent of their knowledge or information are among the most important of these. As he observes:

> The individual can be rational in terms of the organisation's goals only to the extent that he is able to pursue a particular course of action, he has a correct conception of the goal of the action, he is correctly informed about the conditions surrounding his action. Within the boundaries laid down by these factors his choices are rational-goal oriented.[7]

Where the theory of bounded rationality differs fundamentally from the rational actor model is in its denial that there is a simple relationship between ends and means. Simon's decision-makers have to ascribe values to their actions. Central to the theory of rational decision-making is the concept of utility as a homogeneous entity which it is the task of the administrator or politician to promote. Exponents of the theory of bounded rationality discard this notion. Policy-making is seen essentially as a choice between policies that relate to outcomes which are not comparable in terms of utility. Policy-makers have the task of choosing between sets of alternatives, each of which is related to a unique and valuable outcome; the task, therefore, is to find an acceptable outcome in the face of competing demands. In this way rationality is bounded so that decisions are concerned with maintaining each of the valued alternatives at an acceptable level. Consequently there is no notion of maximising outcomes, only of finding acceptable ones. The conception of the decision-maker is thus less Olympian. He or she cannot be expected to know how much utility will be produced by any given decision, nor to compare outcomes in terms of a common measure. In this way policy-making becomes the art of compromise between unknown outcomes and separately valued goals. Simon coined the term 'satisficing' to describe this concept.

Sir Geoffrey Vickers, a theorist of organisations, propounded a broadly similar set of ideas in his theory of appreciative judgement. Here decisions stemmed from both the aspirations of individuals and social and institutional constraints: 'the mental activity and the social process are indissoluable'. Most administrative activity consisted of regulation. There were times, however, when it was necessary to exercise appreciation by viewing the problems afresh and coming up with new ideas or perspectives in order to tackle them. Vickers cites the Buchanan Report on traffic in towns of 1963 as a classic example of such appreciative judgement. Up to then the provision of highways and town planning had been seen as entirely distinct in administrative terms and contradictory policies had often been pursued. Buchanan argued that the two should not be regarded in isolation and subsequently planning took on board this insight. The art of appreciation, Vickers maintained, was to assimilate a major change with the greatest net gain while preserving the value of the existing system.[8]

DISJOINTED INCREMENTALISM

These reflections on the limits of rationality have been taken further by Braybrooke and Lindblom who have constructed an altogether more radical model which is in some ways the polar opposite of the rational actor account. They argue that the latter offers a totally misguided picture of how the vast majority of decisions are taken. In the real world people move cautiously making small or incremental adjustments to the existing pattern and taking decisions on the basis of a low level of understanding. This is how individuals tend to run their own lives and it is how the vast majority of political decisions are made. As they write:

> These decisions, we now see, are the decisions typical of ordinary political life . . . Decisions like these are made day to day in ordinary political circumstances by congressmen, executives, administrators, and party leaders.[9]

Braybrooke and Lindblom use the following diagram to illustrate the process of policy-making based upon two continua:[10]

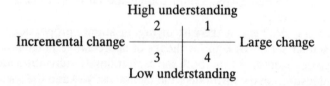

Braybrooke and Lindblom argue that two of these quadrants, (1) and (4), have no explanatory use in reference to political behaviour. In fact they contend that such forms of policy-making are very rare in politics. Quadrant (1) decisions would be those of revolutionary or utopian decision-makers, visionaries who had a high understanding of issues and who wished to effect large changes in society. Quadrant (4) decisions would be the preserve of decisions made at times of crisis or revolution. These situations are rare and untypical and cannot be used to explain normal political activity. Policy-making in politics is usually, if not exclusively, concerned with effecting small changes in society; analytical techniques are therefore concentrated on explaining the decisions in quadrants (2) and (3). Quadrant (2) is the preserve of rational theories of decision-making. The rational theories of decision-making treat this as an area of choice between well-defined and comprehensible options, each related to the attainment of a clear and valued goal. Braybrooke and Lindblom believe this explanation of decision-making to be unsatisfactory because it does not fit the actual behaviour of decision-makers, primarily because the level of information, and thereby understanding, is not that high. A more powerful explanation of the policy process, they believe, is to be located in quadrant (3) where decisions in practice are taken to effect small changes and are taken on the basis of low levels of understanding.[11]

The model of disjointed incrementalism starts from the premise that policy-making is an endless process, exploratory in nature. It does not consist of clearly defined stages in which problems are first identified and then solutions propounded and weighed. It is serial and continuous in nature. Decision follows decision and builds up a pattern. Policy makers tend to trace well-tried paths and have an in-built tendency to avoid costly innovations or departures from the routine. Rather than spending their time identifying goals and choosing policies which seem to offer the best chance of attaining them, decision-makers in practice try to evade and minimise problems. 'In this sense', write Braybrooke and Lindblom, 'it is also better described as moving *away* from known social ills rather than as moving *toward* a known and relatively stable goal'.[12]

Policy-making is therefore incremental rather than synoptic; it attempts to solve problems, piece by piece, modifying the solutions chosen in the light of the evidence about the effects of previous policies. Decision-making according to this perspective is also primarily reactive. Action will be taken when pressure arises. There will be an inbuilt tendency towards the status quo and some kind of political pressure, scandal or dramatic event will usually be needed to galvanise decision-makers into reappraisals.

Whereas the rational actor model assumes that means are subordinated to ends, according to the perspective of disjointed incrementalism the reverse is more often the case. Changes in technology or the methods of delivering services may prompt a radical rethink about the objectives of a policy. Changes in the technology of nuclear weapons and their delivery systems, for example, may be the prime motive factors in changing defence strategies.

Not only is decision-making seen as incremental: it is also fragmented or disjointed. Thus decision-makers will often utilise first one policy for moving away from a social ill, then, when the effects of this are seen, change to adopt another policy. Policy-making is a process of oscillation or evolution. Equally, the incrementalist model emphasises the very large numbers of actors and institutions which are involved in the formation of policy. Whereas the rational actor model tends to assume a hierarchy of decision-making with clear chains of command, incrementalism emphasises the plurality of decision-making in a complex modern society. This would be the case even in a single area of government, such as education. Not only the Department of Education and Science but the Treasury, local authorities, teachers' unions, professional associations, universities and colleges, think-tanks, and voluntary bodies would all play an important part in the formation of policy. This would be even more marked in a broader area such as policy for the inner cities which could involve a vast range of departments and interests.

The exponents of disjointed incrementalism claim that their model provides a far more powerful explanatory theory of decision-taking than the rational-orientated models. The latter may be suited to explain limited areas of decision-making or very technical or special-ised areas of policy-making, but cannot cope with the complexities of political behaviour. By contrast incrementalism is seen as particularly well suited to a rapidly changing environment, characterised by limited information, an increasingly unclear comprehension of the linkages between policies and outcomes, confusion over the central values to be pursued and an ever shifting ranking of social ills. It can cope with the obvious point that policy-making will differ from situation to situation, from issue to issue and from time to time; the rational synoptic ideal treats these as parameters, whereas disjointed incrementalism axiomatically sees them as variables.

Lindblom termed his theory the 'science of muddling through'. Incrementalist theories, he claimed, offered a better means of understanding the decision-making process than rational ones.[13] It is, however, important to realise that for Lindblom and many other incremental theorists the model moves quickly from a descriptive to a prescriptive position. It is no less normative than the rational actor model. In Lindblom's eyes rational theories are positively harmful because they are simplistic and mislead actors in the political process. Disjointed incrementalism provides us with a better way of running the world. Once we abandon the chimera of authoritarian centralised rationalism we will be better placed to improve the quality of policy-making. The accommodation of a variety of interests, and the recognition that analysts do not have to agree upon a single ultimate goal if they are to produce good policies, is, it is claimed, a prerequisite for satisfactory government in a pluralistic (Western) democracy. Lindblom describes the interplay of forces in the decision-making process as a partisan mutual adjustment. Such wide-ranging participation in the decision-making process, such fragmentation, such disjointed adjustments, will guarantee a measure of stability and liberty in the polity. In 1979 he wrote:

> The connection between a policy and good reasons for it is obscure, since the many participants will act for diverse reasons . . . In many circumstances their mutual adjustments will achieve a coordination superior to an attempt at central coordination, which is often so complex as to lie beyond any coordinator's competence.

Far from sadly accepting incrementalism as a second best given the impossibility of rational approaches, we should positively relish it.

> Many critics of incrementalism believe that doing better usually means turning away from incrementalism. Incrementalists believe that for complex problem-solving it usually means practicing incrementalism more skilfully and turning away from it only rarely.[14]

From this it appears that the implications of disjointed incrementalism are profoundly conservative. Indeed the model fits conservative pluralist views of democracy like a glove. Policy-making is portrayed as diffused and democratic, allowing most interests in society to have a say. There are shifting majorities rather than a single exploitative majority. Society does not need radical reconstruction to improve the quality of its decision-making, and long-term visionary thinkers can have only a limited role in improving the quality of politics – indeed they are likely to be positively disruptive and damaging. Many of the critics of incrementalism have homed in upon these points. It has been pointed out that some important viewpoints of underprivileged or minority groups are filtered out of the policy process and that the model does not address itself to the issue of how fair and just a society is. Disjointed incrementalism concentrates unduly upon the style and process of decision-making rather than upon its substance. Others suggest that even in complicated pluralistic societies like those of the United States and western Europe serious economic, social or environmental problems may arise which positively call out for strategic appraisal. Yehezkel Dror has claimed that Lindblom's theories constitute 'an ideological reinforcement of the pro-inertia and anti-innovation forces prevalent in all human organizations, administrative and policy making'. Although unrealistic in its pure form, Dror asserted that:

The 'rational-comprehensive' model has at least the advantage of stimulating administrators to get a little outside their regular routine, while Lindblom's model justifies a policy of 'no effort'.[15]

Other criticisms have directed their fire less upon the normative desirability than upon the empirical or descriptive validity of the model. It has been claimed that Lindblom and others have underplayed the degree of strategic planning and prioritisation in government. Lindblom recognised the existence of large decisions outside the quadrant of disjointed incrementalism but dismissed these in advanced Western polities as being rare and untypical. Whilst this may be true, some have suggested that this is seriously to play down their significance. From time to time in a polity there may be fundamental decisions made in a rational-comprehensive manner which will have profound consequences for all other areas of policy-making. The decision to go to war is an obvious example.

Similarly it may be possible to trace the impact of sudden changes in values or of advances in technological or scientific knowledge which necessitate widespread policy reviews. Changing attitudes towards racial questions in the post-war period, for example, led to the abandonment of segregation in the American South and the profound rethinking of policy in a host of areas. Over the last few years an appreciation of the problems of global warming has led all Western governments to a strategic rethinking of energy and environmental policies, with ramifications throughout the range of policy arenas. The change resulting from the signing of the Single European Act is another example of such large or fundamental change occuring as a result of strategic or rational planning as opposed to the science of muddling through.

The incrementalist plays down ideology in favour of pragmatism. Indeed it is a familiar view that radical governments always end up adopting pragmatic solutions. But critics of incrementalism claim that it goes too far in writing off ideology. The Thatcher Governments in Britain in the 1980s could be cited as ones which displayed a strong strategic sense based upon firm sets of ideas.

Finally, the disjointed incrementalist model shares a serious defect with the rational models of decision-making. Because it is essentially a theory to link decisions and outcomes, it does not consider the ways in which the process of making policy can influence outcomes. The models are all essentially 'black box' theories of decision-making in the sense that the structures and processes internal to policy-making are obscured from view. They are not seen to be integral to the explanation.

THE ORGANISATIONAL PROCESS MODEL

Any attempt to get inside the 'black box' of decision-making will have to examine the organisational structure within which decisions are taken. It is a writer on international relations, Graham Allison, who has most clearly illuminated this aspect of decision-making. In his seminal study of the Cuban Missile Crisis Allison identified three distinct models which purported to explain the decision-making process.

The study of international relations or diplomacy is traditionally one which has placed great emphasis upon the interaction of sovereign states. Individual states tend to be seen as sovereign rational actors. It is easy to personify them – as when in popular parlance we say, 'America's aim in the Middle East is such-and-such' or 'France's overriding objective at the forthcoming meeting of European Community heads of state is to achieve this or that objective'. At its crudest, international relations may be pictured as if states were controlled by individuals playing a board game such as *Diplomacy* or *Risk*.

The Cuban Missile Crisis of 1962 was the greatest conflict of the 1945–90 period of superpower rivalry and almost certainly the nearest the world has come to nuclear conflagration. Soviet missiles were placed on Cuba which led to a furore in the United States and a subsequent American blockade of Cuba. In his study Allison identified three key questions: why were the Soviet missiles placed on Cuba?; why did the United States respond with a blockade?; why did the Soviet Union withdraw its missiles? In adopting what he termed a rational actor perspective Allison found it difficult to match behaviour to goals convincingly. He believed this form of explanation to be severely limited because it failed to deal with certain factors in the policy-making process. Specifically, he criticised the assumption that policy was the result of policy-making by one actor, the state. He contended this was a vast oversimplification of reality. Policy-making is not the output of a monolith; there is simply no one, single body within a society which makes policy. Rather, policy-making emerges from sets of organisations and from the bargaining between these organisations. Allison offered two alternative models for explaining policy-making which made sense of the Cuban Missile Crisis: the organisational process model and the bureaucratic politics model, both of which were attempts to take account of the importance of bureaucratic organisations.[16]

Allison's organisational process model sees policy as the output of organisations. Most policy is usually the outcome of separate organisations each working to standard operating procedures. These routines pre-exist any rational assessment of the problem and its appropriate solution. In applying this model to British politics, we would focus upon the ways in which departments are organised. If the Foreign Office is traditionally geared up to concentrating on relations with the largest powers, for example, then relations with a smaller country like Argentina will receive a low priority, and the department may be ill-equipped to formulate policy in this area. Again, certain groups or interests in the state may exert more influence than others simply because there is a government department to push their interests; hence farmers in Britain have been more influential than the electorally larger group of old-age pensioners. A classic example of this phenomenon was the almost total absence of interest of successive British governments in Northern Irish affairs before the advent of the 'Troubles' in 1969. This was because responsibility was devolved to the Stormont Parliament and there was no department at Westminster to concern itself with Northern Irish affairs; Scotland, by contrast, enjoyed the benefit of its own department.

Another feature of the organisational process model is the emphasis it places upon the differing ideological attitudes of different departments. Each department or agency of government is seen as having its own view of the world or its own values. In this connection various former civil servants and politicians in Britain have drawn attention to the importance of what Lord Bridges, a former head of the Civil Service, once described as departmental philosophies. These are the frameworks through which policy questions are viewed and which may in effect screen out policy options.[17] One of Bridges' successors, Lord William Armstrong, reflecting upon his days at the Treasury in the 1960s, expressed this very lucidly:

> We . . . had a framework for the economy [which was] basically neo-Keynesian. We set the questions which we asked ministers to decide arising out of that framework so to that extent we had great power . . . We were very ready to explain it to anybody who was interested, but most ministers were not interested, were just prepared to take the questions as we offered them, which came out of that framework without going back into the preconceptions of them.[18]

It is not difficult to find examples of such departmental points of view or frameworks. The Department of Transport, for example, has traditionally interpreted improved transport to mean more and wider roads rather than either better public transport facilities or a more integrated system of transport. In recent years considerable disquiet has been voiced about the large number of fatal or serious accidents involving cyclists on Britain's roads. The Department of Transport has persisted in viewing the problem as one of cyclists' behaviour rather than that of motorists' driving or of the design of roads. Thus the emphasis has been placed upon encouraging cyclists to wear bright coloured clothing or crash helmets, rather than upon curbing speeding motorists, educating motorists as to the vulnerability of cyclists or designing junctions and roundabouts which take into account the needs of cyclists.

From time to time the prevailing framework of policy within an organisation may change as a result of a political impetus, the impact of new fashions in ideas, or some scandal or major event. In the late 1970s and the 1980s the Treasury's neo-Keynesian framework was undermined by the impact of monetarist ideas and the desire of New Right politicians to change economic policy-making radically. But from the organisational process perspective such shifts in frameworks are usually painful. The student of organisational processes will emphasise the inherently conservative outlook implicit in organisations. It is almost invariably easier to carry on following existing patterns of behaviour than to work out new ones.

Allison's organisational process model also places a good deal of emphasis upon the implementation stage of policy-making. Politicians or senior officials may take a policy decision but the actual content of that policy will be refracted by the administrative mechanisms available to carry it out. Many examples may be cited of incoming governments' policy aspirations coming to nothing because of the failure to provide adequate administrative machineries for their implementation. A particularly well-documented case is the failure after 1964 of the incoming Labour Government's Land Commission. The idea here was to prevent speculation in land prices, by setting up a new government department with powers to buy up land. However, as Richard Crossman showed in his diaries, the whole basis of the new ministry was undermined by the strenuous and successful struggles of his own Ministry of Housing and Local Government to retain powers over land planning.[19] The whole policy of controlling land prices as a result was a colossal failure. Another example from the same period was the failure of the much-vaunted Department of Economic Affairs to make much headway, given the Treasury's control over so much of the implementation of policy.

Social policy, which usually affects large numbers of citizens, involves many government employees and depends upon vast and complicated administrative machinery, is particularly susceptible to difficulties in the implementation process. Two examples may be given. After the Second World War a comprehensive new system of social security was established designed to sweep away the old Poor Law, but many years later vestiges of Poor Law practices could be found retained in the system of social security. Again the establishment of the National Health Service (NHS) was, amongst other things, intended to provide for a rational system of resource-allocation to all those in need. But for the first 30 years of its existence the NHS failed to develop any explicit principles for resource-allocation to regional health authorities. The rhetoric of policy in these cases soon came to be at odds with administrative practice which was determined by the standard operating procedures.

The organisational process model therefore stresses the multifarious nature of the decision-making process. Rather than being a central directing force, government is made up of a network of different organisations. Each will tend to have its own set of procedures and values. Although there may well be hierarchical relationships among the organisations, they will all tend to have their own way of doing things, their own standard operating procedures.

BUREAUCRATIC POLITICS MODEL

Allison's other model of the decision-making process which he gleaned from the Cuban Missile Crisis, the bureaucratic politics model, shares a great deal in common with the previous perspective. Indeed later Allison attempted to merge the two. However, although both share a recognition that bureaucracies are of key importance, the emphasis is shifted considerably. According to the bureaucratic politics model, policy emerges not as a rational choice by a central actor but as a result of bargaining between key personnel in the policy-making process. These individuals represent different bureaucracies within the government structure and propose or oppose various policies in terms of their own bureaucracy's interests or their own personal career prospects. Government is thus composed of a myriad of competing groups, each seeking to promote its own interest and to defend its own patch. Policy may thus emerge as the preferred option of one or more groups in the governmental structure who happen to be powerful at a particular time or with regard to a specific issue; or, more commonly, it may be the result of a compromise between various proposals. Clearly such a perspective ill fits the rational actor model since it cuts across the central assumptions of that model.

Applying this perspective to British politics, it is easy to find many examples of inter-departmental tensions and conflicts which derive from competing bureaucratic interests. They feature frequently in the Crossman and the Castle diaries, those authoritative insider accounts of decision-making at the top. Mrs Castle reflected how she expected, when entering the Cabinet, to engage upon a seminar on how to carry out the policy and manifesto of her party; instead she found herself facing a collection of 'departmental enemies'.[20] Crossman again and again lamented how he was unable to take a broad view of government policy but was over-preoccupied with concerns of his own department.

The bureaucratic politics model in general ascribes a higher degree of influence and power to the Civil Service and official advisers than, for example, the rational actor approach to decision-making. But it would be an over-simplification to read it in terms of bureaucrats controlling political leaders. Of course it is possible to find many examples of elected politicians becoming mere stooges of their official advisers when they achieve office; but the bureaucratic politics model is more subtle than this. It is not so much a question of politicians being outmanoeuvred or 'going native' as of having a natural tendency to fight their corner. The celebrated aphorism 'where you stand depends on where you sit' captures this well. In government it comes naturally to a politician or official to promote the interests or put forward the views of the organisation to which he or she belongs. In British political history it is easy to find examples of politicians who completely change their views on an issue after being reshuffled. It will be apparent that the bureaucratic politics model greatly plays down the importance of ideas or ideology as contributory factors in decision-taking. Such motivating forces are seen as very much subordinate to concrete sectional interests or to considerations of prestige or institutional self-aggrandisement.

The bureaucratic politics and organisational process models have themselves been the subjects of considerable criticism. It has been pointed out that they can only be of importance to the extent that governmental structures are bureaucratic – which is not invariably the case – and that the role of organisational procedures in altering policy is a function of the leadership's attention to the impact of that policy. Bureaucratic and organisational explanations may be more powerful in accounting for certain types of policy-making, namely those specifically involving inter-bureaucratic conflict and those middle- and low-level governmental decisions which involve routine and well-understood rules.[21] Critics have also pointed to the tendency inherent in the bureaucratic model to over-concentrate on the micro level, or on the specifics of particular decisions, so that the wider framework of policy-making tends to be ignored; for example the influence of powerful external pressure groups in directly or even indirectly influencing the decision-makers, or the ideological parameters which rule certain policy options off the political agenda. By concentrating upon how specific decisions are taken – upon what actually happens – the bureaucratic politics model, like the rational actor model, ignores the lessons to be learnt from the decisions which do not reach the governmental agenda. We shall return to this point later. The merit of the bureaucratic politics model is that it recognises the fragmentary character of any government with its host of competing interests. It is, however, a model which needs refinement. Bill Jenkins and Andrew Gray suggest that it is too facile to see actors' behaviour as solely determined by the position they happen to hold. In any bureaucratic organisation the common interests and values it exemplifies will be limited by extrinsic differences of value, interest and perspective which 'arise from the divergent backgrounds and developments of individuals and groups'. Such extrinsic differences run alongside the intrinsic differences which will be generated within a bureaucracy by such factors as the division of labour, prescribed rule-bound behaviour and hierarchical patterns of authority generated from within government organisation itself. Complete explanations of how bureaucracies operate must take both extrinsic and intrinsic factors into account.[22]

IDEOLOGY AND PERCEPTION IN THE DECISION-MAKING PROCESS

Organisational and bureaucratic models focus on the actual business of decision-making, something which rational and incrementalist models leave out. But as we have seen, to concentrate exclusively on the policy process also omits key elements, in particular the ideology and perceptions of those involved. Decision theorists have pointed out the importance of the world images and general perceptions held by those involved in decision-making. The clearest statement of this argument is to be found in Kenneth Boulding's book *The Image*.[23] Boulding claims that individuals need intellectual mechanisms to filter the data that they are faced with in order to make any decision. The sheer volume of information facing a British cabinet minister is well attested to by the insider accounts of Crossman and others. Some of the filtering will be institutional and bureaucratic in nature, the function of 'gatekeepers' in government, who protect their seniors from being submerged by the clamour of supplicants for attention.

However, Boulding's most powerful point is that information cannot be selected randomly; rather it is selected according to the existing notion of the world held by the individual and his or her advisers. Information which challenges the prevailing image of the world is less likely to be accepted than that which supports it. Thus decision-makers, in formulating policy, will evaluate the information facing them according to a well-defined image of the issue, although this is usually a subconscious process. Given that the image consists of perceptions of fact and value, it constitutes a very powerful filter, which may fundamentally affect the ways in which policy-makers sift the evidence. Hence, for example, it is common to find policy-makers who hold a particular policy goal to be of vital importance ignoring evidence or data which suggests that that policy is not working or is having adverse consequences or unintended side-effects. Boulding's theory stresses that political choices are made according to the political and social values of those making the decisions. Such an emphasis undermines the rational decision-making approach which sees the outputs of policy emerging after a comprehensive weighing-up of all the inputs. But it is equally subversive of bureaucratic theories of decision-making which are inspired by incrementalist ideas. These latter can, as we have seen, dangerously undervalue or ignore the values of decision-makers which are extrinsic to the bureaucratic organisations.

Work on the psychological basis of policy-making also indicates how policy-makers may, because of the images they hold, fundamentally misperceive the issues involved; this misperception is then fed directly into the policy-making process. In a compendious survey of the causes of misperception, Robert Jervis shows the impact of belief systems and images on policy-making. Central to his argument is the impact of ethnocentrism, the tendency to make assumptions about the targets of policy on the basis of beliefs held by the group making the decision. In other words policy-makers, both individually and as a group, may consistently misperceive the information they receive. They may regularly make unsupported assumptions about the likely impact of past and future decisions on groups in society, and may often impute to the demands and behaviour of groups within that society motivations and desires that those groups do not possess.[24] The Gulf crisis of 1990–1 offers an interesting illustration of how conflicting perceptions on the part of protagonists can colour their behaviour. The Americans perceived Saddam Hussein almost exclusively in terms of a second Hitler, a power-crazed dictator keen to gobble up one state after another, for whom the appropriate treatment was military intervention: the lessons drawn upon were therefore those of appeasement in the 1930s. The Iraqi leadership by contrast had a view of the world deeply influenced by Ba'athist ideas of pan-Arab struggle and nationalist liberation from élitist Western stooges. A reading of history was adopted which perceived the Western powers as responsible for so-called artificial political divisions within the Arab world and for colonialist policies which apparently maintained the state of Israel.

It is no accident that much of the work on perceptions and misperceptions has tended to stem from the field of international relations where the scope for such clashes is far greater. Irving Janis, in his book *Victims of Groupthink*, produced an interesting application of psychological explanations of policy-making to the decision-making process. Janis argued that the outcome of the policy-making process can often be explained by the phenomenon of what he termed 'groupthink'. This related to the desire among policy-makers to maintain an *esprit de corps* and an amiability in the policy-making group; this in turn resulted in an unwillingness to voice doubts and reservations as to the wisdom of certain policy options if these seemed to be enthusiastically endorsed by the rest of the group. Strong pressures for conformity would emerge simply because each individual would want to remain part of the group, for psychological as well as professional and career reasons. The result, moreover, was that the policy-making group emerged as an 'in-group' with a clear coherence based on an unquestioned moral and ethical superiority to those outside the group.[25]

Few, if any, attempts have been made to apply Janis' idea to domestic politics, part of the problem perhaps being that empirical evidence is hard to come by or to assess. There is some anecdotal evidence, however, of the difficulty which members of a Cabinet have sometimes felt in raising doubts about a policy especially if enthusiastically endorsed by a leading cadre. However, it may be hard to separate the groupthink factor from more purely institutional factors, such as the power of the Prime Minister to manipulate the agenda or the difficulty of ministers speaking outside their departmental remit. However, anyone who has experienced committee membership at any level will almost certainly be able to bear witness to the existence of groupthink, however trivial in nature.

IMPLEMENTATION, NON-DECISIONS AND POWER

The ideological framework may be an important constraint or contributing factor to decision-making. Many writers have stressed that the question of belief systems is also intimately related to the broader issue of power. As we have said, one of the weaknesses of the simple rational model of decision-making is its failure adequately to take account of the way the implementation of policy-decisions feeds back into the decision-making process. Policy analysts who tend to concentrate on the way in which choices are made may ignore the critical issue of the problems of implementing these choices. Policy-making, however, must also take account of the difficulties of actually implementing policies upon which decision-makers may have decided. Clearly, this issue is central to any explanation of the relationship between governmental activity and society. This has been excellently illustrated in Pressman and Wildavsky's book *Implementation*.[26] The authors show how a policy, in this case urban renewal in Oakland, can be significantly affected at the implementation stage. In this case the particular policy was uncontentious at the decision-making stage, being agreed upon as desirable and necessary by all those involved in the policy-making process. Yet, once made, the decision was never properly implemented. The authors cite a variety of reasons in explanation but their key general conclusion is that in examining the link between policy-making and society, it cannot be assumed that implementation will follow as a natural and logical consequence of decision-making. The implication of this is that merely to concentrate upon the ways in which a decision is arrived at is to run the danger of omitting the actual link between government and society, namely the implementation or non-implementation of that policy.

Another key factor which relates to this link between politics and society is the issue of power. Accounts of policy-making necessarily focus upon observable conflict and debate. It has been forcefully argued that this focus is at best a partial one and at worst misleading. This has been widely discussed in the debates over community power structures. Pluralists, like Robert Dahl, argued that it was possible to assess the concentration of power in a community by observing who wins in decision-making conflicts.[27] His explanation that power was shared by groups in society has indeed been challenged, but the salient criticism here is that his method distorted his findings. In other words, it can be argued that to focus on who wins in policy-making is to miss out the critical processes by which the agenda is set, the aspirations of the competing parties are shaped, and the resources available to the various interests are determined.

A major critique of pluralist accounts of power is contained in two articles by Bachrach and Baratz.[28] They argue that focusing on observable conflict omits consideration of the role of power in preventing issues coming onto the agenda. Because policy-making can, naturally, focus only on those issues and options discussed by decision-makers, it cannot cope with the whole range of political issues which the same decision-makers do not wish to deal with. This relates to our earlier discussion of the role of images and values. There is clear evidence that, because of shared belief-systems and values, decision-makers will not make policy over certain issues; therefore policy-making has to be seen as one area only of political activity. The failure of politicians to take up an issue or to act on something may have a major impact upon society. In this sense a concentration on decision-making is significantly limited by a number of assumptions: first that it is only by making policy that politicians affect society and, secondly, that their interests only extend to those areas where they take decisions. Policy-making thus only presents one side of the coin. Against this, however, it may be argued that a policy-making approach is very useful in explaining the actual behaviour of government and, indeed, is an essential component of any account of how politics and government work. It may not cover the whole range of the exercise of power in a society, but, because it is so obviously a central part of governmental activity, and because it is far more amenable to analysis than any conception of non-decision making, it must rank very highly in any discussion of politics.

The debate is taken a stage further by Steven Lukes in his discussion of power.[29] Lukes notes that, in addition to those limitations inherent in concentrating upon the observable conflicts, there are also other limitations in the view of power put forward by Bachrach and Baratz. He argues that political activity is not only limited to exercises of either observable conflict or non-decision making. There is in addition a third dimension of power, one whereby the very nature of society mobilises bias in such a way as to prevent observable conflict arising in the policy-making process. This view implies that even if no one prevents an issue appearing on the agenda, and even if there is no non-decision, there may still be a conflict of real interests between those in power and sections of society; thus conflict remains latent, that is to say, it exists objectively but is hidden, maybe even from the individuals concerned, by the operations of social forces and institutional practices. These forces and practices operate to prevent individuals and groups not merely from raising grievances, (in which case either of the first two perspectives would account for their fate) but even from feeling them. Their perceptions and beliefs are shaped by society to such an extent that they remain unaware of their real interests.

Discussion of such points moves this survey far away from its starting point. A central consideration here, however, is not that a discussion of decision-taking is negated by these considerations, but that it should be seen within this context. Clearly, any discussion of the role of power in politics has to cope with the various uses made of it and the forms it may take. We do not pretend that the case-studies presented in this book are total explanations of the political activity subsumed in each issue area; what is claimed is that they focus on what remains the central issue of political activity, namely the formulation and implementation of policy.

SABATIER'S MODEL OF POLICY CHANGE

So far we have examined a range of theories. Some, such as the rational actor theory or that of disjointed incrementalism have concentrated upon the nature of decisions in the abstract; others such as Janis' concept of groupthink have been more concerned with specific aspects of the policy process. Others have been concerned with broad questions of ideology and power in society. Obviously some theories are more mutually compatible than others: for example the concept of bureaucratic politics fits the more general idea of disjointed incrementalism better than the idea of rational synoptic decision-making. However, it is wrong to see all the theories as rivals, since they are sometimes attempting to explain different things. All the theories we have examined are general in character and tend to tell us little about the operation of any particular political system. They tend also not to concentrate very much upon explaining change in politics (although Vickers is concerned with this at an abstract level). It may be useful to conclude by looking at one example of a recent, general model of policy-making, rooted in empirical research, which focuses on policy change. The model is advanced by the US political scientist, Paul Sabatier.

There has sometimes been a tendency for those explanations of policy-making revolving around belief systems and those rooted in bureaucratic or institutional explanation to talk past each other. Sabatier has attempted to create a comprehensive model of the policy process which integrates traditional concerns with political resources and interests on the one hand, with concerns for the role of knowledge, policy information and values on the other hand. His model is based upon research into air-pollution policies in the United States, but it is intended for broader application. Although it is rooted in a study of American politics, it is particularly interesting from our point of view because it draws upon so many of the abstract ideas which we have touched upon.[30] Sabatier complains that political scientists 'have traditionally perceived policy change as primarily the product of a power struggle among groups with different resources and values/interests operating within a given regime structure and a changing socio-economic environment'.[31]

Too often it was assumed that actors were motivated by short-term interests and that policy-making emerged out of short-lived coalitions of interest. He believes this dangerously underplays the role of ideas in the political process.

In contrast to those approaches which see the key focuses of policy-formation in institutional terms, for example administrative agencies, legislative committees and interest groups (the famous 'iron triangles' of American political science), Sabatier has developed the idea of a 'policy subsystem'. Policy subsystems comprise the above groups, but should also be seen to include journalists, researchers, academics and policy analysts; indeed such people played a vital role in 'the generation, dissemination, and evaluation of policy ideas'.[32] The very fluidity of these subsystems, he believes, reflects realistically the actual world of policy-making where individuals rapidly move from one position to another as a matter of course.

Within the various policy subsystems Sabatier posits the existence at any time of various competing advocacy coalitions. Such coalitions comprise collections of people, who share a common set of beliefs but who might be scattered around a variety of organisations. In addition to these advocacy coalitions may be found a number of policy brokers, generally those who have a vested interest in minimising conflict for the sake of political or administrative convenience.

Sabatier believes this concept of advocacy coalitions has several strengths. It recognises that individuals move frequently from one organisation to another; it accommodates the fact that there is often 'huge variation in behaviour among individuals within the same institution'[33]; and above all it provides a better framework for analysing the dynamics of actual change in policy over a period, an aspect of policy-making which institutionally-based explanations find difficult to account for. It is indeed this dynamic aspect of the policy process which Sabatier finds most interesting and regards as most important.

Advocacy coalitions act within a given ideological framework, or way of looking at the world. They aim to have this framework adopted when policy is defined. They seek to convert others to their particular perspective. Drawing upon the work of writers on belief systems Sabatier suggests it is possible to conceive of three layers of belief which members of an advocacy coalition will share:

1 Deep core beliefs (e.g. fundamental ideas about human nature or religion).
2 Basic political values or strategies relating to a policy area.
3 Applications of policy in specific areas.

It will be far easier to effect changes in the third level than in the second; the first level of fundamental beliefs, however, will be extremely resistant to change. Sabatier also assumes that public policy may be conceptualised in the same manner as individuals' belief-systems.

In his analysis of the dynamics of the policy process Sabatier maintains that the actors in a policy subsystem will be constrained by two exogenous factors. The first comprises such relatively stable parameters as the distribution of natural resources, the nature of the problem area, the social structure, fundamental cultural values, and the basic constitutional structure. These tend to change only rarely or slowly. Secondly, there are the more dynamic factors which tend to change more quickly or more often. These include, for example, changes in economic or social conditions, technological innovations, changes in politics (i.e. in the governing coalitions), the impact of changes from other policy subsystems and the feedback from earlier policy decisions within the subsystem.

Such are the constraints and resources which affect the policy subsystem within which the advocacy coalitions operate. How does Sabatier explain the dynamics of policy-change and the role of decision-makers? Here he develops Hugh Heclo's ideas of 'social learning'.[34] As well as being the product of exogenous factors of change, policy development must be seen as due to the interaction and gradual learning of small groups of specialists within a particular policy area. Sabatier draws upon the work of Carole Weiss concerning the 'enlightenment function' of research. Policy-makers judge social research through their own construction of reality; élites will filter evidence to fit their beliefs and will be reluctant to abandon assumptions in the face of empirical evidence. These are ideas which, as we have seen, are shared with Jervis and Janis. However, Weiss maintained that this was not the end of the story. In a study of the responses of 155 decision-makers in the field of mental health in the United States, Weiss and Michael Bucuvalas found that empirical research did not merely serve a purely practical or applied purpose. It filtered into the policy-makers' field of reference in many ways. By offering ideas and concepts for making sense of experience it could gradually alter or enlighten the decision-makers' views. The perspectives of whole agencies or groups of policy-makers could be affected over time by the cumulative effects of research work.[35]

Drawing all these threads together, Sabatier constructs the following model of the policy-making process (see Figure 1). In any policy subsystem there will be a small number of competing advocacy coalitions. On major controversies within a policy subsystem, where core beliefs are concerned, the line-up of allies and opponents will be relatively stable over periods of a decade or so. There will be a greater consensus among the actors in an advocacy coalition on issues pertaining to the policy core than to the application of the policy (the third level of the belief-system); weaknesses in these secondary aspects of the policy system will be acknowledged more easily than those in the policy core. The various policy élites within the advocacy coalitions will seek to understand the world better in order to identify means to achieve their more fundamental objectives. They will search to improve the techniques for applying their ideas.

Policy brokers will be responsible for mediating between the advocacy coalitions and for the detailed implementation of decision-making, but there will normally be a dominant advocacy coalition in any policy subsystem. Moreover, the core attributes of a governmental programme are unlikely to be significantly revised so long as the advocacy coalition that instituted that programme remains in power. It will generally be external forces – either from the stable or the dynamic quarters – which will drastically weaken core beliefs or which will lead to the undermining and downfall of an advocacy coalition. The role of minority advocacy coalitions within the subsystem is not, however, a negligible one. They will have opportunities to influence the secondary levels of policy, as opposed to the core. Such minority coalitions too will have every incentive to improve their relative resources and to 'outlearn' their adversaries. It may be that the policy-learning that goes on will provide opportunities for a minority coalition to bring about substantial changes in the secondary aspects or even undermining the credibility of the core programme supported by the dominant coalition: 'In a world of scarce resources,

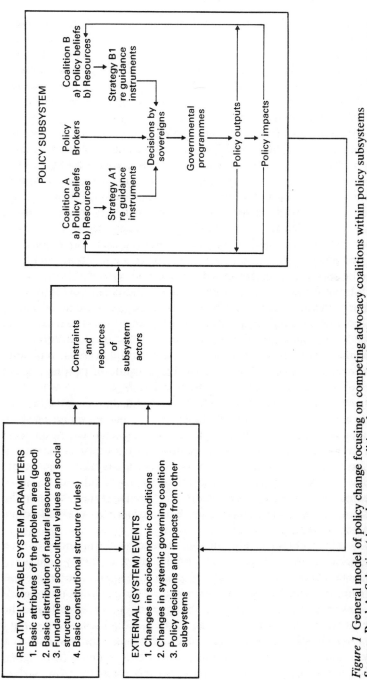

Figure 1 General model of policy change focusing on competing advocacy coalitions within policy subsystems
Source: Paul A. Sabatier 'An advocacy coalition framework of policy change and the role of policy-oriented learning therein',
Policy Sciences, 1988, vol. 21, p. 132.

those who do not learn are at a competitive disadvantage in realising their goals'.[36]

Policy-orientated learning occurs both within belief-systems and between rival belief-systems: 'The former is relatively unproblematic: members of an advocacy coalition are always seeking to improve their understanding of variable states and causal relationships which are consistent with their policy core'.[37]

Competing advocacy coalitions rooted in different belief-systems, by contrast, will tend to indulge in a dialogue of the deaf, especially when they engage in frontal assaults upon each other's core positions. However, there may be opportunity for learning across coalitions at an intermediate level of informed debate. Such learning will also take place most fruitfully in forums which are relatively free of political content and which are dominated by professional norms.

Several general qualifications may be made of Sabatier's model. In the first place, as he himself recognises, the concept of policy-learning may be most appropriate in a technical and scientific arena where performance indicators are quantitative rather than qualitative and where professionals in rival advocacy coalitions may the more readily find common ground for debate. It is significant that his own examples come from areas such as the debate over air pollution in California and deregulation of US air fares. It may be less fruitful in areas dominated by the social sciences, for example, the question of poverty, where controlled scientific experimentation is less feasible and where the subjects of research can get up, move about and themselves start participating in policy strategies. Again, the model would seem to be more appropriate to limited policy subsystems whose boundaries can be fairly narrowly and clearly drawn – for example control of pollution, transport – and less so to broader areas such as economic policy or foreign policy. These latter will be likely to be more affected by sudden outside events and circumstances, so that the decision-maker may be less of a strategist and more concerned simply to react to events.

Another problem facing Sabatier is that his terminology can be somewhat vague and imprecise. The fluidity of advocacy coalitions, although advantageous in some respects, can also make definitions difficult. It is hard to see how it is empirically easier to identify belief-systems than interests. Moreover, Sabatier pays little attention to the role of the policy brokers. As he himself recognises, these cannot always be distinguished from policy advocates: the distinction is a continuum – 'many brokers will have some policy bent, while advocates may show some serious concern with system maintenance'.[38] Again empirical definition is scarcely likely to be easy or disciplined and there is always the danger of tautology. Sabatier's concentration upon the long time-span and the importance of ideas may be a corrective to over-institutional analysis, but it may be in danger of ignoring actual decision-making at the expense of broad policy change. Some would challenge his assertion that 'it is shared beliefs that provide the principal "glue", of politics'[39], on the grounds that it dangerously downgrades such haphazard forces as self-interest, envy, incompetence and the desire for power. Finally, it may be that Sabatier's ideas are more suited to a decentralised political system than a centralised one, and to a consensual political tradition than to an adversarial one. In which case they may fit Great Britain less easily than countries such as the United States or Sweden.

CONCLUSION

We have outlined Sabatier's model at some length partly because it succeeds in drawing together so many of the theories we have already examined and partly because it has not yet become familiar in any of the textbooks on British politics. It is also significant in that it rescues elements of rationality in the decision-making process. Sabatier is well aware of all the pitfalls which surround the crude version of the rational synoptic model: the diffusion of power centres, the competing of bureaucratic agencies, the incremental nature of much politics, the difficulty of separating policy-making from implementation, the filtering effect of belief-systems and so on. But at the end of the day he suggests that his model of competing advocacy coalitions and policy learning places some sort of premium on rational analysis. Information and policy analysis is seen as important for a variety of reasons. It is perceived threats to core values or interests of decision-makers which motivate them to expend scarce resources in policy debates. Information and rational analysis alerts people, including potential allies, to the extent to which a given situation or development may advantage or disadvantage their position. Analysis can then further be used in an advocacy fashion to justify and elaborate the position of actors in the policy process. Finally, it is rare in a pluralist political system to find actors in a position to exercise raw power; they will find it advantageous to engage in analytical debate in order to convince other actors of the soundness of their position with regard to a particular problem. In summary, Sabatier concludes that:

Despite the partisan nature of most analytical debates and the cognitive limits on rationality – actors' desires to realize core values in a world of limited resources provide strong incentives to learn more about the magnitude of salient problems, the factors affecting them and the consequences of policy alternatives.[40]

Whether or not we accept the precise claims and formulations of Sabatier's theory, we ought to recognise the value of his general approach. His analysis builds on the different insights into decision-making that we have set out in this chapter. The appeal of the rational actor model is tempered with a recognition of both its lack of empirical foundation and its theoretical narrowness. At the same time, the determinism of bureaucratic or organisational models is qualified by acknowledgement of the political importance of both ideology and information.

Neither Sabatier's theory nor any general theory of decision-making can be so precise as to account for behaviour in all political systems. General theories of decision-making must be intertwined with theories about the particular operation of specific political systems. It is this level of theoretical analysis to which we now turn. What theories are used to account for decisions within the British political system?

3 Models of British politics

INTRODUCTION

In the preceding chapter we considered some general theories of decision-making. These were concerned with the behaviour of decision-makers in the abstract. In this chapter we continue to examine some theoretical approaches to the decision-making process, but our emphasis is now upon the models which relate directly to decision-making in British politics. These theories attempt to shed light into the 'black box' of the decision process. Naturally, we are only able here to give somewhat simplified or truncated versions of the models.[1] Our aim is to delineate the variety of perspectives from which the British political system can be viewed rather than to examine the detailed debates which have taken place among the adherents of the various schools.

DEMOCRATIC SOVEREIGNTY MODEL

Western democracies are based upon the assumption that citizens have the ultimate say in how they are governed and what decisions are taken in their name. The mechanisms for the translation of popular will into legislation and policy-making will differ from one political system to another, but direct plebiscitary devices are rare. The institutions of representative democracy are seen as both the most practical and the most desirable methods of giving effect to the popular will. Elected representatives at various levels of government are seen as having the role of enacting the people's will. A select group among them are chosen to exercise leadership which will involve steering the ship of state to the chosen destination with suitable deviations to avoid the various shoals, currents and storms which history will raise along the way.

Such is the conventional view of the British political system. It has been especially influential in Britain because of the constitutional importance of Parliament. Unlike most other Western democracies there were only conventional and not constitutional restraints upon Parliament's power. Parliamentary sovereignty was indivisible and Parliament was the sole law-giving body. The classic constitutional statement was put forward by Dicey in 1885: this stressed the centrality of a representative parliament accountable to the people and to public opinion, with the executive and judicial arms of the state subordinate to it.[2] Dicey's work is still widely viewed in the academic study of law as the definitive description of the British Constitution. This 'liberal' view of the constitution is, of course, a normative more than a descriptive view. It had developed in the early and mid-nineteenth century as a vision of how a liberal political system should be constructed and as a contrast to the aristocratic government of the day. As A. H. Birch has pointed out, the liberal model of the British constitution never wholly succeeded in displacing a rival interpretation, the Whitehall model. This latter emphasised quite a different set of values: the power and authority of the Crown, the need for government to be responsible and its duty to provide good and effective administration.[3]

As a realistic description of the policy-making process the liberal democratic sovereignty model is shot full of so many gaping holes that it is unnecessary to spend much time in criticism. For a brief period between the Reform Acts of 1867 and 1885, (ironically when the democratic franchise was extremely limited), the model bore some semblance to political reality. Then both Parliament and municipal councils initiated many social reforms and MPs exercised some control over the formation of ministries and had a voice, albeit restricted, on some of the important decisions of foreign policy. However, the democratic sovereignty model finds it hard, if not impossible, to come to terms with most of the political developments in Britain since 1880, namely: the rise of well-disciplined parties; the increasing influence of the bureaucracy; the growth of government; the tendency towards delegated legislation; the mushrooming of interest groups; and the increasing technical expertise necessary for government. These are factors which affect all Western democracies, but it could be argued that Britain has fewer opportunities for the exercise of democratic rights than most – certainly fewer in comparison with the United States, Germany or Sweden. One only has to point to the decline of local government, the absence of federalism or checks and balances and the weakness of mechanisms both for popular participation and for rendering administration accountable. At a more general level the idea that the populace is knowledgeable about or interested in politics or that it behaves along rational lines was exploded immediately political scientists began to research public opinion.

Parliament does, of course, retain vestigial exclusive rights over a limited range of policy areas, such as abortion or capital punishment. These issues are seen as matters of conscience, rather than of party or ideology, where policy is largely determined by legislation. Parliament continues to play a major role in the political system; but to concede this is not to endorse the democratic sovereignty model. Parliament is seen by most political scientists as one actor in decision-making, rather than as playing any leading role. The extent of its power and influence will vary according to the type of issue and the political circumstances of the day. It is possible that some measures of radical constitutional reform might in the future render the democratic sovereignty model marginally more realistic, but many of the general qualifications we have made would still cast doubts upon its explanatory capacities. In any case the tendency towards the growth of supranational centres of decision-making in the context of Europe is likely to render the model even less realistic.

The democratic sovereignty model does allow some degree of modification. It can be seen to allow the aspirations and pressures of the citizens to penetrate into the world of the political élites. It is possible to build pressure groups, political parties, accountable government departments and various non-elected government agencies into the model. However, such attempts remind one of the desperate efforts of the Ptolemaic astronomers to incorporate into their system ever more complicated epicycles in order to meet the awkward findings of empirical research rather than to surrender their entire model.

The democratic sovereignty model would scarcely seem to merit any consideration were it not for a paradox. Despite its empirical weakness, it retains an exceptionally potent hold upon the minds of the practitioners of politics. Politicians at whatever level almost invariably present themselves as the servants of the public charged with translating popular wishes into decision-making. Unelected officials, in public at any rate, also appear generally happy with this picture and it is one with which the media is most at home. Reforms in the political process also tend to be couched in terms of this model. Thus moves for electoral reform are supported in order to achieve a fairer representation of the electorate's views. In short the model provides the dominant language of political discourse. Most citizens feel that this is broadly speaking how the policy-making process should operate, and this in turn provides a powerful incentive for political actors at least to go through the motions of following its precepts.

THE PARTY GOVERNMENT MODEL

The model of government by competing political parties developed historically out of and within the democratic sovereignty model and indeed may be largely seen as an adaptation of it. The advent of the mass franchise in the 1880s witnessed the rise of the party machine. Democratically-organised political parties sought to bundle up the policy aspirations of their supporters into coherent manifestos for government action across the board which, once the party had captured power, would be implemented into legislation. The party faithful in the country would monitor the progress of the party leadership and call them to account for any backsliding. Such was the philosophy of the National Liberal Federation in the 1870s and 1880s. An essentially similar view of the political process was adopted by the early Labour Party, although here the coherence of party was cemented by the concept of class solidarity.[4] This is always a view of the political process that has appealed more to the radical left than to the conservative centre or right. Labour Party leaders such as MacDonald and Attlee strongly and successfully resisted any such attempts by the Party rank and file to dictate to them, but this vision of 'intra-party democracy' has remained powerful. In the early 1980s it came to the fore in reaction to the disappointments of the 1974–9 Labour Governments. Moves were then made to introduce constitutional devices to strengthen the influence of the grass-roots activists, efforts which were thwarted in the late 1980s under Neil Kinnock.

As a vision of the policy-making process this version shares many of the deficiencies of the simple democratic sovereignty model: overemphasis upon both the rationality and the commitment of the electorate; underplaying of the influences of bureaucracies and pressure groups; and an overemphasis upon the role of legislation as a key determinant in the policy-making process. It is, however, possible to make out a much stronger empirical case for supporting the model's emphasis upon political parties as key actors in decision-making. In this respect, moreover, the importance of parties can rest independently of the normative elements of democratic theory which gave rise to the model. Let us put this more simply. In the mid-twentieth century democratic theorists put forward a model of the democratic process in which the electorate played a less noble or heroic role. The most important theorist here was Schumpeter who applied an economic analogy. The electorate was pictured more passively as a consumer of politics and policies. It was the competing political parties which presented the electors with different policy options in broadly the same way as firms offered rival products to the consumers.[5]

It is not necessary to adopt a view of democracy which sees policies being projected from below, from the party rank and file, in order to accept that parties are an important factor in the policy-making process. The British political system is characterised by an exceptionally adversarial style in which party competition is ascribed pride of place. The tradition of government and opposition and the conduct of the House of Commons emphasise this, but it is also reinforced by the existence of a strong two-party system and the centralised nature of the polity. In Britain, political parties also dominate local government. Striking contrasts may be drawn here between Britain and other Western democracies, notably the United States and Germany. In Britain, political parties are presented as essentially vehicles for the formulation, development and transmission of policies.

It is at elections that the claims of the party government model tend to be especially dominant. A more restrained version of the party government model is generally adopted by academic political scientists and indeed probably by most thinking politicians when away from the mind-numbing excitements of the hustings. According to this view political parties are one of many inputs into the decision-making process, the chief others being: pressure groups of various kinds; the Civil Service or other bureaucracies; other agencies of governments; direct public opinion; foreign governments and international and supranational bodies. Policy-making may be seen in a series of stages: policy germination – policy formulation – decision making – policy execution – and policy fulfilment. Different forces will come into play at different levels and different policy areas may show different patterns. Political parties, however, are ascribed key roles simply because they are adept at operating in the various institutional frameworks and because in a democratic system it is generally the case that the key decisions will be made by members of the political élite. Nigel Forman, himself both a politician and a political scientist, presents this view very clearly.[6]

According to this perspective parties can effect the germination of politics by their presence in the country at large (although the Civil Service also plays a key role at this stage). Policy formulation consists of the translation of germinal ideas into coherent programmes and here again political parties play a key role. At the decision-making stage parties are present in the guise of the ministers who take part in Cabinet or the Cabinet system. Legislation and the monitoring of legislation offer parties ample scope for influence in the Parliamentary forum. Clearly, there will be some areas where party influence is weaker than others but they are generally key actors in the decision-making process. It is held to be impossible to make sense of British politics without an appreciation of the workings and nature of British political parties.

THE ADVERSARIAL POLITICS MODEL

The style of British political debate is particularly adversarial, graphically illustrated by the seating arrangements in Parliament. Added to this is the fact that historically the two main competing parties have represented very different interests in society and presented contrasting policy programmes on a range of economic and social issues. Such considerations led several commentators in the 1960s and 1970s to develop an extreme variant of the party government model, the 'adversary politics model'. The thinking here was that British politics was particularly marked by discontinuities in policy-making resulting from the alternation of politically different governments. Thus, for example, industries like steel – nationalised by Labour, then denationalised by the Conservatives – became political footballs at the mercy of the electoral process; similarly areas of social policy, such as pensions, which required long-term planning, suffered from inconsistencies of policy. S. E. Finer was the foremost exponent of the adversarial politics view.[7] It was an ideologically committed view since such writers perceived this adversarial system to be one of the key factors engendering Britain's decline. Its exponents advocated a series of reforms such as proportional representation and decentralisation in order to reverse these tendencies. Such views came to be enshrined in the electoral programme of the centre parties in the 1980s.[8]

For our purposes the adversarial politics interpretation represents an extreme example of the application of the party government model. It argues that the actors in British politics are the parties. It further contends that in such circumstances the one factor affecting party behaviour is the activity of opponents. Parties simply devise policies, not on the basis of what is in the public interest, but rather to oppose their rivals. Not only does the model assume parties have clear cut views on policy areas but that they can also crystalise these views into coherent policy programmes; and that these are implemented and the consequences are apparent in society at large and to the electorate in particular. Finer and the 'adversarial politics' school took a gloomy view of such a process; but it is, of course, possible to see it through altogether more rosy spectacles. This after all is the view taken by most political leaders in the two major parties. At elections the distinctiveness of their approaches along with their confidence in their ability to govern better than their opponents is trumpeted on every advertising hoarding and in every party political broadcast. A disciplined party, a firm majority and a clear mandate are seen as key ingredients in successful policy-making.

Many political scientists have cast doubts upon the empirical validity of these interpretations. Gamble and Walkland, for example, studied a range of economic policies over the last decades and concluded that policy shifts did not correspond in any way with the alternation of parties in office; quite the reverse, the most dramatic changes tended to occur mid-term. If this was true in an area of traditionally high political salience, it was likely to be all the more so in other areas where party conflict was less marked, for example foreign policy or technical and scientific policies.[9]

Another school of writers in the 1970s took a rather different view of the adversarial political process. In their opinion political parties were the victims as much as the manipulators of the democratic process. Parties were forced to engage in a series of competitive bids in order to maximise their electoral support. This in turn led them to become dependent upon a series of powerful groups and interests within society. This form of coalition building led to incoherencies or inconsistencies in policy. Anthony King saw this as leading to 'overload', governments becoming overcommitted with responsibilities which it was difficult for them to deliver.[10] Samuel Beer saw the process as one of 'pluralistic stagnation' which threatened the coherence of the balanced political system which Britain had enjoyed in the 1950s.[11] Samuel Brittan saw the competitive bidding as leading to economic unsoundness and disaster.[12] This diagnosis was supported by the more theoretical New Right views of Mancur Olson. Olson has maintained that the older and more developed a democracy is, the greater the density and strength of interest groups. These groups effectively prevent the state from adapting to changing economic forces.[13] The result is economic decline. Such

views differed from conventional party models in so far as they stressed
the importance of interest groups within the political process. They
nevertheless assumed that it was the policies of parties – or the failures
of policy-making by parties – which were major determinants in the
political process, if only by default.

The democratic sovereignty model, the party government model
and the adversarial politics model are all clearly descended from
the same root. In our case-studies we will have an opportunity to
assess their application or validity. But at this point it is sufficient to
note that they fit well into the framework of explanation offered by
rational decision-making. They all assume a degree of rationality in
the political process in so far as policy goals can be weighed against
policy means. They assume that it is possible to identify clearly who
the decision-takers are in society and that these decision-takers come
primarily (although not exclusively) from the arena of the political
élites. They assume that it is possible to separate policy areas from
each other and easy to determine responsibility for their conduct.
They assume that the policy process has some kind of a beginning
and end.

However, it has been argued that this is to impose far too rigid
a framework on what is essentially a fluid process. Hogwood and
Peters, for example, have pointed out that policy innovation is less
common than is usually recognised. Many 'new' policies are old
ones adapted and are accordingly constrained. 'Policy succession' is
a better way of viewing the policy-making process: policies gradually
evolve and this is a pattern which is becoming more marked.[14] Such
a perspective casts doubt upon the capacities of political systems to
change direction given the commitments of resources, organisational
arrangements and values centred upon the politics of the past. If this
is so then it is a mistake to place too much emphasis on the activities
of parties and the system within which they operate. Other models of
the policy-making process in Britain attempt to take these issues on
board.

THE CABINET GOVERNMENT MODEL

There is a well-established view in the British political tradition which
is sceptical of the claims of democratically-focused interpretations.
Stemming from a Tory view of the importance of the King's government, this has emphasised the power and autonomy of the Whitehall
central executive. Responsible rather than representative government
is the key. A classic account of British politics from this perspective

was provided by Leo Amery in *Thoughts on the Constitution* published in 1947 and which still repays reading today.[15]

The argument is that the organs of the state at the Centre provide the dynamo of policy-making. The Cabinet is the key coordinating force in British politics. It rests at the summit of a vast network of government committees and agencies. It is the meeting place of the great bureaucratic organisations of the state and the world of party politics. The democratic side of politics – parties and Parliament etc. – are mere accoutrements: they may on occasion play a key role in policy but this will be on a limited range of issues and never in a sustained manner, usually affecting the timing and the details rather than the substance of policy. Whereas the liberal or democratic models of politics see the lines of initiative coming upwards from the electorate through parties and Parliament to the Cabinet, with the Civil Service carrying out policy, the Whitehall oriented models see lines of command and initiative usually going in the other direction.

The Cabinet should not simply be understood as the formal Cabinet meeting of Prime Minister and twenty or so leading members of the Government. Since the time of Lloyd George an elaborate and systematic network of Cabinet Committees has grown up. These comprise both the key standing committees and a large number of *ad hoc* committees appointed to deal with particular issues (termed MISC or GEN committees). It is estimated that Mrs Thatcher appointed some 200 of these, although only about fifteen are likely to exist at any one time. It has long been the convention that the decisions taken in subcommittees are binding upon the Cabinet as a whole. The committees offer a very flexible means of conducting business and their membership is extremely elastic. They are serviced by the Cabinet Secretariat whose power and size has grown considerably during the past twenty years.[16]

The simple vision of a handful of largely unbriefed men and women sitting down once or twice a week to take decisions has never corresponded to the reality since 1900, although when faced with international crises this may be how the Cabinet behaves. The key question is whether the growth in its institutional apparatus has strengthened or undermined the nature of Cabinet government. Various answers have been put forward to this question. One is that Cabinet cliques have tended to dominate the proceedings of the Cabinet. Another, extremely influential since the 1960s, has been that British government is now prime ministerial. This latter view has led to a debate which is singularly lacking in intellectual rigour, consisting largely of the trading of anecdotal material. It is necessary, after all, to examine which factors increase prime ministerial power at the expense of the Cabinet as a whole – such as the personality of the Premier, his or her political standing, and the type of issue. There is no doubt that the changes in the media and in the pattern of international diplomacy are among the factors which have tended to increase the political salience of the Prime Minister. We do not wish, however, to enter into this debate here since both Cabinet government and prime ministerial exponents share the basic assumptions that it is the Cabinet Office and the Prime Minister in Cabinet that are the key coordinators of policy.[17]

BUREAUCRATIC DISPERSION

An alternative view of Whitehall stresses the weakness of the Cabinet system in coordinating policy. According to this perspective the great departments of state each largely determine policy in their own areas with only minimal coordination from the Treasury and the Cabinet Office at the centre. The Cabinet appears less as a 'Board of Directors' intent on a common enterprise than as a collection of competing departmental heads jostling for resources and jealous of their own autonomy.

It is easy to find many examples of interdepartmental tensions and conflicts and the key roles which departments play in making the Cabinet system work. It is a theme which runs through the Crossman and the Castle diaries.

These bureaucratic conflicts may be traced deep inside the British Cabinet system with its interlocking Cabinet and official committees. Some commentators claim that the striking feature of the British system of government is not the dominance of the Prime Minister but the weakness of the centre. Sir Burke Trend, a former Secretary to the Cabinet, for example, drew attention on his retirement to the 'hole at the centre'.[18] British government could thus be likened to a vast polo mint, with powerful vested interests, such as education, defence, agriculture and employment forming the ring and determining the behaviour of those at the centre. There are, of course, countervailing centralising or coordinating forces such as the Prime Minister, the Cabinet Office and the Treasury – but the inherent force is a centrifugal one. Another ex-senior civil servant, Sir Douglas Wass, in his Reith Lectures of 1983 also considered the Cabinet to be lacking in strategic capabilities. He urged the creation of some sort of review staff 'to offer bold and provocative advice about the balance of policy' in order to strengthen the collective capacities of the Cabinet.[19] Those impressed by the lack of coordination inherent in the Whitehall system believe it is particularly difficult to achieve coherent decision-making on policy areas which cross a number of departmental interests. One such example would be policy towards inner cities which might involve the concerns of the Treasury, the Departments of the Environment, Trade and Industry, Social Security, Transport and the Home Office, as well as local authorities and a host of other non-departmental agencies.

Some writers have suggested that a segmented decision model is the best way of explaining how the Cabinet works. The Prime Minister has considerable power in a limited range of key areas, such as foreign affairs, defence and economic policy. However, in a range of other areas, especially of a technical nature, the Prime Minister's capacity to influence policy will be weak. These will be the province of the bureaucratic departments with coordination where necessary taking place in the bureaucratic machine. Even in the strategic areas of policy-making, for example foreign affairs and economics, the Prime Minister's power will be circumscribed by the interests and influences of the specialists in those areas.[20]

But just as models which concentrate on Parliament and the parties might be criticised for ignoring the administrative system, so those models which emphasise the importance of Whitehall in one way or another have been criticised for over-concentrating on the central government and neglecting the contribution of agencies and groups outside the formal political sphere.

THEORIES OF POLICY COMMUNITIES AND POLICY NETWORKS

Pressure groups in Britain have always been seen as especially important. There is a long tradition of active pressure group involvement in politics going back to the late eighteenth century. In recent years theories have been devised to link the ideas of bureaucratic politics to those concerning the role of interest groups in society. Jordan and Richardson's explanations of British politics in terms of 'policy communities' have been particularly influential in this respect. Writing on the eve of Mrs Thatcher's accession to power in 1979 Jordan and Richardson criticised the 'still widespread view that British policy-making is a process played out between the electorate, Parliament and the Cabinet'. In their book, *Governing under Pressure*, which they subtitled 'The Policy Process in a Post-Parliamentary

Democracy' they argued that the true focus of important decision-making was not the formal party or parliamentary arena – what was popularly perceived to be the realm of politics – but the more hidden world of relations between government departments and interested pressure groups. The Civil Service and pressure groups were not adjuncts to the recognised political process but its very core. The parliamentary and party arena might still be the centre of controversy but controversy rarely centred on important issues except in a few policy areas of high political salience.[21]

Such views were not particularly original, what was novel was the stress Jordan and Richardson placed upon the fragmented nature of the policy process. British politics was divided into a series of 'policy communities'. Such policy communities, like defence, education, transport, welfare etc., typically had as their focus a government department but also incorporated a wide range of interested parties in the broader community. Thus the transport policy community, besides the Department of Transport, included *inter alia* the Automobile Association, the British Road Federation, the Society of Motor Manufacturers and Traders, the National Council of Inland Transport, the Freight Transport Association, the Road Haulage Association, British Rail, Transport 2000 etc. Of course, not all members of the community exerted the same influence. A radical group like Transport 2000 would tend to be at the periphery compared to the influential Automobile Association, but the pattern was flexible and could change in time. Different policy communities had their own inherent characteristics. Thus the defence community was small in number and closed in character, comprising not much more than the Ministry of Defence, diplomatic advisers, the intelligence networks, various institutes or academic advisers and leading arms manufacturers. The education community, by contrast, was very extensive including all manner of professional bodies and associations as well as trade unions and local authorities.

Very extensive consultation was the hallmark of the decision-making process. Policy-making was a process of government bodies feeling their way. Extensive consultation was necessary both to help the production of viable decisions and equally important to commit the policy community itself to these decisions, thus assisting both the implementation of policy and the creation of a degree of consensus within the policy community. Jordan and Richardson concluded, moreover, that notwithstanding the adversarial style of formal politics in Britain, more marked than in any other Western democracy, 'the main feature of the British system is that ongoing problems and constraints force successive governments into very similar policy positions'.[22] Problems are handled similarly irrespective of what government is in power. The development of the policy community process ensured the smooth operation of consensus politics. Without perhaps being conscious of it, Britain had 'decided' on a policy system aimed at maximising agreement where 'the incrementalist-humdrum style of policy-making' was appropriate and the 'process of accommodation' was of 'paramount importance'.[23]

The combination of adversarial formal party politics with consensual and pluralist policy-making was remarked upon by various other writers who observed Britain in the late 1970s. The American political scientists, Douglas Ashford and Samuel Beer, both independently noted it, although both drew less sanguine conclusions. Ashford concluded that adversarial Parliamentary politics, although based upon a remarkable degree of élite consensus, was too introverted and insufficiently geared towards assessment and criticism of the policy process within the administration. Beer, for his part, gloomily mused about the possibility of pluralistic stagnation in Britain, especially dangerous in the face of the structural economic problems.[24]

No sooner had Jordan and Richardson published their book than they were faced with a radical government, determined to smash the post-war consensus in policy terms and possessing an inbuilt and almost pathological dislike of vested interest groups. Returning to the question in 1987, in *British Politics and the Policy Process*, they insisted that the main structure of their model remained surprisingly robust. Certainly, a few instances, such as the Government's handling of the miners' strike of 1984, give a different picture and the Thatcher administrations consciously kept at arms length certain professional 'producer' groups, such as teachers, lawyers, opticians, or health service employees who were seen as wielding undue power at the expense of the consumer. But in many instances it was possible to find that radical objectives, such as the creation of Enterprise Zones or changes in unemployment policy, 'became compromised in the process of bargaining and implementation'.[25] Policy-making in Great Britain, as well as being unpredictable and complex, was simply variable and most political issues were resolved in the relatively private and specialised world of policy sectors. In their interviews with civil servants they were impressed by 'the sheer weight of consultation – quite at odds with the so-called "Thatcher style" – and the readiness of civil servants to use the language of political patrons to the groups "in their patch". They were referred to as "customer groups", "client groups" – even "constituency groups"'.[26] The Thatcher Governments had proved to be an exception to the 'normal' style of British decision-making 'only to a degree, and in some areas'.[27] This 'British style' was the consequence of deal-seeking behaviour between realistic groups and consensus-seeking civil servants. It was a 'standard operating procedure of government', a 'procedural ambition', even if it was not always possible to carry it out in all circumstances.[28]

Writing in 1990 Richardson concluded that the pattern of policy-making in the Thatcher years was often a period of 'confrontational style' followed by one of indecision after which the government-group bargaining process reasserted itself at some stage. Where the government had made up its mind on radical reforms it was often the case that the very groups which had been challenged were consulted and bargained with over the practicalities of policy implementation. In other cases, such as privatisation for example, government set out from the beginning to bargain with the chief interests involved in order to make the policy a success.[29]

Another influential writer who has adopted a broadly similar perspective to Jordan and Richardson has been Rod Rhodes. The focus of his interest was initially relations between local and central government and his researches led him to stress the high degree of mutual dependence of the one upon the other. Rhodes has concentrated upon the sheer extent and complexity of the mass of government agencies in what he terms 'sub-central government'. In his book *Beyond Westminster and Whitehall* of 1988 he points out the inappropriateness of the picture of the centralised state as the focus of decision-making. In the first place, the British state was highly fragmented with multiple centres of policy-making. Secondly, the central agencies of the state were constrained because they did not for the most part carry out executive functions: they were heavily dependant on a variety of other governmental units who were the real workhorses of administration. Thirdly, key factors in policy-making were the enormous range of networks of organisations' including large numbers of professional organisations. The metaphor of the 'machine' of government was not really appropriate: British government was more like a 'maze or a labyrinth'.[30] It was not simply the structure of government which was fragmented, the very problems of government were themselves 'factorised' into semi-independent component parts. Moreover, policies themselves interacted and fed upon each other: 'Interdependence amongst policies increases faster than our knowledge, and unanticipated consequences proliferate'.[31]

In order to understand the way British government worked it was therefore necessary to analyse the very wide variety of policy networks. Rhodes suggested the following classification. There were the policy communities vertically integrated, centred around a government department, and insulated from each other. These had restricted membership. Whereas these were functional in character – based on a policy area such as education or transport – a second group were territorial communities concerned with major geographical interests such as Scotland or Northern Ireland. A third category comprised the issue networks. These lacked a common institutional focus, a single central department, and were composed of a more varied and atomistic membership; the leisure area was a good example of this. Professionalised networks were those dominated by a single profession able to determine through their expertise important policy areas; examples are the water engineers and architects. A fifth category comprised the intergovernmental networks representing the interests of local authorities, characterised by informal relations with each other. Finally, there were the producer groups dominated by economic interests.[32] There was no one, single pattern for all policy areas. The centre was the fulcrum of policy networks and could manipulate them; but it faced critical limitations upon its power. Rhodes, therefore, constructs a much richer, more complex picture of the way decisions emerge. He accepts neither the simple executive model nor the interest group model, but seeks instead to combine both in a variation of the policy community model.

Other writers have, however, been unimpressed by the concepts of policy communities and policy networks. Brian Hogwood, for example, has suggested that such theories overemphasise the degree of containment of policy within particular areas. They ignore the way in which issues get shunted aside and tangled up. He quotes with approval the 'garbage can' model put forward by March and Olsen. This 'draws attention to situations where the raising of an issue provides an opportunity for other problems to be considered'. At any time not only are there problems awaiting solutions but also pet solutions looking for a problem. 'The raising of a new issue may result in some of these other issues being dumped in the same decisional "garbage can" because some angle or relationship with the new issue is perceived'.[33] Hogwood also stresses the extent to which the policy process in Britain varies. Such variation occurs principally across departments or areas, but it may also be found within the same department; thus foreign policy may be distinguished in terms of high and low policy arenas. In turn, this may force re-emphasis of the role of the centre. A flexible Cabinet system can provide a fruitful opportunity for integration within the British executive: an inbuilt counteraction to the tendency for fragmentation inherent in policy communities.[34]

The concept of policy communities or networks can misleadingly underestimate the extent to which central government is able to confront such interests head on, bypass them or reorganise the machinery of government. J. A. Chandler, in particular, has attacked the power dependency view of relations between central and local government in these terms. Bargaining is only possible if both sides have resources but local authorities had become almost bereft of these. 'It is a frequent but pathetic fallacy in political analysis to believe that power necessarily accrues to those who habitually walk with the great.'[35] It is this argument, that the power at the centre is considerable, which lies at the core of much New Right analysis of British politics.

NEW RIGHT PERSPECTIVES

During the 1980s the political theories which have had greatest novel impact, apart from those of the Green movement, have been those of the New Right. As normative political theories their scope lies largely outside our concerns in this book. However, because of their influence upon conservative administrations on both sides of the Atlantic, observers have begun to wonder whether any general lessons about how the political system works may be gleaned from assessing their impact. In this connection Madsen Pirie, President of a leading British New Right think tank, the Adam Smith Institute, has produced an interesting study of the relationship between ideas and policy in his book, *Micropolitics*.[36]

New Right ideas are borrowed from the public choice school of theorists, but are given a particular ideological twist. Put simply, such theorists have stressed the similarities between political and economic behaviour. In politics individuals or groups seek to maximise their advantage. They trade their support or their votes for benefits particular to them. Politics thus becomes a pattern of horsetrading or 'log-rolling', with the result that the interest of the public suffers. What motivates interest groups also motivates bureaucrats. Bureaucracies have a vested interest in their own growth and aggrandisement and jealously promote the programmes which they administer. They are in a particularly powerful position in the polity. Government comes to oversupply goods which are themselves organised more in the interests of the producers than the consumers. Thus education is dominated by the educational profession, just as the Health Service is run primarily in the interests of the health professionals. To roll back the frontiers of the state and to give back to the consumer real power and choice is the ambition of the New Right ideologue and the promotion of the free market economy is a key goal.[37]

Pirie is interested in the mechanism for the translation of ideas into policy. He maintains that the simple common-sense view that great thinkers produce original insights which are popularised by their disciples and then implemented in the practical world, is wide of the mark. It represents an oversimplified view of the relationship between theory and practice, since most theory is in turn moulded by practice. This view also ignores the key importance of the 'policy engineers', people who can work within the political system to effect radical ideological shifts in the application of policy. Just as the scientific community undervalues the engineer in comparison with the pure scientist, so it has been in the world of politics. Policy engineers are needed to make machines out of theory; more than this the policy engineers themselves create innovations which refine theory.[38] Pirie contrasts the failure of the Heath and Nixon administrations to implement radical free market mechanisms in the 1970s with the successes of Thatcher and Reagan in the 1980s. Such a striking contrast was to be attributed not to earlier failures of political leadership or faults in the free market philosophies themselves, but rather to inadequate attention having been paid to the importance of policy engineers and to the tactics of policy implementation or change. For Pirie the whole governmental machine and the complex network of interest groups attached to it, had an inbuilt and irrevocable bias against New Right solutions. Victory in the realm of ideas was not enough. It was necessary to come up with different detailed mechanisms for the injection of New Right ideas into the policy process in such a way as to maximise their popularity and to minimise opposition from the vested interests within the state. Independent think tanks of the late 1970s and 1980s, which worked outside the governmental machine, had played a key role in elaborating such tactics.[39]

Pirie has coined the term 'micropolitics' for the general process by which policy gets changed. The essential hallmark of this approach is to work on a piecemeal and gradual basis; this is in contrast to 'macropolitics' which attempts sweeping changes across the board which are rarely implemented properly and which take insufficient account of political reality, of the decisions made by individuals and groups which trade for advantage in the political market.

Examples of micropolitics in action under the Thatcher Governments are: the sale of council houses to tenants; the education reforms – including giving parents more choice of school, devolving budgetary power to heads based upon numbers taught and increasing the management powers of headteachers and governors; and the piecemeal privatisation techniques. These policies are incremental in character. They work within the existing system injecting new thinking and practices within it. 'Heroic' or comprehensive radical reforms in these areas – for example, dismantling the council house system, introducing education vouchers for use in a wholly privatised educational structure, and wholesale denationalisation – would, Pirie argues, have maximised opposition, have proved difficult to implement and have courted political unpopularity. Micropolitics is presented as limited in its operation. 'It does not win converts through ideas, but wins supporters by conferring advantages.' It operates on a small rather than a grand scale. It works in a cumulative manner. It achieves partial rather than comprehensive solutions. Policy-making appears as a process of learning whereby key policy engineers, highly ideologically motivated, experiment and where successful devices have an impact because of their success.[40]

As a model, micropolitics suffuses the governmental process with a somewhat roseate hue. Success is assumed to be readily verifiable, politicians appear rational, and the political market forces are held to be as predictable and consistent as those of economics. The model plays down the inconsistencies, muddles and confusions inherent in administration. Pirie paints with a very broad brush. Although he presents many examples, he avoids detailed examination of the process of decision-making. Reading his book alone, one would scarcely realise that civil servants or interest group leaders played any role in decisions. It is interesting in this respect to contrast his conclusions with those of Jordan and Richardson. Critics might also take issue with some of his examples. The convoluted story of privatisation could be equally well cited as a story of muddle and simple pragmatism as one of the triumph of micropolitics. Pirie does, however, draw attention to a phenomenon of the Thatcher era, the existence and influence of a network of ideologically-inspired think tanks, small groups of intellectual strategists intent on influencing the framework of decision-making and of providing a source of policy advice, often at a detailed level, from outside the confines of the bureaucracy, the political party or the conventional pressure group universe. As a member of one such group Pirie has a vested interest in magnifying their influence, and empirical assessment of the actual claims of such groups is a well-nigh impossible task. In this respect Pirie's model goes along with that of Sabatier in suggesting that many accounts of decision-making have tended to undervalue the role of such groups as researchers, academics, journalists and writers. Not only do such groups have a direct influence on decisions, they are also indirectly significant in so far as they set the climate of opinion or determine the intellectual hegemony of the time.

MARXIST-INFLUENCED PERSPECTIVES

The radical right's interest in the ideological framework within which decision-making takes place is mirrored on the left. Socialist perspectives on British politics have always stressed the central importance of questions of power and of the ability of the powerful élites to shape the intellectual framework within which decision-making takes place. There is a great variety of Marxist approaches but they all share the assumption that the real battle in society is between competing classes rooted in economic interests. A key factor in politics is the ability of those dominant interests to set the agenda and to create conditions under which their goals are both achieved and legitimated. Such a perspective inevitably places only limited emphasis on decision-making in government. The real battle for resources is determined elsewhere.

Within this general Marxist approach, there are, however, many variants. These stem from disagreements about, among other things, the nature of the interests at work within society. For more traditional Marxists, economic interests are decisive in determining the character of public policy. The key resource in society is capital, and the key power is the ability to use capital to generate profit. A string of dependence relationships are created: individuals come to depend on capital for work, and governments depend upon it for economic growth to finance their policy programmes, which in turn support capitalism through welfare provision, education, road building and so on. The interests of capital can, therefore, become the public interest of society. Policy decisions get taken as a means of advancing this interest. The analysis of decision-making has to be set, says the Marxist, in this wider context.[41]

This broad picture is, however, not universally shared on the left. Critics point out that capital does not come in one form, nor do the interests organised around it necessarily seek the same end. Important distinctions need to be drawn, for example, between finance capital and manufacturing capital, between domestic, foreign and multi-national capital. And within such categories there are yet further demarcation lines to be drawn – for example, the interests of the small business and the large business may be quite different. Equally, a small business in the south of England may not experience the same conditions as those experienced by a Scottish small business. These differences within capital, it is argued, require a modification of the basic economic model, with the emphasis being shifted to the political importance of economic interests. Nonetheless, this approach still seeks to explain public policy by reference to the way it advances dominant economic interests. Although such analysis inevitably focuses on economic and industrial policy, it can equally be applied to decisions about the welfare state and foreign policy. For instance, Britain's relations with Iraq, after the execution of a British journalist and before Saddam Hussein's invasion of Kuwait, were undoubtedly influenced by the extensive trade links between the two countries. The political process, by this account, becomes a servant of the economic process.

Some Marxist-influenced policy analysts, while accepting the general framework, are unconvinced by the idea that economic interests are the only forces at work. They argue that political interests need also to be incorporated into the picture. The state does not simply reproduce the values of the economically powerful, it also injects interests of its own. These include its desire for legitimacy. For the state to be able to act in a liberal democratic system, it has to be able to claim some popular authority. This authority may be manufactured, through the mass media, through parliamentary rituals and through elections, but this is not to deny that resources have to be devoted to these tasks. The state's interest also can stem from its very existence. The people working within the state, the capital invested in the state, all have an interest in increasing the power of the state. Either of these sources of interest may well be at odds with those of the economic interests at play. The study of public policy, therefore, requires an account of both the political and economic interests at work in the policy process. Such thinking can be detected in the emergence of corporatist accounts of British politics. Writers on the left (Alan Cawson) and the right (Keith Middlemas) concluded that the policy process was dominated neither by capital nor by competing interest groups nor by the state, but rather by a particular combination of each. Power was concentrated at the centre, but its exercise was negotiated by the representations of labour, capital and the state (most especially the Treasury). These powerful interests set the agenda for policy-making and determined which other groups would be consulted or considered.[42] While in recent years Labour's fortunes have declined, it is still possible to argue that the basic corporatist strategy, of incorporation and agenda-setting, still stands as a general model for policy-making.

Further variants of the Marxist picture are added by those who argue that the interests of women and of ethnic groups are also systematically suppressed. There is considerable debate here as to how to explain such oppression, but this does not detract from the central point being made: that the wider social processes are expressed in, and reinforced by, micro-level decisions. Welfare state policy, for example, cannot be understood separately from ways in which the family, and the role of women within it, is represented. This wider context for understanding the policy process can be linked to the work of writers like Andrew Gamble. In *Britain in Decline*, Gamble sets the rise of Thatcherism, and in particular its policies for limiting the economic and welfare role of the state, in historical perspective. He argues that these policies have to be seen as part of a longer process of adjustment to a new world order where Britain is no longer in the vanguard.[43]

Emerging from these variants of Marxist analysis is a new school of British policy analysis. While retaining the structuralist character of Marxism, it rejects the reliance on a materialist base which allows interest to be independently identified. Patrick Dunleavy, a leading exponent of this radical approach to policy-making, argues that interests are created rather than given. Parties create constituencies for their policies, and they use those policies to build a constituency. There is, he suggests, nothing inevitable about the sale of council houses being a Conservative policy; it was merely made to seem that way.[44] Equally, Dunleavy argues that the state does not itself have any fixed character. It too is constantly changing, with its various institutions and agencies taking on different shapes and forming different relationships. Explaining decision-making, therefore, re-quires an account which recognises the many elements involved. It also means accepting no one, definitive story. There is no simple 'truth', hidden somewhere in a Whitehall filing cabinet. Instead the understanding of decision-making means looking in detail at many different policy areas, while at the same time looking across the different policies to see how variations might be explained and compared.[45]

Dunleavy's argument can be read as a plea for a kind of structured eclecticism, in which competing interpretations are built from a thorough study. He writes: 'Political Science is inherently a multi-theoretical discipline in which issues of interpretation are of central intellectual interest.'[46]

In this chapter we have described some of the competing accounts of British policy-making. We have seen some of the criticisms to be made of them and some of the differences between them, but our main aim has been to demonstrate their range and character. We have not argued that there is one overriding, comprehensively correct thesis. We share with Dunleavy the view that our understanding of political processes depends upon applying these theories and comparing the results. The next six chapters, each of which concentrates in detail upon a single policy or policy area, are an attempt to provide such an approach. They provide, we hope, a means by which the student of politics may assess the competing ideas and accounts which we have outlined in this chapter and the previous one.

4 The response to AIDS

INTRODUCTION

Almost every decision taken by government contains some element of risk, uncertainty and ignorance. But it is important to notice that the extent of the unknown varies between decisions. Whereas the uncertainties contained in abolishing the Civil Service Department (chapter seven) were confined to only a few aspects of the decision, uncertainty pervades every aspect of the decision to counter AIDS (Acquired Immune Deficiency Syndrome). Initially, nothing was known about AIDS' existence; then nothing was known about its transmission; then nothing was known about its cause; then nothing about its incidence; and then nothing about how people could be stopped from acquiring it. And even though major gains in knowledge about AIDS have been made since the early 1980s, there remain substantial gaps in understanding of both key medical and sociological aspects of the disease. The Minister for Health, David Mellor, told Parliament in early 1989, 'we are all on a learning curve in this matter'.[1]

Lack of knowledge about the disease (and indeed ignorance about what is not known) pose very real problems for decision-makers. It can incline them to do nothing, until all the facts are known. Or, alternatively, it can provoke panic, as ignorance allows the spread of irrational fears. Because of the possibility of these radically different responses, this chapter focuses considerable attention on the timing of the decision to take action on AIDS. There is no equivalent of the Argentine invasion of the Falklands to prompt action; there are no manifesto commitments or key political goals to determine policy. The interesting question is, therefore, what determined the Government's decision.

In stressing the role played by ignorance and uncertainty in AIDS, there are two important additional points to be made. Firstly, ignorance about AIDS is not simply an objective fact. The state of knowledge is itself a variable over which government may exercise considerable control. At one level, the Government may make itself more or less accessible to certain sources of information. Its ignorance may, therefore, be a consequence of not choosing to listen. At another level, the lack of knowledge may be a result of a decision not to spend more on research. So while AIDS policy-making may be characterised by considerable ignorance, the degree of that ignorance is itself an object of the political process. The second important point to be made about AIDS policy is the different areas of political life into which it intrudes. Combatting the spread of AIDS is not simply a matter of delivering a magic bullet, a cure or a vaccine. Rather, it involves the government in decisions about research, about public health education, about Health Service funding, about discrimination in employment and about issues of compensation and insurance.

There has not been a single AIDS policy, but a series of policies, each dealing with different practical and political concerns. The Government has been involved with a wide variety of AIDS-related interest groups (e.g. the Terrence Higgins Trust, Body Positive, Frontliners, the Haemophilia Society), with health and social service workers, with the Medical, and Economic and Social Studies Research Councils, with insurance companies, and so on. The Government, as a result, is expected to make decisions about what research to fund, what resources to allocate to the Health Service, what rules to make about immigration, screening, and many other issues. In short, AIDS entails a considerable policy network, although as we shall see the key decision-makers are few in number.

Not only is AIDS policy characterised by diversity, it is also subject to changes in priority. Since the British Government's initiation of an AIDS policy in 1985, that policy's public profile has altered greatly. The first campaign received relatively little attention or funding. The second, started in late 1986, was quite different. It was announced by the formation of a special Cabinet committee to deal exclusively with AIDS. The policy reached a peak in public attention in late 1986 and early 1987.

By January 1987, it was very hard not to notice that the British Government was worried about the spread of AIDS. There were advertisements on television exhorting people, albeit rather enigmatically: 'Don't die of ignorance'. Every home in Britain was sent a leaflet on how AIDS was transmitted and how it could be avoided. Ministers spoke publicly of safe sex and condoms with a familiarity they typically reserved for the rate of inflation. After this flurry of publicity and the impression of intense endeavour, the public face of AIDS policy faded slightly, only to reappear several months later in another public education programme which shifted the focus from the general public to the young and to intravenous drug users. This time pop papers carried full page adverts warning of the dangers of shared needles. Fashionable magazines like the *Face* and *Q* contained mirrors with the slogan 'Now you know what the typical AIDS carrier looks like'. Encouraged by the DHSS (Department of Health and Social Security), the Independent Broadcasting Authority lifted its ban on television advertising of condoms. As well as the changing profile there has also been the changing focus of the policies. For instance, the public health campaign, which is now the responsibility of the Health Education Authority, has changed its target to include the young, holiday makers, heterosexuals, gay men and bisexuals.[2]

This response has been to a virus which had killed 1,612 of the 2,830 people who had contracted AIDS by December 1989. A further 11,676 people were known to be HIV (Human Immunodeficiency Virus) positive, and therefore susceptible to the illnesses characterised by AIDS. The total number of people who were HIV positive was estimated to be 50–100,000.[3]

The British Government has been applauded nationally and internationally for its response, but there has also been criticism: that the publicity has been less explicit than that of, say, the Dutch Government, and that insufficient funds have been allocated to research or to the Health Service. The House of Commons Select Committee on the Social Services' report on AIDS, published in May 1987, praised many of the Government's initiatives, but it also spoke of a lack of political coordination and a shortage of resources.[4] Criticisms too could be heard in Parliament. Labour MPs have called for more provision for, and protection of, those with AIDS. Alternatively, a group of Conservative backbenchers expressed the view that the Government was not doing enough to protect us from the 'extreme danger' posed by AIDS 'to our civilisation'.[5] And yet, despite these voices, AIDS has remained largely uncontroversial in Parliament, if not elsewhere. Certainly, political reactions to AIDS – whether consensual or controversial – are an important feature of any account of AIDS policy, and explaining the Government's response to AIDS means analysing both the ideological issues the disease has raised as well as the particular decisions that have been taken in an attempt to cope with it. To that end, this chapter outlines the political story of British AIDS policy. It focuses on those issues of particular interest to students of decision-making and British politics: the way the problem was defined and the agenda set, the interaction of interests and information in the construction of policy, and the organisation of the political process.

THE FORM OF AIDS POLICY

The main resource involved in AIDS policy is money – money for research, treatment and education. This is transformed into practical form by various institutions, operating inside and outside government: the Medical Research Council (MRC), the National Health Service, advertising agencies, the Terrence Higgins Trust, etc. government decisions are substantially a matter of determining the size of the financial contribution and the priorities to be recognised in its distribution. But the Government's contribution is not purely financial. It is able to determine or, at least, influence the public profile and perception of AIDS; it can set the agenda by distinguishing, for example, between types of patient: between haemophiliacs, who have acquired AIDS through infected blood products, and homosexuals, who have got AIDS through sexual activity. In doing this, the authorities create different degrees of blame and responsibility for contracting the disease.[6] Through its access to the media and its role in Parliament, the Government is able to shape the way AIDS is understood, i.e. the 'problem' its policy is intended to solve.

The first death from AIDS in Britain, at least as far as anyone knew at the time, occurred in 1982.[7] AIDS was a recognised syndrome, but its cause was unknown. It took another year before the virus was isolated and another two years for a test for the virus to be developed. By 1985, it was understood that the transmission of AIDS took place through blood and semen, and in that year the Government's AIDS policy began to take shape. Although those groups deemed to be at risk, most notably homosexuals and bisexuals, had been asked not to donate blood since 1983, systematic screening only became possible in 1985. From then onwards, the Government's AIDS policy emerged, albeit in piecemeal fashion.

In late 1985 the Government announced a package of AIDS measures, including £2.5 million for publicity and a special allocation of an extra £680,000 to those health regions where AIDS patients were most concentrated (Greater London in particular, where about 80 per cent of patients were being cared for). By 1986–7, the contribution to health authorities had risen to £6.3 million. But the major increase was in the publicity budget, for which £20 million was set aside.

The sum allocated to the health authorities from central funds was increased to £7 million. It was less than had been asked for. Although the bulk (£4.4 million) went to three London authorities, one of these, North West Thames, estimated that AIDS treatment cost it £2.4 million in 1987. Increases were also made in the AIDS research budget. In 1986, only £400,000 was given to the Medical Research Council; in 1988, the allocation was £6 million.

In 1989, the then Minister of State for Health, Virginia Bottomley, summed up the Government's AIDS strategy:

> First, to stem the spread of HIV infection; second, to increase understanding of the nature of HIV in order to counter effects; third, to help those affected by the virus; and fourth, to foster informed sensible and caring attitudes within society to create the conditions in which action can be effective.[8]

These four elements – education, research, treatment and prevention – form the basis of our analysis of AIDS decision-making.

Education

The programme of public education is the element of AIDS policy that has been given the most attention and money. In 1986 Barney Hayhoe, as Minister for Health, explained to Parliament that 'Government funding on education on AIDS has been primarily directed towards informing the general public about the AIDS virus and the precautions that can be taken to minimise its transmission'. In January 1987 the Secretary of State, Norman Fowler, re-emphasised Hayhoe's point: 'public education is the only vaccine we have'. But it was a vaccine that ministers wanted to use cautiously. Fowler's junior minister, Edwina Currie, explained that the Government had to find 'a way of telling people what the risks are and what they should do without shocking them so much that they switch off entirely'. At the same time, the Government limited itself to behaviour rather than morality; as Tony Newton, another DHSS minister, admitted, 'we frankly don't have time to rely on changing the moral climate'.[9] Although the style of advertisements has changed with time, the strategy has remained the same.

The education campaign has been run in distinct phases (see Table 1). While the first two campaigns were largely directed at the general population, the later ones have been more precisely focused: first on the young and on intravenous drug users, and then on heterosexuals. All these campaigns have been designed to increase awareness of

AIDS first and then to change behaviour. As one Cabinet minister commented: 'Just as it would have been unthinkable to fit children with gas masks until the Second World War made it acceptable, so steps to stop AIDS spreading could be tolerated only if public opinion was mobilised beforehand'.[10]

The first campaign merely sought to publicise the advice the DHSS had been giving since early 1985. This could be found in the thirteen different leaflets and documents on AIDS which it distributed that year. The publicity campaign itself was based on newspaper advertisements. It gave an accurate, if undramatic, account of current wisdom on AIDS. One of the adverts was headed, 'AIDS. NEED YOU WORRY?'. The copy began with an injunction to 'Please read this carefully' and was signed by the Government's

Table 1 Publicity campaigns

Date	Audience/location	Theme
March 1986	National press	Information
Dec 86–Feb 87	TV, press, posters, leaflets to all homes	Don't die of ignorance
Feb 88	TV, youth magazines (men and women)	You know the risks; the decision is yours
Summer 88	Posters in airports, ports, stations, etc.	Holidays
Dec 88–March 89	National press	You're as safe as you want to be
March 89	Gay press, listings, magazines	Men who have sex with men
April 89–June 89	Young women's magazines, young women, ethnic press	Young women
Summer 89	Posters at airports etc., radio, ads in inflight magazines	Holidays
Dec 1 1989	Ads in national dailies, Sundays, and ethnic press	World AIDS Day
Dec 89–March 90	Ads in youth press (men and women), radio	Young people
Feb–March 90	TV, national press	Experts on HIV and AIDS

Source: HEA, *Strategic Plan 1990–1995*

Chief Medical Officers. It went on to explain what AIDS is, how it is spread, and how it can be avoided: 'Using a sheath can help reduce the risk of catching AIDS. So can cutting out casual relationships'. The only illustration was a picture of an AIDS leaflet.

The second campaign was more direct and more extensive. It too used the newspapers, but it also entailed circulating leaflets to every home in the country, poster and billboard advertising, and TV and radio slots. The second campaign was also much more expensive, costing more than £10 million (compared to the £100,000 spent on the first). Its intention was to encourage safer sex which was defined as sticking to one partner and/or using a condom. Not only did it use explicit newspaper adverts, it also coordinated a national and local radio campaign, and local and national telephone helplines. Perhaps most noticeable, though, was the decision to use television as the key weapon in the campaign.

One of the most intriguing features of the Government's response to AIDS was its initial reluctance to use television to carry its message, a reluctance that could still be detected in the rather coy advertisements shown in January 1987. Their main purpose was to notify the public of the leaflet that was being sent to every home. The telephone helplines, together with the leaflet, were to provide the detailed information. The advert itself was rather enigmatic. There was no AIDS patient to shock us, no familiar face (no face at all) to guide us; just an anonymous pair of hands drilling the word AIDS into a block of stone. The message was 'Don't die of ignorance'. But while the TV campaign was rather elliptical, the leaflet it advertised was very direct. It spoke about anal and oral sex and about the use of condoms. It seems that the Government originally intended to use a more explicit campaign, but decided against it. This was partly because of the fear (expressed by the Prime Minister, among others) that people might be offended. In fact, research published in the *British Medical Journal* in April 1987 indicated that a majority of people felt that explicit language should be used.[11] Nonetheless, the higher political profile given to the education campaign did fuel arguments about the content of the campaign. There was, for example, a clash between the Government and the Health Education Authority (HEA) over a schools AIDS education pack. The pack was scrapped after the Department of Education and Science (DES) objected to the lack of a suitably strong moral message. A spokesman for the DES explained that the pack was not consistent with the Government's general policy on AIDS public education in schools.[12]

These political concerns aside, the British campaign stood in stark contrast to the very cautious attitude to any concerted national campaign in America, where the AIDS epidemic was even more serious. Despite pressure from high-ranking medical officials, President Reagan remained reluctant to back a national campaign. His hesitancy was reflected elsewhere. Justifying a decision not to broadcast condom adverts, the Vice-President of the CBS television network said, 'We believe birth control messages – of any kind – would be an intrusion on the moral and religious beliefs of our audience'. In Britain, condoms are advertised, albeit without any sight of the product itself.

How successful was the education campaign? Because the intention was to change attitudes, awareness and behaviour in areas typically deemed to be private (and outside the typical responsibility of government), assessing its effectiveness has not been easy. The DHSS has employed eight different research organisations to look at the impact of government policy. Most reports suggest that the first campaign was not a great success, at least among heterosexuals who did little to change their behaviour even where they were more aware of the risks. Advertising executives were not surprised. One remarked of the campaign: 'We are talking about changing a way of life. There is no point buying one page in a paper to discourage permissiveness when the other 24 promote it'.[13] There was some evidence, however, that gay sexual behaviour did change; it is less easy to tell whether this was a function of government policy or of their particular circumstances.

By contrast, the second campaign was much more explicit and was claimed as a success. The Government reported that 69 per cent of people said that they had seen the press advertisement and that 73 per cent of people questioned said that they now knew how to avoid the disease. But the detailed results were more ambiguous. Respondents were classified into three groups: 'adult', 'gay' and 'youth'. All of these groups displayed a major increase in knowledge about AIDS. On the other hand, there was limited evidence of actual changes of behaviour among heterosexuals. Although the young and the gay sample both now put AIDS as a greater risk to them than lung cancer, it was only the gay respondents who had changed their behaviour significantly. A Marplan poll of 18–24 year-olds confirmed this pattern: while 15 per cent of respondents said that they had given up casual sex and 36 per cent said they favoured monogamy, only 2 per cent said that they used condoms. Equally worrying, the campaign seemed not to have altered the view that AIDS was something that affected other people and was, furthermore, their fault.[14] These results help explain the targeting of the third campaign on particular groups; and also the fourth campaign's concern to remove complacency among heterosexuals.

The Government's own attempt at public education has run parallel with – and against – considerable media interest in AIDS. This too has played a part in shaping popular reaction to AIDS. Sometimes this coverage has sustained the government campaign. In February–March 1987, all four television channels agreed to coordinate an AIDS campaign. Each organised programmes – some 'specials', some part of its normal programming – over a single week.[15] At other times, the coverage has worked against government policy. The tabloid press has spoken luridly of the 'gay plague' and played down the risk to heterosexuals. Television documentaries have also cast doubt on the 'official' version of the spread and cause of AIDS. The Government, and agencies like the HEA, have as a result been forced to counter such propaganda. In short, the AIDS education policy has been made in the context of media coverage of AIDS in general.

Research

For some people, research holds the key to AIDS policy. They argue that only this can provide the fundamental understanding which will allow for greater control of the disease. The question remains, though, as to what kind of research is appropriate. Should it be directed at finding a vaccine and/or a cure for AIDS? Or should it be focused on the spread of HIV? Or on the behaviour of individuals and groups? In fact, much of the research effort has been concentrated on vaccines, with some epidemiological work on the transmission and spread of HIV.

With each year, the sums allocated to research have increased substantially. Having given only £400,000 in 1985, the DHSS found £14.5 million in 1987 for the MRC. It may not be a coincidence that this big increase was made just before the general election. Critics also observed that the British contribution to research was considerably smaller than that made available in the USA. A member of the British Institute of Cancer Research claimed that the Government's research strategy was to let the Americans spend their money so that the British could buy the result when the breakthrough arrived.[16] Outside biomedical research, things moved yet more slowly.

It was only in 1987 that the Government backed research into the sexual behaviour of homosexuals. Previous work in this area by a

London consultant was not published in the Government's *Health Trends* at the insistence of Barney Hayhoe because it was thought to be 'politically sensitive'.[17] The DHSS subsequently committed £700,000 to epidemiological research and clinical trials. This work was eventually supplemented in 1988 when the Economic and Social Research Council (ESRC) announced a £1.5 million research programme into sexual behaviour. But when the ESRC planned a major national survey of sexual behaviour this was blocked by the Prime Minister.[18] (The research was subsequently picked up by a private foundation.)

The decision to allocate research funds is not as simple as it might seem. There are clearly complex questions to be answered about where the funds should go, how they should be spent and what sort of work should be done. Because of their intrinsic complexity, a political process emerges by which these questions can be resolved. Departments of state, research bodies and industry are linked in a political process, the result of which leads funds to be allocated in particular ways. In the case of AIDS, it is noticeable that clinical medical interests have tended to dominate the process.

Treatment

Although the public education campaigns and the search for a cure have received most attention, the Government has also been involved in decisions about the management of the epidemic itself. At one level, this means deciding on funds for treatment. The cost of treatment has, of course, increased as the disease has spread, and it might be guessed that the potential escalation provoked the Treasury to push the Government to respond to AIDS in the first place. At another level, the Government has had to resolve questions of who should be screened and under what conditions and about how the terminally ill should be cared for.

In deciding on the treatment of AIDS, it is noticeable that non-clinical needs have received a low priority. This is most apparent in the small allocation of funds to the counselling of people who are HIV positive. Although nurses and doctors involved in the treatment of AIDS argue that counselling is a crucial feature of the screening process, little money has been provided. In 1985 only £150,000 was given for the training of AIDS counsellors (who are responsible for helping AIDS patients to come to terms with their condition); and only £20,000 was allocated to the special training of nurses. When Norman Fowler announced the provision of £20 million for the AIDS public education campaign, he explicitly ruled out extra money for clinics for sexually transmitted diseases. Subsequently, there has, in fact, been a dramatic increase in the funds for such clinics, and they have been transformed from forgotten institutions into plush new buildings.[19]

The bulk of the Government's treatment policy is concentrated on the hospital services. Estimates of the cost of treatment per patient in 1987, according to the DHSS, ranged from £10,800–£20,000 per patient; in 1988 the estimated cost had risen to £30,000. The difficulty in giving a more accurate figure stems from the unknown cost of new methods of treatment. In the light of this, between £12 and £24 million was made available to the Health Service in 1987 for the treatment of AIDS patients. Costs, in other words, had to be roughly estimated. They could not be rationally assessed. As a result, some health regions have complained that they have not had enough money to cope with AIDS while others have been able to use the extra AIDS funds to refurbish their service as a whole. It has also been claimed that there is a regional bias in the distribution of funds, with Scottish health authorities receiving less per patient than their English counterparts. The central allocation for an AIDS patient in Yorkshire is £52,500, whereas in Lothian it is £20,000.[20] As with research, the decisions being made are not based on straightforward calculations of objective need. Not only are judgements made about what can be afforded for the hospital service, but also about the priority accorded to AIDS. A further set of judgements are made in the decision to allocate funds through hospital-based treatment, rather than some form of community care. The Government has been reluctant, for instance, to commit itself to providing special hospices for AIDS patients.

Prevention

For as long as the research into AIDS fails to produce any positive results and for as long as the costs of treatment increase, the Government's only other resort, apart from the high profile education campaign, has been prevention – i.e. the direct use of government resources to counter the disease's spread.

Since October 1985 all donations of blood have been tested for HIV. Prior to this there was no commercially available test, and so the policy was to request 'at risk' groups to refrain from making donations. Between the request and the testing, 41 people became HIV positive from blood transfusions.

Apart from the screening of blood, there has also been the possibility of testing the population in general. Without such testing, it is argued, the spread of HIV can neither be known nor monitored. But to decide on such screening requires decisions on a number of other issues: should it be mandatory and universal? Should it be voluntary? Should it be anonymous? Each of these questions, and the general issue of testing, have been the subject of considerable argument. The debate has led the Government to proceed cautiously. Issues of cost, practicality and confidentiality have provided arguments for inaction; these claims have been reinforced by various interest groups. The Government ruled out the screening of all hospital patients, for example, on the advice of the Public Health Laboratory Service. There is rarely only one source of advice on an issue, and government has had to mediate between competing forms of expert advice. Opinion has been divided over the value of national screening (the Royal College of Obstetricians and Gynaecologists have been opposed; the British Medical Association in favour, albeit with reservations and internal divisions). Sometimes interested parties accord: the Foreign Office and the European Community both opposed screening at borders or airports/ports.[21] The outcome of these various debates was the eventual decision to adopt a system of anonymous testing of the general population from January 1990.

One way of preventing the spread of infection through the sharing of needles in drug use is to provide free needles and needle exchanges. The Chief Medical Officer and the Home Office's Advisory Council on the Misuse of Drugs have advocated a national needle exchange scheme. The Government has been cautious in following this advice, preferring to rely on local initiatives which have varied in success, depending on the way the system has operated. The recommendation, endorsed by probation officers, that the same system should operate in prison has been rejected by the Home Office. It argues that the incidence of intravenous drug use is small and that distributing free needles would, in fact, exacerbate the problem.[22]

The best physical protection against the sexual transmission of HIV is the condom. While the Labour opposition has advocated the free distribution of condoms, the Government has not followed this advice, although the Army did make them available to troops serving in Africa. Individual hospitals and family planning clinics distribute condoms, but there is no government policy here, and in fact funding for the Family Planning Association has been severely reduced. The only explicit government decision is not to distribute condoms in prisons, on the grounds that this would only encourage dangerous homosexual practices, which are, in any case, illegal in prison. The Government has also taken no steps to monitor the production of condoms or to insist on new standards of safety. This has been left to the market.

Another aspect of the process of preventing the spread of AIDS, it can be argued, entails 'normalising' the disease. For as long as AIDS is the object of fear, stigma and prejudice, the harder it is for the disease to be prevented. There have been reports of people who are HIV positive having their houses set on fire by their neighbours. Some of the Government's decisions and policy pronouncements can be seen as attempts to normalise AIDS and to counter such prejudice. The Princess of Wales was encouraged to visit a hospital ward containing people with AIDS. No legislation, however, has been introduced to prevent discrimination against those that are HIV positive, although the Department of Employment introduced a pamphlet on 'AIDS and employment' which indicated that the dismissal of anyone because they were HIV positive would be unfair under the terms of the existing legislation. After extensive lobbying by various interested parties, the Government has also chosen not to act against life insurance companies and private medical insurers who refuse cover to those who are HIV positive.[23]

This brief account of the decisions the Government has taken includes instances of as many choices not to act as to act, to ignore interest groups as to accommodate them. This process of selection and action is most sharply focused by looking at the timing of AIDS policy – why did the Government choose to act when it did?

THE TIMING OF AIDS POLICY

Any study of decision-making can be illuminated by asking why a decision was made at a particular time. In this case, why did the Government move so decisively on AIDS in November 1986? One of the leading AIDS counsellors offered this critical judgement on the timing of the Government's response: 'The government had plenty of time to act. It did not, until now [November 1986], because of a fear of losing votes. That has meant that people have already needlessly lost their lives'. The Prime Minister, by contrast, argued that such criticisms fail to recognise the Government's problem: 'Governments cannot stop people from getting AIDS. They can give the information which enables them to prevent themselves getting it'.[24]

The doctor accused the Government of negligence; the Prime Minister wanted to limit the Government's liability. To reach some conclusion about the timing of the Government's response, we begin by examining the reasons the Government had for not acting.

The first factor is the uncertainty surrounding AIDS. In 1983, a year after the first British AIDS death, the DHSS report 'On the State of Public Health' could still announce that: 'the cause remains unknown, but is likely to be a viral agent transmitted by sexual contact, transmission of blood and certain blood products'.

It had taken two years to uncover how it was transmitted. As late as February 1988, the science journal *Nature* reported that, on the question of the rate of transmission, 'the data on infectivity and incubation time which are now to hand are too meagre to sustain a useful guess'. In January 1986 Parliament was told that government had no detailed evidence on the spread of AIDS among drug users. It is now part of the established wisdom that a condom is one of the most effective methods of guarding against the sexual transmission of AIDS. But even this piece of common sense took time to emerge. Tests on the effectiveness of commercial brands of condom were not reported until 1986.[25] The first clinical trials of possible AIDS vaccines only began in 1986–7. Meanwhile evidence about variations in susceptibility to the disease, about the percentage of people who were antibody positive who developed the full-blown syndrome, and about the precise course of the disease, all were constantly being revised and challenged. To add to this, a second virus, with similar consequences but of different biochemical structure, was discovered in the late 1980s.

This medical uncertainty was compounded by ignorance about the incidence of AIDS, the least reliable information being about the number of people who were HIV positive. Even as late as 1990, official reports were reaching substantially different conclusions.[26] Estimates of the rate of transmission were also vague. There was no established knowledge about, for example, people's sexual habits. As *The Lancet* commented, 'Medical science knows more about the molecular structure of the HIV virus in a lycocyte than it knows about human sexual behaviour in the bedroom'. This ignorance and uncertainty furnishes an excuse for hesitation, although governments are in a position to rectify some aspects of this ignorance. Whether or not the Government was at fault for not causing certain research to be done sooner, it still faced a familiar dilemma: whether to act before all the facts are known and risk criticisms of over-reaction or to wait until the evidence is clear and risk the accusation of complacency.

To translate the dilemma into another form: between 1982 and November 1987, AIDS killed 517 people in Britain. In that period there had been more than 200,000 deaths from lung cancer, and some 25,000 road deaths. If the Government's responsibilities are defined by the size of the problem, then it could be charged with irresponsibility for devoting so much attention to AIDS and people's sexual habits, and so little attention to road safety and to people's smoking habits. On the other hand, the Government also had to consider the prospect of a future in which a million people may be HIV positive and thousands may have died from AIDS. Duncan Campbell offers this judgement:

> The cost of failing to curb AIDS and HIV disease will be somewhere between £5 and £20 billion, quite apart from the loss of 20,000 to 50,000 people, mostly now in their 20s and 30s.[27]

These contrasting statistics emphasise that decision-makers face two questions to which there is no definitive solution. First, there is the question of priorities, of how, under conditions of scarce resources, one problem is to be compared against another; and secondly, there is the matter of not knowing exactly what the problem itself consists of. Within such uncertainty, it is possible for less scientific factors to come into play, if, that is, they are not at work already. Here, if an excuse is needed, is a place for prejudice and ideology to shape the problem that the Government sees. Political and social values are no less real than statistical data for policy-making and policy-makers.

AIDS has been linked with a variety of images and fears, and these have created opportunities for inaction. Democracy is not typically a source of radical change. It encourages hesitancy. Where popular opinion is known or thought to be conservative, elected politicians will tend to act cautiously. There is evidence that the emergence of AIDS was accompanied by a new wave of prejudice against homosexuals.[28] Put crudely, there seemed to be few votes (irrespective of what the future brings) in fighting AIDS. The Thatcher Government's initial reluctance to act accords with the behaviour of its predecessors. Where the issue is seen as one of morality or sexuality, governments have typically chosen to avoid direct responsibility.

The moral and electoral arguments for non-intervention were supplemented by the general ideological predisposition of the Thatcher Government. Mrs Thatcher made much of her commitment to ideas of the traditional family, the market and individual responsibility. She was also closely associated with reform of local government legislation which made it illegal for local authorities to 'promote homosexuality'. AIDS could (and can) not be separated from the particular ideology and the general practices of policy-making. It constituted a further reason for acting cautiously, or rather for not acting. John Mackay, Under-Secretary of State for Scotland, told Parliament in April 1986 that: 'AIDS is a totally self-inflicted illness, and it is so much more morally reprehensible when it is inflicted on children . . . It is a moral question which comes down to people reviewing their living habits'.[29]

The same argument was taken up by right-wing moralists such as Paul Johnson in *The Spectator* and Sir William Rees-Mogg in *The Independent*. While such views may not have been shared by all on the right, their presence served as a dead-weight against those inclined to a more interventionist strategy.

The inclination to inaction was further reinforced by relative invisibility (seen from particular vantage points) of the problem. It is a familiar, if frustrating, feature of political life, that the visibility and the character of a problem, rather than its seriousness, may determine the response (or lack of one) that emerges from a government. There are some interests or causes which do not appear on the agenda because they are not visible or rather because they are not made visible.

The initial attention paid to AIDS in the West stressed its association with homosexuality. This conditioned official and other responses. The AIDS threat was not seen as a threat to society at large, but as an affliction of homosexuals and drug users – who elicit little public or political sympathy. And in the case of the sexual transmission of AIDS, it was ascribed to a type of social group not a type of sexual behaviour. Dennis Altman writes of the American experience: 'The high concentration of [AIDS] cases among certain groups and localities means that a few people have felt a disproportionate amount of personal loss'. In so far as the experience of AIDS has been concentrated, this not only makes it less visible in 'straight' society, it also influences the response of that society. 'For most people', argues Altman, 'it has been fear of contagion rather than experience of loss that has made the disease a reality'.[30] Seeing the disease as a threat from the outside is very different from seeing it as a common problem. Over 70 per cent of those known to be HIV positive have acquired AIDS from homosexual contact. Over 80 per cent of British deaths from AIDS have been among homosexuals.[31] The apparent group specificity of AIDS, when combined with prejudice against homosexuality, provides a basis for the idea that while some people with AIDS are the 'innocent victims', most are responsible for their own infection and are guilty of passing it on. Making such distinctions will tend to provide an excuse for inaction.

The concentration of AIDS amongst a particular social group is further exaggerated by geographical factors. A majority of AIDS patients live (or are treated) within the Thames health regions, the rest being concentrated in Scotland. This may, therefore, have made AIDS appear less of a national problem.

The potential marginality of those with AIDS is further encouraged by the fact that, after homosexuals, the other main social group identified with the disease are drug users (with Scotland containing the bulk of the drug-related patients). While not attracting the moral disdain imposed on homosexuals, drug users are, by virtue of their life-style (and the laws against drugs), on the fringes of society and are unable to command the sympathy that their condition might otherwise engender.

All these dispositions for inaction are framed by the policy process itself and the established common sense of Whitehall. Rudolph Klein writes:

> Britain's tradition of social policy making is paternalistic and, more generally, the ideology of British government has tended to be interventionist. Yet when it comes to dealing with the problem of individual life-styles, and the prevention of disease, British government has shown a reluctance to intervene'.[32]

This pattern has a long tradition. William McNeill wrote of epidemics in the nineteenth century:

> 'In England . . . a libertarian prejudice against regulations infringing the individual's right to do what he chose with his own property was deeply rooted; and as long as theories of disease and its propagation remained under dispute, clear imperatives were hard to agree upon'.[33]

In short, the general approach of Whitehall gave some weight to those who favoured caution and who saw AIDS as a consequence of private behaviour.

But even if a decision-maker was resolved to act, they had one further reason for holding back. What was to be done? Medical science had not produced an answer. The disease had no known cure; there was no vaccination against it. This biomedical gap was compounded by the greater ignorance about sexual behaviour and about the factors causing changes in sexual practice.

So, we can see that a considerable argument could be mounted for not acting on AIDS. It is this background which we need to hold in mind when analysing the Government's eventual decision to act. Why was 1986–7 the time when the arguments against action were overcome? What determined the decision to act? Doctors and others had been calling upon the Government to act since 1982. To them, the Government was complacently ignoring British reality and American experience.

We need first to recognise that the argument for inaction was not invulnerable. Uncertainty does not always constitute an incontrovertible case for inaction, as the Falklands War showed. Besides, steps can be taken to reduce ignorance about the relevant facts. Similarly, the risk-of-error argument does not point conclusively to present caution. Governments over-supply electricity on the grounds that the cost of excess generation is not as intolerable as the cost of energy shortfall. It is not, in fact, clear what counts, in the case of AIDS, as the cautious strategy – is it doing nothing until the evidence and/or risks are known? Is it acting now to avoid possible future consequences? The same is true of how the risks are measured and weighed. There is no single way to account the cost of a disease. For these reasons there is no neat, simple explanation for why and how the Government responded to AIDS. Death, or rather the threat of death, can be a powerful incentive. In explaining government response to an earlier epidemic, William McNeill wrote: 'To do nothing was no longer sufficient; old debates and stubborn clashes had to be quickly resolved by public bodies acting literally under fear of death'.[34] But in the case of AIDS, talk of an 'epidemic' did not reflect reality. For any individual the chance of dying from AIDS was very small.

What did change, however, was the perception of those affected. The emphasis shifted to the heterosexual transmission of the virus. In drawing attention to this, we need to recognise that, well before 1986 and the launch of the Government's first campaign, it was acknowledged that AIDS was not confined to homosexuals, although the DHSS's official estimate was that only 3 per cent of AIDS cases occurred as a result of heterosexual contact. Nonetheless, it appears that the Chief Medical Officer and officials within the DHSS focused on the possibility of heterosexual spread both because that risk was not being taken seriously by the general population (particularly the young) and because – cynically – it provided a good argument for extracting money and action from ministers.

It is noticeable, too, that the political ideology that might previously have worked against a major initiative, now worked for it. Sir

Nicholas Bonsor, speaking for the Conservative MPs who wanted the Government to do more about AIDS, argued that treasured values and institutions were threatened. 'Obviously there is substantial drug-taking and homosexuality', he observed, 'and we have to decide how we can protect people from the undesirable activities of their neighbours'.[35]

These general shifts in the perception of the problem were given a sharper focus by the welter of mass media interest. The *Health Education Journal* noted that AIDS received 'unprecedented coverage' in the two months before the second campaign was announced in November 1986.[36] The respected current affairs programme, *Weekend World*, devoted several hours to the disease. The media could be seen to legitimate government action, and then to provide the channels through which that policy was implemented. Prior to this, the press had done much to focus on the scare factor in AIDS and to publicise the 'shock-horror' view of the disease. This was especially noticeable in the coverage of the deaths of a prison chaplain and of the film star Rock Hudson. The net effect of press and TV attention was to establish a climate of opinion which required government action, or gestures of action.

THE MAKING OF AIDS POLICY

Explaining the timing and implementation of AIDS policy cannot be the end of our analysis. We also have to consider the form of the political machinery and its effect on the policy. The administrative structure both reflects and enforces a particular reading of the problem to be solved. The interpretation of illness, and especially sexually-transmitted disease, is not simply a matter of medical science; it is also a matter of social science. As Allan Brandt puts it, 'disease is socially constructed . . . practice and policy are fundamentally influenced by the symbols we attach to a particular disease'.[37] Certain meanings are attached to illness through the political response to it. The administrative machinery is an attempt to impose a particular understanding of the disease, in order to make the problem appear manageable.

One example of this phenomenon in AIDS policy is its politicisation. Although AIDS policy has been organised for the most part through the DHSS (or Department of Health, as it is now), a shift in responsibility occurred with the creation of a special AIDS Cabinet Committee in late 1986. Rather than being an official secret, this particular committee became a publicly boasted achievement. The committee, under Lord Whitelaw and then John Moore, brought together ministers from the DHSS, the Home Office, the Foreign Office, the Ministry of Defence and the Scottish, Welsh and Northern Ireland Offices. Its creation usurped some of the power of the DHSS, and in particular the AIDS Expert Advisory Committee that had been in operation since February 1985. It also caused a further marginalisation of groups like the Terrence Higgins Trust (THT) which had, until then, worked closely with the DHSS. One THT worker reflected ruefully: 'once the government itself started intervening in AIDS, the Trust gradually lost influence and relations became more formal'.[38] The new Cabinet Committee signified a higher political profile for AIDS, but this politicisation of the decision-making process constrained the range of options available.

While the net outcome was a large increase in funds and a major public education campaign, the Cabinet Committee reinforced the priority given to publicity, as against research. The DHSS committee was more receptive to both medical and social science expertise, together with counselling and other AIDS-relevant skills. The new Cabinet Committee added a new set of (political) criteria to the policy deliberations.

Furthermore, while the Cabinet Committee signified a change in the political priority given to AIDS, it threatened to make the issue a party political one. There were signs of a restriction on the flow of information: briefings were refused to the opposition; Mrs Thatcher declined to name Lord Whitelaw's successor as chair of the Cabinet Committee; and greater emphasis was laid on political expediency (e.g. the decision not to allow condoms in prisons). Dr Mukesh Kapila, Deputy Director of the HEA's AIDS programme, summed up the effect of political involvement:

> it is clear that UK government leadership has been an important driving force to get things going and, in general, our politicians have made wise decisions. But it is also true that in countries in which political expediency dictates social policy, the personalities and personal beliefs of key individual politicians and civil servants have profound influence on how programmes evolve, including their tone, credibility, public and professional acceptability and ultimately their impact.[39]

In fact, the political consensus has survived largely through the bipartisan work of the House of Commons Select Committee on the Social Services. The Committee has been a rich source of information on AIDS. This has been supplemented by the educational role played by the All Party Group on AIDS, another bipartisan organisation, which produces a regular AIDS newsletter.

Even after the takeover of AIDS policy by the political leadership, the principal administrative burden for coping with the disease has continued to fall upon the health authorities, especially those in the Thames region. These regions have had to depend on central decisions about the availability of funds to meet the spread of AIDS, but the real policy has been made within these lower-level administrative structures. There has been, in other words, a centralised policy initiative with a decentralised implementation process. Such a pattern is echoed in the consultative structure.

Where in the USA gay interests have been part of the policy process from the beginning, in the UK it is the medical profession which has been regarded as the main source of expertise and information. The Terrence Higgins Trust, a primarily gay organisation which has built up considerable knowledge about AIDS and about the daily experience of those with AIDS, has not enjoyed the same intimacy with policy makers as the medical profession. No one from the DHSS attended the first two conferences on AIDS organised by the Trust. Although the Trust received £100,000 in 1986–7 from central government, this only just covered its printing bill and, while its grant quadrupled in the next four years, it still depended for two-thirds of its income on private sources. Rather than treating the Trust as a source of expert advice, the Government has preferred to use it as a conduit into the gay community, and as an adjunct of policy implementation not formulation. It is important, though, to notice that different ministers have varied in their contact with the Trust. Although Norman Fowler had few dealings with it, David Mellor visited the Trust on several occasions.[40]

For the most part, it is biomedical interests which have been most prominent in the consultative process, with the result that AIDS has been defined as a medical (or medical science) problem, rather than a social problem. This emphasis has shifted slightly, following the recommendations of the Commons Select Committee and lobbying within the DHSS. Behavioural questions featured more prominently on the agenda, even though the thrust of policy continued to be medically led. It is noticeable too that within the medical lobby certain disciplines predominate. It has been the clinicians (who deal in certainties), not the health educationalists and epidemiologists (who deal in probabilities) who have dominated the consultative process and the public forums.

But while a narrow range of interests have been consulted,

and while this has had the effect of undervaluing AIDS' social dimension, there have been some hidden benefits. As Dennis Altman observed of the American experience, the gay movement's ability to claim legitimacy for its life-style affected – and probably distorted – early research on AIDS.[41] Had there been no identifiable community to which the disease could be attributed (by those so inclined), there might have been less inclination to look for life-style causes of the disease. By the same token, the exclusion of gay groups in the UK may have left less excuse for prejudice and delay within government.

The same rather exclusive consultative process may also have worked to minimise the effect of moral majority groups. While in the USA such groups have managed to hamper attempts to speak explicitly and act decisively about AIDS, in Britain their equivalents have been almost wholly ineffective. Their lack of success may also be explained by the lack of public outrage – the DHSS received only 187 letters of complaint about the national AIDS leaflet; over half of these came from people who had not opened the offending document.

It might be surmised, therefore, that the same political system which allows for the broadest range of interest-group involvement provides less favourable conditions for an effective response. This is not, however, the end of the story. Consultation is only one element in the process. Implementation is equally important, and the British record on this has been criticised for lacking the very centralist inclinations that the consultation process displayed. The Commons Select Committee heard many witnesses argue that there was a serious lack of central coordination and planning. Too much discretion, they contended, had led to duplication and to a confusion of priorities, particularly to the detriment of scientific research. The existing mechanisms were described as 'politically expedient', '*ad hoc*' and 'crisis management'.[42] MPs took up the Select Committee's theme when issuing a call for a Minister for AIDS.

Whatever political structure is appropriate, it is evident that political and ethical values have played an important part in the shaping of AIDS policy, and that their role has increased with the politicisation of the policy process. The response to AIDS can be seen as part of the Government's general political strategy: in the way that the policy is dependent upon Health Service funding and administration, in the way the Government's general science and research priorities are paralleled in AIDS research; and in the ideological emphasis on personal responsibility.

It is noticeable also that the Government has not sought to explore further the problems entailed in changing sexual behaviour, despite the recognition that injunctions alone, however dramatically expressed, do not have the desired effect. Changing sexual behaviour appears to need more than the advertiser's art. Critics have stressed the need for more specific targeting of the public education campaigns, focusing on particular towns, not on the population at large or even general regions.

Finally, it is worth observing that the recognition of the social dimensions of AIDS has not focused on the policy process itself, the way information is collected and collated, or how groups are singled out as high risk, rather than behaviour as risky. This may be an important oversight. The historian Allan Brandt has argued, on the basis of the precedent provided by syphilis, that in themselves education, public health measures, cures and vaccines will not solve the problem.[43] A coherent response depends on providing both a political environment and a policy process which allow for these measures to be effective. Learning not to die of ignorance may mean, therefore, more than issuing instructions and funding medical and sociological research; it may mean learning how political practice and private behaviour interact.

CONCLUSION

What this chapter has demonstrated is the way in which decision-making in British government is affected, first, by the state of knowledge about the problem to be solved; and second, by the way in which information is organised and/or sought. Decisions cannot be seen as just assessments of the available information. What information is available is itself a result of prior decisions, and the structures that frame them. None of this denies the political importance of individual decisions, but it does argue for the need to understand the context in which the decision is made and the process by which the choices are constructed. Knowledge is a crucial political resource. Decision-making is often a process in which competing knowledge-claims and types of expertise fight for superiority. The winners help to define the 'problem' being addressed and the 'solution' that is appropriate to it. AIDS policy amply demonstrates the political importance of information to decision-making.

5 The Falklands War

INTRODUCTION

On 2 April 1982 Argentine forces invaded the Falklands to the consternation of British and world opinion. At a stroke British politics were transformed. For the next three months British politics *were* the Falklands crisis, all other issues being virtually swept from the attention of the media and Parliament. Even the normal workings of Whitehall were dislocated, as a permanent secretary confided to Tam Dalyell: 'it was just not possible to get the concentration of senior Ministers on matters other than the South Atlantic. As far as reaching decisions on other matters was concerned, Whitehall virtually seized up'.[1]

Yet in the months before the crisis broke the issue had been one of low political salience, the concern primarily of a limited section of the Foreign Office, of sections of the intelligence world and of a few back-bench politicians, like Sir Bernard Braine, who took an interest in these far-flung remnants of empire. The Falklands shows how on occasions issues can be transformed: one moment the almost exclusive concern of a coterie of professional diplomats, the next the centre of world drama. As the Falklands question went critical, so the issue itself underwent a metamorphosis. As a consequence the whole pattern of decision-taking was bound to be transformed.

In one sense the Falklands crisis was not typical of British politics. British governments do not as a matter of course have to assess the probability of foreign invasion of British sovereign territory or to launch large naval expeditions to far-flung corners of the globe. In other respects the Falklands crisis provides a rather old-fashioned example of decision-making. It did not encompass considerations of high technology; nor did the process of decision-making involve large numbers of individuals or obscure and cumbersome processes of government. It evolved around the classic issues of diplomacy and the conduct of war, with which Lord Palmerston or Gladstone would have been at home. Indeed after 2 April 1982 it seemed as if British politics had entered a time-warp, with pictures of the crowds lining Portsmouth harbour to cheer the fleet as it slipped away on the high tide to salvage national honour. Like the conflicts of the nineteenth century, the war, when it came, was a remote one which affected the lives of few, and news of which could be carefully controlled. Unlike the confused and opaque guerrilla wars of most of the post-1945 period it was a classic set piece, involving battleships, fighter aircraft and army brigades. The issues were clear, the outcome measurable. The population could watch it unfold with a *frisson* of excitement. Not often were politics such high drama.

Our concern in this chapter is not with the conduct of the war which ensued but with the events which led Britain into the conflict. This is because an account of the military side would involve far too much detail and would be very untypical of peacetime decision-making.[2] However, the authoritative findings of the Franks Committee, which later investigated the Government's conduct, supplemented by the investigations of journalists, have succeeded in laying bare the intricacies of Cabinet decision-making to an extent most unusual in foreign affairs.[3]

Before analysing the decision-making process it will be helpful first to sketch the actors involved in the run-up to the crisis and then to outline the principal events.

THE CHIEF ACTORS

The first to consider is the Argentine Government. The position and views of successive Argentine governments were simple. The 'Malvinas', as they called the Falklands, were an integral part of Argentine territorial inheritance, which in the early nineteenth century had been unlawfully seized by British colonialists and settled 'artifically'. Restoration of the Malvinas to Argentine sovereignty had long been a dream of Argentine governments, but the issue only became practical politics after the mid-1960s with the growth of anti-colonialist and anti-Western feeling in the Third World and the evident willingness, if not desire, of successive British governments to retreat from imperial responsibilities and to concentrate both political and military resources upon the North Atlantic area. For the Argentines 3 January 1983 was held to mark some kind of a deadline for resolving the issue, since this date marked the 150th anniversary of British occupation of the Islands.

If the general strategy was clear, the tactics to achieve it were not. How could negotiation and the threat of force best be balanced? What was to be the future status of the Falkland Islanders? How were the exact intentions of the British Government to be interpreted? What sorts of compromise were acceptable? After 1965 successive regimes found the Malvinas question a convenient means of distracting popular attention from domestic economic and social difficulties, but this in its turn presented dangers: it aroused expectations which it might not prove possible to fulfil. Moreover, Argentine policy-making was itself far from monolithic, especially in the period of rule by military junta after 1976, when the civilian politicians and diplomats at the foreign ministry were frequently at odds with the leaders of the armed services, which were themselves sometimes divided.

By the late 1970s the policy-makers in Buenos Aires had become somewhat disillusioned with negotiations with the British which seemed to be getting nowhere. It was felt that British governments were not averse to reducing their international commitments and would take a realistic approach to old colonial problems. However, it was felt necessary to supplement diplomatic negotiations with the maximum of pressure. By 5 January 1982 the Argentine junta decided to follow a double policy of allowing its Foreign Ministry to increase the diplomatic pressure on Britain, whilst simultaneously the armed forces were to 'analyse the possibility of use of military power to obtain the political objective'.[4]

In one respect the position of the 1,800 Falkland Islanders was clear-cut. They were of British descent and wished to remain under British rule. The vast majority of them wished to have as little to do with the Argentine Government as possible. They viewed with suspicion all attempts by the Foreign Office to negotiate with the Argentine Government. As they were so few in number, comprising for the most part crofter farmers of a peculiarly passive temperament, it might seem that their political position was extremely weak: after all the British Government had in previous years taken no notice of the wishes of the 1,200 inhabitants of Diego Garcia in the Indian Ocean when that island was required to be evacuated for the creation of an American military base. However, the Islands were dominated by the powerful Falkland Islands Company which owned most of the Islands and controlled their economy completely. There were certainly many social tensions on the Islands but poor educational standards and a somewhat pacific temperament among the inhabitants meant that they accepted the vocal opinion-leaders, concentrated in Port Stanley. Such opinion-leaders tended to exaggerate the antipathy of the Islanders to the idea of negotiations. In 1968 the Falkland Islands Company mobilised a parliamentary lobby of a number of backbench Conservative MPs which zealously interrogated successive Foreign Office representatives about the possibilities of a sell-out in what for them became an emotive issue. After 1976 the political complexion of this lobby became more varied with the addition of anti-junta Labour MPs as well as Liberals and Scottish Nationalists. After 1978 the Falklands lobby also spent a good deal of time mobilising support for economic investment in the Islands with a view to exploiting their fishing and geological wealth. This lobby, as we shall see, soon became a major domestic constraint upon successive Foreign Office ministers.[5]

The third major actor in the developing crisis was the British Foreign and Commonwealth Office (hereafter referred to as the Foreign Office) which had inherited Britain's vestigial colonial commitments from the defunct Colonial Office. Here we should note an important contrast. Whereas the previous two groups of actors regarded the Falklands as of major importance, for the Foreign Office they were of peripheral concern. Indeed Lord Carrington is reputed to have told an Argentine representative in New York that they ranked number 242 in his department's order of priorities! Foreign Office ministers and civil servants could only give strictly limited attention to the Falklands, and relations with Argentina were dealt with at junior ministerial level as part of the department's relations with Latin America. For the Foreign Office the Falklands had by the late 1960s become of little more than nuisance value. They had lost any strategic significance and they complicated relations with all of Latin America. The potential commercial and political benefits of good relations with Argentina were, on the other hand, important. From the late 1960s the Foreign Office followed a fairly consistent broad line of policy: to negotiate some sort of compromise over sovereignty which would satisfy Argentine aspirations yet safeguard the 'interests' (not always to be defined as identical to the 'wishes') of the Islanders.

The Foreign Office was the sole government department responsible for making policy on the Islands, and policy options were from time to time discussed in a clear-cut manner within the department. But other government departments had a subordinate interest. The Ministry of Defence was concerned in all matters that involved the deployment of British forces in the area, and the Treasury in policy decisions which would involve the expenditure of large sums of money, for example if it was deemed desirable for strategic or diplomatic reasons to build a modern long-haul airport on the Islands. Neither had any interest in committing resources to the Islands, quite the reverse. The Ministry of Defence was anxious to avoid weakening its forces in what it perceived as its main theatre of operations, the North Atlantic and Western Europe. If the Foreign Office wished to pursue a policy option that required the expenditure of military or financial resources – such as 'Fortress Falklands' – it would have to work through the Cabinet system, which in effect meant securing the approval of the Defence and Oversea Policy Committee of the Cabinet, chaired by the Prime Minister.

Since diplomatic activity depends upon knowledge, mention must also be made of the work of the Joint Intelligence Organisation (JIO). The role of this body, based in the Cabinet Office, was to make assessments of a wide range of external situations and developments based upon: (a) diplomatic reports and telegrams; (b) the views of government departments; (c) intelligence material from MI5 and MI6; (d) signals intelligence.

Current intelligence groups, primarily serviced by Foreign Office and Defence Ministry civil servants on secondment, made assessments on a geographical basis which were considered by the JIO which made weekly reports to the Defence and Oversea Committee of the Cabinet. Again it is important to realise that the Falklands 'were such a back-burner issue as to be off the stove'. Limited resources were inevitably concentrated on the more predictable goings-on in the Eastern bloc.[6]

A CHRONOLOGY OF THE CRISIS

The following is a brief chronological outline of the Falkland Islands crisis as it unfolded. In 1964–5 the Argentine Government renewed its interest in regaining the Falklands and secured a UN General Assembly resolution calling for Anglo-Argentine talks which would end 'colonialism' while securing the 'interests' of the Islanders. The Argentine claim to the Islands was raised when the Foreign Secretary, Michael Stewart, visited Buenos Aires as part of a Latin American tour in January 1966; and in September of that year an unofficial party of Peronist adventurers landed at Port Stanley, although this was disowned by the Argentine Government. Talks were held between Britain and Argentina in 1967, when for the first time Britain indicated that she would be prepared to cede sovereignty under certain conditions provided that the interests of the Islanders were respected. Negotiations at an official level reached agreement on a 'Memorandum of Understanding' in August 1968 whereby London would accept Argentine sovereignty over the Islands, but only when and if it was satisfied that such a transfer was acceptable to the wishes of the Islanders. In 1968 a parliamentary back-bench campaign began to resist any such settlement, and in November 1968 Lord Chalfont, a junior minister at the Foreign Office, visited the Falklands but failed to persuade the Islanders of the advantage of a settlement. In December 1968 the British Cabinet decided not to press ahead with the plan for a long-range negotiated settlement but to work for the development of better relations between the Islanders and the Argentines by fostering communications and trade – a policy of seduction. In any future negotiations Stewart conceded that the Islanders' wishes would be paramount. The Foreign Office hoped that the fostering of ever closer links between the Islands and Argentina would assist assimilation and change the Islanders' perspectives. Relations deteriorated after the return of a Peronist Government in 1973; and throughout the early 1970s the Foreign Office was unable to make progress with various schemes for condominium (joint rulership) or for economic cooperation because of the intransigence of both the Argentines and the Islanders. In 1975 the Labour Government commissioned Lord Shackleton to produce a long-term plan for economic development in the South Atlantic which aroused deep Argentine hostility.

After the military coup of March 1976 Argentine diplomatic pressure mounted and this was accompanied by bellicose actions such as the landing of a small group of sailors for 'purposes of scientific research' on the South Sandwich Islands. Meanwhile in February 1977 the British Government decided to embark on a new round of negotiations, without prejudice to the position of either government with regard to sovereignty over the Islands. By October 1977 Argentina started a series of naval manoeuvres which alarmed the British; so in November the Prime Minister, Mr Callaghan, ordered a small naval squadron of two frigates and a submarine to be sent covertly to the area to buttress the Government's negotiating position. Talks between Britain and Argentina continued on a variety of issues until 1979. These included scientific cooperation in the South Atlantic dependencies of the Falklands, economic development, and sovereignty issues.

The new Thatcher Government in 1979 reviewed all the options and in 1980 started exploratory talks with the Argentine Government, ministers having come round to the view that a 'leaseback' solution was the most practical solution to the problem. Under such an arrangement Argentina would acquire formal sovereignty, but British administration would be guaranteed for a lengthy period into the future. The Foreign Office under the previous Labour Government had concluded as far back as 1977 that such a scheme might be the only practicable solution, although most Islanders seemed hostile to it.[7] Mr Ridley, a junior Foreign Office minister, visited the Islands to try to persuade the Islanders of the merits of negotiations along these lines. However, on his return to London he received a very hostile reception from all sides of the House of Commons. In the light of this the Government felt that it was politically too costly to do other than keep some kind of talks going with the Argentines, while hoping that Island opinion would work its way round to seeing the necessity for some kind of a settlement along leaseback lines. After 1980 the British Government's policy was therefore essentially passive. Meanwhile in late 1981 the Government announced that HMS *Endurance*, the Antarctic ice patrol vessel, was to be withdrawn as part of the Defence Review; while the British Antarctic Survey announced that budgetary cuts would mean closing their base at Grytviken on the island of South Georgia. In December 1981 General Galtieri succeeded as President of Argentina.

In January 1982 the Argentine Foreign Ministry set out proposals for the establishment of a permanent negotiating commission to meet monthly and to try to reach a conclusion by the end of the year. In late February talks were held in New York about the possible nature and operation of such a commission. On 19 March Sr. Davidoff, an Argentine scrap metal merchant, landed illegally on the British Island of South Georgia. Events in South Georgia appeared confusing for a while, but on 22 March the Base Commander at Grytviken reported indications of collusion between Davidoff and the Argentine Navy. HMS *Endurance* was ordered to take off Argentine personnel from South Georgia, but on 25 March intelligence was received of the despatch of Argentine warships to the area. London still believed that it was essential to avoid exacerbating the situation, although some contingency plans were made. Only on the afternoon of Wednesday 31 March did the Ministry of Defence believe that a full-scale Argentine invasion of the Falklands was likely. Such an invasion occurred on 2 April, notwithstanding a last-minute telephone call from President Reagan to General Galtieri in which the President strongly tried to dissuade the General from any such action.

After the invasion events moved fast in Britain. An emergency Cabinet meeting was held on 2 April and the House of Commons met in a special session on the following day – a Saturday morning. Lord Carrington, the Foreign Secretary resigned; meanwhile Britain persuaded the Security Council of the UN to pass a resolution calling for the cessation of hostilities, the withdrawal of the Argentines from the Islands and a diplomatic settlement. Over the next few weeks a large British Task Force was assembled at great speed and sent to the South Atlantic, a 200-mile war zone round the Islands being declared on 7 April. There then followed a lengthy attempt at shuttle mediation by the American Secretary of State, Alexander Haig, which broke down on 19 April only to be succeeded by an attempted Peruvian peace plan. Meanwhile the British Task Force reached the South Atlantic and South Georgia was recaptured. On 2 May the Argentine cruiser, *General Belgrano* was sunk, an event which signalled the commencement of naval and aerial engagements. Some UN peace efforts dragged on until 19 May, but on 18 May the decision was taken to launch a full-scale British military assault on the Islands. A complete Argentine capitulation followed within a month on 15 June. Such then is the bald outline of the diplomatic and military manoeuvres which preceded the Argentine invasion of 2 April 1982. Let us next consider what the case-study reveals about decision-making in British government.

MINISTERIAL CONTROL OVER POLICY OPTIONS

One point which stands out is the remarkable continuity in the general lines of Foreign Office policy during the period 1965–81. No sudden shifts can be discerned after the change of British governments in 1964, 1970, 1974 or 1979. The general strategy was to negotiate in good faith a settlement with the Argentines which would be acceptable to the Falkland Islanders and to parliamentary opinion at home. The details of what constituted that settlement varied from time to time. It might be tempting to conclude from this that here was a departmental policy line promoted by officials who assiduously foisted it upon their political masters. The pro-Falklands lobby of Conservative back-benchers at times appeared to adopt this interpretation. The evidence of the Franks Committee, on the other hand, suggests that this would be a gross over-simplification. On the contrary, the Falklands issue was regularly reviewed at ministerial level. Talks with Argentina occurred for the first time after Michael Stewart's tour of Latin America in 1966. In November 1966 the Foreign and Colonial Secretaries presented a paper to the Defence Committee of the Cabinet on the subject. By September 1967 talks had reached foreign minister level and it was Lord Chalfont, a junior minister, who visited the Islands to explain the Government's policy in 1968. It was a meeting of the full Cabinet on 11 December 1968 which decided not to continue to seek a settlement on the basis of the Memorandum of Understanding on account of adverse parliamentary reaction and the inflexibility of the Argentine Government.[8]

From 1969–74 negotiations on improving cooperation between the two governments on matters of communications and commerce continued in a low-key manner; but the Labour Government, newly elected in 1974, was 'presented with a range of options', and again it was the Defence Committee of the Cabinet which decided 'to consult the Falkland Islands Executive Council on the possibility of initiating talks with Argentina on condominium'.[9] By March 1976 when relations had sharply deteriorated it was the Prime Minister, Mr Callaghan, who decided to undertake a major review of policy. In March 1976 the Defence Committee and the Cabinet approved his proposals for a fresh dialogue on all aspects of the dispute, including both the possibilities of Anglo-Argentine economic cooperation in the South-West Atlantic and 'the nature of a hypothetical future constitutional relationship'.[10] In February 1977 the Foreign Secretary, Mr Crosland, announced the Government's decision to explore more avenues of cooperation and it was Mr Ted Rowlands, a junior minister, who proceeded to visit the Falklands in order to investigate the possibilities for progress. Crosland's successor, Dr Owen, also presented a paper to the Cabinet Defence Committee in July 1977 reviewing future tactics.[11] Following the general election of 1979 the Foreign Office presented the new junior minister of state with a full range of policy options. These included: (a) Fortress Falklands; (b) abandoning the Islands and resettling the islanders; (c) to go through the motions of continued negotiation; and (d) to continue the negotiations in good faith in an attempt to find a solution acceptable to all parties. Franks tells us that:

> Mr Ridley discussed these options with Lord Carrington, and it was agreed that, before the Government decided on the handling of any formal negotiations, Mr Ridley should visit the Falkland Islands and Argentina to sound out views there at first hand.[12]

According to Hastings and Jenkins it was Ridley who took the initiative in all this and who 'briskly set about cohering the options'. Lord Carrington, the new Foreign Secretary, thought the initiative was probably 'right but rash' and the Prime Minister herself responded with an instant dogmatism replying to Carrington who broached the matter to her in a manner described by Whitehall sources as 'thermonuclear'. It was Ridley who persisted in the face of Prime Ministerial hostility, finally gaining leave to have leaseback discussed at the Defence Committee where, with the support of 'Wet' ministers like Whitelaw and Pym, he won approval to prepare a new plan.[13] Following Ridley's parliamentary débâcle in December 1980, policy was carefully reviewed by Ridley on 26 March 1981. Prompted by the British Embassy in Buenos Aires, the Foreign Office decided in May 1981 to embark on yet another round of talks with Argentina; a senior official, Mr John Ure, was sent to visit first the Islands in order to encourage the Island Council to come to a decision and then on to Argentina 'to reassure the Argentine Government of the British Government's wish to make progress towards a solution and to seek to persuade them not to force the pace'. Following these explorations a 'major review of policy' was undertaken on 30 June 1981 at a meeting chaired by Ridley.[14] Policy options were further analysed in a minute to Carrington on 20 July 1981, at a meeting of ministers and officials on 7 September and in a minute by Carrington to the Prime Minister on 14 September.[15] All this seems to vindicate a very orthodox, rationalist view of policy. A single department is responsible for policy on an issue; officials under ministerial direction make periodic reviews of policy options in the light of changing external circumstances; adjustments are made and important initiatives or departures are taken to the relevant Cabinet committee, in this case the Defence Committee, where the key decisions are made. However, this simple picture of decision-making requires some important qualifications. It ignores many of the constraints under which the Foreign Office was operating as well as the impact of broader political considerations.

DOMESTIC POLITICS AND INTER-DEPARTMENTAL WHITEHALL PRESSURES

A critical factor at various times in the Falklands dispute was the power of Parliament. The conventional view is that Parliament plays little role in foreign policy-making and that MPs, even when they are interested in such issues, are largely powerless to influence governments. Yet the representatives of the Falkland Islanders built up a lobby whose political nuisance value was out of all proportion to the power of the interest affected. An early warning of the influence of this lobby was the way in which Michael Stewart back in 1968 was forced to concede that there would be no cession of sovereignty against the wishes rather than the mere interests of the Islanders – a significant distinction.[16] By 1977 the Falklands lobby was engineering about five interventions a year, including in that year two full-scale debates. By that time it possessed a full-time director, Air Commodore Brown Frow, and a budget of some £15,000.[17] Both Lord Chalfont and Ted Rowlands received extremely hostile receptions in 1968 and 1977, which were widely reported in the press. This influenced government policy at subsequent Cabinets or Cabinet committees. But the harshest reception was reserved for Nicholas Ridley in 1980 when he tried to sell the idea of a leaseback. He suffered a savaging from all sides of the House and according to observers left the chamber 'ashen and shaking'.[18] This episode in turn only bolstered up the opposition in the Islands to the concept of leaseback, and, following the rejection of the idea by the Falkland Islands Joint Council, the Cabinet decided not to pursue the plan. This was not the only effect of the parliamentary débâcle. By mid-summer 1981 Ridley concluded that the only policy options were to continue to open negotiations with the Argentine on leaseback, to let Argentina conclude that the British Government was no longer interested in discussing sovereignty or (more positively): 'to embark on a public education campaign to educate Islander and British public opinion about the facts of the situation, the consequences of a failure to negotiate and the corresponding advantages of a sovereignty solution'.[19]

All three Foreign Office ministers discussed this on 7 September. Lord Carrington could not accept this last policy. He later told the Franks Committee 'that, in his view, such a campaign would not have been agreed by his colleagues [in Cabinet] and would have been counter productive'. Domestic political considerations were obviously crucial here – as is made explicit in a personal letter from Mr Fearn, Official Head of the South American Department of the Foreign Office, to the British Ambassador in Buenos Aires of 23 September. It explained that ministers had decided that:

> The domestic political constraints must at this stage continue to pre-vent us from taking any steps which might be interpreted either as putting pressure on the Islanders or as overruling their wishes. Spec-ifically that meant that an education campaign in the Islands and the United Kingdom has, at least for the present, been ruled out.[20]

Why did domestic political considerations weigh so heavily at this time? The answer is to be found in the general political context which it is all too easy to ignore when concentrating upon the development of a single policy area. Since 1979 Lord Carrington and the Foreign Office had spent a great deal of their time wrestling with the problems of Rhodesia and trying to sell a policy of transferring power in that country to Marxist-inclined guerrillas. Relations between the Foreign Secretary and Conservative back-benchers had been, to say the least, far from cordial. Neither the Foreign Secretary nor the Prime Minister had any incentive to add to their difficulties on this score. Rhodesia was a major problem necessitating immediate treatment; the Falklands represented a minor irritant which was far from pressing.

Parliamentary opposition exaggerated the strength of opposition within the Falklands to leaseback. Had the Foreign Office and the Government as a whole possessed the political will to press ahead with this as a policy such opposition might easily have been overcome. The problem facing the Foreign Office was that such opposition was echoed within the Cabinet, especially by the Prime Minister, whose gut reaction was to mistrust the Foreign Office's lack of gumption in this as in other fields. The political price for any Foreign Office initiative was a high one and seemed out of proportion to the intrinsic importance of the issue.[21] In September 1981 these considerations inhibited the Foreign Secretary, Lord Carrington, from endorsing the policy of an education campaign for Island opinion. Indeed from September to March 1982 Carrington preferred to keep the Defence Committee of the Cabinet informed through a series of minutes, rather than risking a full-blown policy discussion.[22]

Parliament, opinion within the Conservative Party, and extraneous political considerations therefore greatly influenced policy-making in the Falklands. Another powerful constraint was the influence and interests of other Whitehall departments. Several examples may be cited of the Foreign Office's policy lines being disrupted by the actions or inactions of other departments. During the 'Argentine seduction' phase of the early 1970s the Overseas Development Agency, with other more pressing claims on its budget, refused to provide funds for the development of an airport on the Falklands and for other improvements in communications with Argentina. To the Argentines this appeared but a typical example of British perfidy.

Another major clash of interest was between the Foreign Office and the Ministry of Defence (MOD). Even for the Foreign Office the Falklands were a low priority, but for the MOD they were an issue of the lowest possible priority. The MOD took five months to respond to the Foreign Office's request in May 1981 for a short politico-military assessment of the UK's ability to respond to a range of Argentine actions.[23] If war is the extension of diplomacy by other means, then to be credible in situations of tension diplomacy needs the sanction of force. It was in the interests of the Foreign Office to maintain an adequate defence force in the South West Atlantic, but this ran counter to the MOD's interest. After 1974 the Foreign Office continually had to fight hard to ensure that the ice patrol vessel, HMS *Endurance*, was not withdrawn from the area. Such a withdrawal in fact was agreed in June 1981 to take effect the following year, notwithstanding the protests of Carrington and Ridley. This was interpreted in Argentina, in the words of an intelligence report from Buenos Aires: 'as a deliberate political gesture; they did not see it as an inevitable economy in Britain's defence budget since the implications for the Islands and for Britain's position in the South Atlantic were fundamental.'[24]

Similar misleading signals were given to the Argentine leaders by the new British Nationality Bill, sponsored by yet another Whitehall department, the Home Office, which was aimed primarily at preventing an influx to Britain of Hong Kong Chinese, but which had the effect of denying rights of full British citizenship to Falklanders who did not have British-born grandparents; even the Gibraltarians were spared this ignomy by virtue of an amendment in the House of Lords.[25]

THE TENDENCY TO DRIFT AND THE FORECLOSING OF POLICY OPTIONS

With the benefit of hindsight it is easy to see that early March 1982 was the last opportunity for the British Government to have dispatched a naval force, given the naval passage time of 20–25 days. Ministers at this time were certainly worried at the deteriorating situation in Anglo-Argentine relations and at the increasingly intransigent mood of both government and public opinion in Argentina. On 8 March the Prime Minister raised the question of contingency planning, and on 5 March officials told Lord Carrington of the action taken by the Labour Government, in 1977 in dispatching a small naval force of frigates and a submarine in similar circumstances. Lord Carrington still declined to accept that the prospect of continuing negotiations at that time was hopeless.[26] Even if Carrington had taken a less sanguine view it would not, as Hastings and Jenkins have pointed out, have been easy for a Foreign Secretary in these circumstances to have secured assent from the Defence Committee of the Cabinet:

He will find the Ministry of Defence averse to the cost and dislocation of ships. The Treasury will likewise be unsympathetic. He will therefore need substantial evidence of a threat to national interests, presumably in the form of a JIC assessment from Cabinet Office. He will need to square the Prime Minister in advance.[27]

In early March Foreign Office officials and ministers felt that they lacked the necessary intelligence evidence to justify such a request which would have been particularly inopportune at a time when Whitehall inter-departmental relations were dominated by budgetary considerations in the wake of Sir Geoffrey Howe's strict policy of cash limits.

The Falklands episode illustrates very well the workings of the Cabinet system in Britain. Although Falklands policy was the responsibility of the Foreign Office, all important initiatives had to be approved by the Defence Committee or by the Cabinet itself. As many of these initiatives required the support or action of other departments or had broader political ramifications it was difficult to secure any progress. Conversely a policy of passivity meant that the question escaped Cabinet discussion. This was the situation after September 1981 when Lord Carrington vetoed within the Foreign Office the idea of an education campaign in the Falklands and the UK. Similar considerations dissuaded Lord Carrington from applying for a nuclear-powered submarine to be deployed to the South Atlantic in March 1982 in view of the deteriorating situation. What ensued in the first three months of 1982 was a period of paralysis. As the Franks Report has noted:

> Government policy towards Argentina and the Falkland Islands was never formally discussed outside the Foreign and Common-wealth Office after January 1981. Thereafter, the time was never judged to be ripe although we were told in oral evidence that, subject to the availability of Ministers, a Defence Committee meeting could have been held at any time, if necessary at short notice.[28]

The next time the Committee discussed the Falklands was 1 April on the eve of the invasion. The episode reveals very clearly the tendencies to passivity of the British political system. Meetings on a subject tend to be held only if a decision is required. Whether a full discussion of the situation at Cabinet level would have made much difference to the outcome is impossible to judge although Franks concludes:

in our view, it could have been advantageous . . . for Ministers to have reviewed collectively at that time [September 1981], or in the months immediately ahead, the current negotiating position; the implications of the conflict between the attitudes of the Islanders and the aims of the Junta; and the longer-term policy options in relation to the dispute.[29]

In surveying the history of the Falklands dispute between 1965 and March 1982 one cannot help but be struck by the way in which the policy options open to the Foreign Office in reality gradually foreclosed, despite the fact that formally speaking a range of options were rationally weighed and considered at various stages. In one sense the initial decision to open up talks with Argentina in 1965–6, albeit not on sovereignty at that stage, conceded that there was a problem and that an Argentine case existed. Hereafter any resort to a Fortress Falklands policy would appear to be illogical as well as too costly in military and financial terms. The longer the policy of pursuing a generally accepted negotiated settlement was pursued, the less feasible it became to change to one of the two alternative radical policy lines: Fortress Falklands or unconditional withdrawal. At first the broad category of a negotiated settlement provided plenty of leeway; but in the words of Franks:

> the picture that the history of the dispute presents is one in which the negotiating options were progressively eliminated until only one – leaseback – was left that might eventually satisfy the aspirations of Argentina on the one hand and the wishes of the Islanders on the other.[30]

One can certainly trace the steps by which the options were narrowed. At first, 1966–8, the objective was talks to decrease friction. After 1968 it was clear that any settlement would have to be acceptable to the wishes not just the interests of the Islanders. From 1969–74 the objective was to further the cultivation of good communications and understanding between the Islanders and the Argentines while avoiding the issue of sovereignty. From 1973–4 the idea of a condominium was explored but was found to be unacceptable to the Islanders. From 1976–9 the policy was to promote dialogue between Britain and Argentina not excluding consideration of sovereignty, the strategy being:

> To retain sovereignty as long as possible, if necessary making concessions in respect of the Dependencies and the maritime

resources in the area, while recognising that ultimately only some form of leaseback arrangement was likely to satisfy Argentina.[31]

After 1979 the situation had deteriorated so that the active pursuit of a settlement on the basis of leaseback became the goal of the Foreign Office. This prospect received a major setback as a result of the parliamentary furore in 1980 and the subsequent rejection of leaseback by the Island Joint Council. The only positive option that then seemed open was to embark on the education of Island and domestic opinion. Once this had been ruled out by Lord Carrington (on account of the domestic political dangers) in September 1981 there was in his own words of 14 September 1981 'little we can do beyond trying to keep some sort of negotiation going'.[32] After this date the Foreign Office was completely boxed in. All it could hope to do was to stave off Argentine pressure by attempting to buy time in the hope of simultaneously appeasing the Argentines and persuading the representatives of the Islanders of the need for some flexibility. This was its position in the talks in New York in February 1982.[33] Meanwhile ministers and officials had much more pressing matters, as is shown by Carrington's visit to Israel on the very eve of the invasion. Viewed at from this perspective, policy-making on the Falklands appears far more incremental than one might at first glance suppose. The Foreign Office at any time could have pressed for policy initiatives such as military reinforcement or a compromise settlement such as leaseback, but the political costs of such initiatives were so high as to rule them out.

THE IMPORTANCE OF PERCEPTION

A final feature which emerges from the story of the invasion is the importance of perception in the processing of information. The most striking examples of this are to be found on the Argentine side. The Argentine junta simply misread such incidents as the planned withdrawal of HMS *Endurance*, the passage of the British Nationality Act, and the apparent passivity of the British Government as signs of the weakening resolve of Britain to defend her tiny far-flung colony. Later they misread diplomatic and intelligence data coming from London at the time of the South Georgia incident, concluding that Britain was about to reinforce the Islands. This encouraged them to press ahead with a full-scale invasion. Finally, they badly underestimated the strength of opinion in Britain and the political will of British Government.[34]

Equally striking examples are to be found on the British side. British intelligence persistently failed to give adequate emphasis to the political context of military activity in Argentina. As G. M. Dillon has pointed out, British decision-makers assumed a stable rhythm in the Falklands question whereby peaceful negotiations regularly alternated with periods of tension and pressure. This played down the changing nature of Argentine politics, with the advent of a volatile military junta and a surge in nationalist sentiment. The significance of the coming to power of the hawkish and unpredictable General Galtieri in December 1981, in particular, was ignored.[35] It was also naturally difficult for the British to appreciate the gulf that sometimes existed between the civilian Argentine Foreign Ministry and the military junta. Although the Latin American Current Intelligence Committee met eighteen times between July 1981 and March 1982, it did not once discuss the Falklands, presumably being more occupied with Central America and Belize. Politicians, for their part, found it hard to enter into the mind-set of South American military leaders. Lord Carrington in the very final days, when suggestions were made that he should postpone his visit to Israel, simply:

> Found it hard . . . to imagine that a civilised and pro-Western country such as Argentina would take up arms against another Western country with which she had long-established ties over a trifling argument about who owned some islands in the South Atlantic.[36]

The misreading of intelligence data in the six months or so before the invasion provides a particularly good example of problems of perception. The JIO provided regular assessments of Argentine intentions, although understandably on a low-priority basis. Full-scale reviews took place, in November 1975, November 1977, November 1979 and July 1981. In March 1982 work started on a new assessment which was never completed. The July 1981 assessment was 'particularly important because . . . it had considerable influence on the thinking of Ministers and officials'.[37] This review examined the options open to the Argentine Government and concluded that it would 'prefer to achieve [its] objective by peaceful means' and use force 'as a last resort'. The review considered that there would probably be an escalating series of Argentine actions: first increasing diplomatic pressure in the UN and elsewhere; then fuel and air embargos on the Islands; then actions against British interests in Argentina along with harassment of British trawlers and shipping; then some sort of landing on South Georgia to show the flag; then a series of pin-prick incidents on the main islands; then an official action in some remote parts of the Islands; and only finally a full-scale invasion.[38] Later evidence suggests that this assessment was a fair reflection of the intentions of the civilian ministers and officials at the Argentine Foreign Ministry, notably Costa Mendez, who was unaware of the junta's military planning exercise when he prepared his diplomatic initiative in January 1982.[39] The interesting point to note is that all the incidents of March 1982 leading up to the sudden invasion could be read into this pattern.

A 'freelance' activity on South Georgia by a scrap metal merchant was still quite a long way down the list of Argentine actions. Coupled with this was the conviction, based upon further intelligence reports, that the Argentine effort would be timed towards the end of 1982 in order to have some tangible achievement before the 150th anniversary of British occupation of the Islands in January 1983. In early March a number of intelligence reports indicated that military action was not contemplated in the immediate future. If no progress was made on the sovereignty issue the Foreign Ministry was likely to try to get some declaration at the UN. On 10 March it was reported that 'all elements of the Argentine Government apart from the Navy favoured diplomatic action to solve the dispute and that the military option was not under active consideration at that time'. It seemed unlikely that the naval belligerence would prevail. On the eve of the South Georgia incident some conflicting assessments were made, and there were indications that the situation had deteriorated but there was no reason to think that the July 1981 assessment was invalidated.[40] The South Georgia incident itself was confused and gave rise to a variety of interpretations.[41] With the benefit of hindsight it is easy to see that British intelligence badly underestimated not only the likely effect of bellicose press and popular opinion upon the junta, but also the degree to which General Galtieri and Admiral Anaya would be able to override the more cautious leanings of Costa Mendez and civilian officials at the Argentine Foreign Ministry.

The South Georgia episode at the end of March seems, if anything, to have had a mesmerising rather than a galvanising effect upon both the Foreign Office and the intelligence networks. The extent of official Argentine naval involvement in Davidoff's activities remained somewhat obscure. Thought was being given to contingency military planning from the end of the first week of March but the threat was perceived as late as 20 March to be the cutting-off of sea and air links to the Islands rather than a full-scale invasion. Only between 28–30 March did the worsening situation begin to give serious alarm, and indeed it was only on 26 March, after three days of discussions, that the junta finally made the decision to go for a full military option and to bring forward its invasion plans.[42] As late as the morning of 31 March the current intelligence group in Whitehall dealing with Latin America was still reporting that there was no intelligence to suggest that the junta had decided upon invasion. Signal intelligence was becoming copious at this time but such data is raw and needs careful interpretation based upon previously existing perception. Decision-makers in London perceived such intelligence in terms of their expectations of a slowly escalating Argentine military activity designed to strengthen a negotiating position. They were anxious neither to overreact, as was thought to have been the case in 1977, nor to take any precipitate hostile actions which might provoke Argentina into a pre-emptive strike.[43] On the Falkland Islands themselves, so ingrained was the expectation of limited Argentine military action, that as late as 31 March the Governor, when warned by London that an Argentine submarine was on its way, 'thought there would be a bit of a scrap on the beach and then we would all have a glass of sherry and I'd tell them to go away, and jolly well not come back'.[44] Indeed only on the evening of 31 March as a result of further signal intelligence, did the penny finally drop even in London that a full-scale invasion was under way. By then all the British Government had to fall back on was the persuasive powers of an American President, whose grasp of foreign affairs was notoriously sketchy, speaking on a long distance telephone line to a General, whose command of English was poor.

DECISION-MAKING AFTER THE INVASION

In contrast to the pre-crisis period when the Cabinet processes had kept the Falklands off the agenda because no decision was needed, after the crisis broke in Whitehall on 31 March the flexibility and coordinating powers of the British Cabinet system came into their own. On 31 March a meeting was held in Mrs Thatcher's House of Commons room attended by some key ministers, senior civil servants and intelligence figures and the First Sea Lord, Sir Henry Leach. Next morning the Defence Committee of the Cabinet met, and the Cabinet itself met twice on 2 April. Thereafter a War Cabinet was set up; this was formally a subcommittee of the Defence and Oversea Committee but reported directly to the full Cabinet. Subordinate to this was the Committee of Chiefs of Staffs which met daily, the link between the two being Sir Terence Lewin, the Chief of Defence Staff, who had been visiting New Zealand when the crisis broke. The permanent membership of the 'War Cabinet' was not at first made public but comprised the Prime Minister, Nott, the Defence Secretary, Pym, the new Foreign Secretary, Whitelaw and Parkinson, Paymaster General and Chairman of the Conservative Party.

Several conclusions can be drawn about the workings of the machinery of government over the next few weeks. First, the Prime Minister played a critical role in all decisions. Secondly, the composition of the War Cabinet, in particular the appointment of Parkinson, reflected political considerations, the desire of Thatcher and Nott for support against the potentially 'Wet' combination of Pym and Whitelaw. Thirdly, the War Cabinet effectively made the key decisions as far as the British Government was concerned. Arguments once resolved in the War Cabinet were not then gone over again in the full Cabinet to which the War Cabinet reported every Tuesday; nor was sensitive information relayed which might cause damage by leaks. Fourthly, the composition of the War Cabinet was flexible. The permanent members were from time to time supplemented by other members of the Government, such as Sir Michael Havers who was called in to give advice on legal aspects and by officials and military advisers.[45] The effectiveness and cohesiveness of the British machinery impressed Haig and the American mediators who contrasted it favourably with the 'irrationality and chaotic nature of the Argentine leadership'. Haig at one point is said to have declared that in Argentina:

> there seemed to be 50 people involved in decisions. If he reached some sort of agreement on one of the points at issue with a member of the junta, this was invariably countermanded by a corps commander entering the room an hour or so later.[46]

If the War Cabinet can be identified as the focal point of British decision-making, it would on the other hand be wrong to jump to the conclusion that it operated in a vacuum or without constraints. What other factors or forces were significant? One such was the power of public opinion. In the wake of the invasion the Thatcher Government's standing was at a low ebb in this regard. Firm and decisive action of some kind seemed necessary. But beyond that it was difficult to know what was required. The public wanted resolute action but early signs were that they also wanted to avoid the loss of British life. It was impossible for ministers to know how this might change in the course of the conflict if ever casualties were suffered. For this reason alone it is wrong to think that ministers set out on 2

April with a clear-cut policy on the use of force.[47]

Another important factor was the force of Parliamentary opinion. Anyone who heard the House of Commons debate on Saturday 3 April, even on the radio, could not fail to recognise that here was an historic debate comparable to that which preceded the fall of Chamberlain in 1940. The mood of the House was cross, outraged and xenophobic. Calls came from all sides, including such figures as Michael Foot, for resolute action. In his book, *Iron Britannia: Why Parliament Waged its Falklands War*, Anthony Barnett goes so far as to claim that the responsibility for the sending of the Task Force and the waging of war rested with Parliament itself. The debate, according to this view, was highly charged and to some extent stage-managed so that dissenting voices were not allowed an opportunity to express themselves. At the beginning of the debate Mrs Thatcher's announcement that a Task Force was in preparation was made with 'nervousness rather than self-confidence'. After the debate, 'it became instead an Armada sailing at the behest of the House with the Prime Minister at the helm: the Commons nationalized Thatcher's style of leadership – it was an Iron Britannia that emerged'.[48]

This case is overstated but it has the virtue of focusing attention on the domestic political situation. The 3 April debate and the Conservative parliamentary party meeting which succeeded it showed the importance of Conservative back-bench opinion, while the support of the opposition for the sending of a Task Force strengthened the Prime Minister's negotiating position in many respects.

At this point it is important to assess the implications of the decision made on 31 March to assemble a Task Force. For it is all too easy to conclude that on this date the Thatcher Government 'decided' their policy and resolutely saw it through to the bitter end in San Carlos Sound and Mount Tumbeldown. This is to read history with the benefit of hindsight; although later, for perfectly understandable reasons, this became the orthodox, official Conservative Party version. For one thing the initial decision reflected the interplay of political and bureaucratic forces. According to the full account of the meeting in Mrs Thatcher's Commons room on 31 March given by Hastings and Jenkins the initial reaction of the ministers gathered there – Nott, Whitelaw, Atkins and Luce – was one of caution. Nott, the Defence Secretary, argued 'the logistical difficulties of the sort of operation necessary to retake the islands in the event of an Argentine invasion'. This reflected the earlier policy position in March before the invasion: the assembling of a task force had then been deemed to be impractical. It would have taken up to three weeks to assemble and another three weeks to reach the Islands. It would have denuded NATO and have been extremely expensive to mount. Somewhat by chance, the First Sea Lord, Sir Henry Leach, had come to the Commons in full naval uniform after a day at Portsmouth. Finding the latest briefing material on his desk at the Admiralty, he had hurried along to see Nott at Westminster, and finally found his way, with some difficulty, to the meeting. Once there he forcefully expressed the opinion that a large balanced fleet should and could be mobilised quickly and that such an action would have an immediate effect upon the Argentine admirals.[49] As Leach later put it: 'I think that I sensed, when I went in, that the sort of advice she had been getting prior to that had tended to deflect her from doing anything beyond negotiating, and putting the screws on with words again'. Most participants later considered that Leach's forceful views made a marked impact by undermining Nott's hesitancies. The effect was to ensure that any task force would be a large one and that it could and should be mobilised by the weekend. The decision was then taken to begin to prepare such a task force, although without commitment as to whether or not it should actually set sail.[50] Leach and the naval lobby, smarting under the savage naval cuts which Nott had planned and which would have destroyed their capacity to deploy forces outside the NATO area, saw the Falklands as a heaven-sent opportunity to reverse current government defence policy. They enthusiastically pressed the idea of sending a major Task Force to the South Atlantic.[51] Far more than the future of the Falklands was at stake. There were, therefore, powerful forces within the government machine pressing the Government to undertake a forward policy and such sentiments were music to the Prime Minister's ears.

From 31 March on into late April, until the sinking of the *General Belgrano*, it is possible to see the military policy of the Government in terms of momentum. At first the question was one of mobilisation; it could be presented as a naval as much as a political matter. In the words of Hastings and Jenkins:

To many present, [on 1 April] a task force already seemed the only garment with which they could cover their political nakedness should the worst occur. The fleet was accordingly to be put on the fullest state of alert. Still no one seems to have believed that it would come to blows. Indeed, ministers' readiness to accede to the alert was partly conditioned by its unreality. There was no discussion of rules of engagement, strategy or the likely balance of advantage against the Argentine fleet.

By the early hours of 2 April the task force was already being mobilised
and units were sailing although no such expedition had at this stage
been approved by either the British Cabinet or Parliament.[52]

Hopes of a diplomatic initiative to stop the invasion through
American pressures were still evident on 1 April, although these
faded rapidly as the day wore on. However, at its second emergency
meeting on the evening of 2 April the Cabinet endorsed the sending of
a Task Force. The momentum of the previous few days was one factor,
another was the need to have taken some action when facing what
was bound to be a traumatic session in the Commons the following
day. Equally significant, however, was the feeling that the sending
of the Task Force was a useful adjunct to the intense diplomatic
activity and economic measures which were also to be taken. The
task force could be seen at this stage as simply a supportive gesture
of resolve. All Hastings' and Jenkins' informants agreed 'that on 2
April no Cabinet minister believed for a minute that the outcome of
their decision would be open war'.[53] Sir Nicholas Henderson confirms
this interpretation:

> When the British task force was despatched to the South Atlantic
> few of those responsible for the decision had any idea how the
> Argentines were going to be ejected by force from the islands.
> According to my information, nobody involved in that decision
> thought at the time that it would be bound to lead to an open war.[54]

The Parliamentary debate on 3 April gave further momentum to
the moves to a military conflict. In both Britain and Argentina
popular passions had been aroused on the issue which geared up
its political significance so that the decision-makers' freedom of
manoeuvre was constrained. By later that week the previously unclear
military objective had become clear – the recapture of the Islands
by means of an amphibious assault, and this military advice further
narrowed the options.

Between 4 April and the commencement of hostilities in earnest
after the sinking of the *General Belgrano* military and diplomatic
pressures were exerted in tandem. During this month the constraints
upon the Government of one kind or another were considerable.
The more the Task Force advanced, the greater the momentum.
For the Government to do a 'Grand Old Duke of York' without any
compensating diplomatic achievement would be tantamount to committing political suicide. Various factors came into play. The first was
the time factor. The closer the Task Force sailed, the more were the

chances of military activity simply occurring. Moreover, the Argentine military had every incentive in letting British troops roll about the increasingly stormy southern seas. There was a narrow window of opportunity for military action. The Government was advised that the Task Force could only sustain operations for six months from the date of sailing, and would face progressive deteriorations in effectiveness after three months.[55] Then there was the pressure from the Americans. American support was crucial not only in the diplomatic area but also in terms of covert military support. The amount of 'kit' which the Americans supplied, though never made public, is said by authoritative sources to have been vital. The British Government therefore had every reason not to take precipitate action which would alienate the American Government, a factor which was specially important given the divisions between the 'Anglos' and the 'Latinos' within the American bureaucracy and administration. British public opinion was equally uncertain. It was a matter of guesswork as to how it would respond in the event of British casualties. Finally, there was the problem of the War Cabinet effectively ensuring adequate lines of communication with its forces and above all ensuring that there was effective political control over the military effort. The subsequent revelations concerning the sinking of the *General Belgrano* show that this was no mere academic problem.

6 Nuclear power decisions

INTRODUCTION

For those who suspect that British government can be both incompetent and undemocratic, the story of Britain's nuclear power programme is a persuasive example. In 1979, *The Sunday Times* commented: 'For a quarter of a century Britain's nuclear future has been a story of muddle, indecision, and bitter controversy'. Nearly ten years on, little seemed to have changed. *The Independent* observed: 'The history of nuclear power in Britain has been a history of dithering and of decisions made and then unmade and then remade.'[1]

Rational decision-making has been obscured by the clouds created by political pragmatism, institutional self-interest, and contradictory advice. The nuclear power decisions did not simply emerge from Cabinet discussion, manifesto promises, or scientific assessment. Instead, government operated in a world defined by a mass of diverse pressures and interests. The decision to launch and promote nuclear power is neither a case of adaptation to technological progress nor a case of purposeful policy-making.

The conventional approach to political decision-making is to treat the duly-elected government as the sovereign body in society (see chapters two and three). By this view, Britain's nuclear power programme would emerge in a very straightforward way. It would begin with a party commitment or a national need; it would be followed by the identification of a range of possible options to meet this commitment or need; and it would end with the selection and implementation of the most appropriate of these options. Thus, in the case of nuclear power, the problem would be a potential energy gap; the options would involve the further exploitation of existing energy resources or the development of new ones or a strict policy of energy conservation; the outcome would be the decision to use nuclear power as the most economic and efficient means; and the practical result would be the commissioning and building of nuclear power stations. We would have a simple chain of events: problem → options → policy → implementation.

Not surprisingly, government decision-making is rarely this neat; and in the case of nuclear power, this chain of cause and effect is buried – if it exists at all – under many layers. These layers result partly from the complexity of administration in any modern industrial society and partly from the particular problems posed by nuclear power. Nuclear power is expensive, technically complicated, and long-term.[2] For these reasons alone, we are not dealing with a situation in which the problem is starkly obvious, the possible options clearly defined, or the political actors purely rational. The course by which Britain came to develop its considerable nuclear power programme is correspondingly tortuous.

To follow the long and winding road along which nuclear power has travelled, it is as well to begin by pointing out some of the important landmarks. There are three sets of features which need to be described in brief. They are the major institutions involved; the broad outlines of the policy adopted; and the main issues around which the political conflicts were fought.

THE INSTITUTIONS

First then, let us consider the institutions and the relations that connect them. According to the traditions of British democracy, authority stems from Parliament. For nuclear power, this authority is very limited, and the principal location of supreme command lies with the Department of Energy and the Cabinet. Following the privatisation of electricity, the organisation of electricity production and supply has changed considerably, although the responsibility for nuclear power remains relatively little altered.[3]

The final authority in deciding whether a nuclear power station should be built has traditionally rested with the Secretary of State for Energy. The Department of Energy oversaw nuclear power policy; it announced the plans to build reactors; it decided the size of the programme; and it held the purse-strings.[4] But the responsibility for implementation and formulation of the policy has been more widely distributed than the formal line of authority suggests. Were we to examine the inner workings and politics of the Department of Energy alone we would emerge with only a partial picture. For the Department of Energy relies on a number of other bodies, all placed at various distances from the formal centre of political power. The most important of these other institutions has been the United Kingdom Atomic Energy Authority (UKAEA).

The UKAEA was established by government in 1954, and since then it has come to occupy a unique and powerful place in the creation of energy policy. It was unique in that it was neither an administrative department nor a nationalised industry: it contained elements of both without representing a typical example of either. It was powerful in that it was almost the sole provider of information for government decisions about nuclear power. Roughly, its responsibilities broke down into five categories:

1 Research and design for nuclear reactors.
2 Training personnel for the management of these reactors.
3 Advising the Electricity Boards which commission the reactors.
4 Procuring the materials essential to the operation of the reactors.
5 The manufacturing of the fuel for the reactors.

These last two tasks were subsequently assigned to British Nuclear Fuels Limited, which is responsible for the Windscale (Sellafield) Reprocessing Plant.[5] The UKAEA has been financed by government, and in this sense it has operated as a typical Department of State, but without the formal system of control normally associated with such an arrangement. It has cost the taxpayer about £100 million a year.[6]

The UKAEA provided the theoretical side of Britain's nuclear power programme. The practical side emanated from two groups, the electricity generating boards and the industrial consortia. The latter were formed by a combination of companies which between them provided the wherewithal for building nuclear power plants. In the early days of the nuclear programme, there were four such organisations. In theory these consortia were expected to compete for contracts to build power stations; in practice the contracts were distributed in strict rotation. In the early 1970s this system was rationalised, so that there was a single consortium, the National Nuclear Corporation (NNC) and its subsidiary, the Nuclear Power Company (NPC). The NNC was jointly owned by the General Electric Company, which was responsible for its day-to-day management, the UKAEA and British Nuclear Associates, a collection of companies with interests in the manufacturing of nuclear power plants.[7]

The building of a nuclear reactor results from a commission, which may either come from UKAEA (for experimental or military purposes) or from the electricity boards (for civilian purposes). There were two such boards: the Central Electricity Generating Board (CEGB) and the South of Scotland Electricity Board. The boards were responsible for the provision of electricity for domestic and industrial consumers. Their interest in nuclear power was supposed to be determined by the economic and practical efficiency of nuclear power stations. In reality their interest sometimes stemmed from offers that were difficult to refuse.[8]

Whatever was the case, the electricity boards' plans were dependent on the approval of the Department of Energy and the Cabinet, since the capital expenditure involved was provided by government. The boards made proposals on the basis of the planned demand for electricity; these were then accepted or rejected depending on a variety of considerations, not least of which was overall government planning.[9] Because of the potential danger of a nuclear reactor, a further body was involved in the assessment of such proposals. This was the Nuclear Installations Inspectorate whose job has been to licence nuclear reactor designs and to check their safety once in operation.[10]

Last, and usually least, of the bodies involved has been Parliament. While its Members are the formal authorising agents for all expenditure, the reality is, of course, rather different. Certainly, debates in the Commons have played little part, but the Select Committee responsible for investigating this aspect of government policy has had its moment of glory. Select Committee reports have led to changes in policy.[11]

Normally, the relations between, and the responsibilities of, these various organisations are much more complicated than we have allowed for here. But for the moment, these bald outlines should suffice. Our next concern is with the broad contours of the policy emerging from this network of institutions.

THE POLICIES

There have been four different major policies or programmes in the story of Britain's nuclear power. The main constituents of these policies have been the number and type of reactors, the amount of electricity they can produce, and the time they will take to come into use. The first programme began in 1955, was modified in 1957, and was completed in 1965. Its purpose was initially to produce approximately 2,000 Mw (megawatts) of electricity, but this figure was later increased to 6,000 Mw. The second programme was supposed to run from 1960 to 1975, but it was not actually finished until the mid-1980s. In the meantime, its output was reduced from 8,000 Mw to 6,000 Mw. The third programme was started in 1974, and *en route* it too was changed, even more drastically. Its completion date was to have been 1978, but all that year saw was another change of direction, and the initiation of a programme that has yet to finish. It is to make the relatively modest contribution of 1,500 Mw. The most recent programme, the fourth, was announced in 1980. It was intended to last for ten years, with a new reactor being built each year. In fact, only one had been started at the end of the decade.

Though these details represent the outlines of the programmes, there is more to them than their timing and their contribution. The content of the debate and the decision-making process obviously included reference to such matters, but the main source of conflict and argument has been the apparently technical question of which reactor to employ in order to produce the required amount of electricity. Five major types of reactor have been examined in the course of the last 25 years or more. They differ technically in their basic mechanism and in their country of origin. Three were designed by the UKAEA, and two came from America. The British models were the Magnox, the Advanced Gas-Cooled Reactor (AGR), and the Steam Generating Heavy Water Reactor (SGHWR). The American ones were the Light Water Reactor (LWR) and the Pressurised Water Reactor (PWR).[12] The various designs obviously differ on all manner of counts, but for our purpose the main differences result from: (a) the means by which the nuclear reaction transfers its energy into heat, which is then used to power an electricity generator; (b) the type of fuel used; and (c) the way the chain reaction is controlled. The Magnox reactor uses natural uranium; the AGR uses uranium in which the content of radioactivity has been artificially increased. Both use gas to transfer heat and both use graphite to establish the chain reaction. The LWR and the PWR, which are variants of the same basic form, use enriched fuel and use water as the means of transforming heat into mechanical energy. The SGHWR uses enriched uranium, a water coolant, and a heavy-water control of the reaction. These re-actors also differ in their construction costs, their efficiency and their safety.[13] The essential arguments that occupy the British decision-makers are technical specification, economic efficiency and safety. The decisions were never wholly exercises in scientific assessment, but these factors appear as the ostensible justifications for the various policies. For the first programme, Magnox reactors were used; the second programme employed AGRs; the third, SGHWRs and AGRs; and the fourth, AGRs and PWRs. Other reactors were considered, but they never featured in the final outcome.

THE STORY

In 1945, the British Government, or more accurately, a select number of the Labour Cabinet, took a decision to build a nuclear bomb. Neither the British public nor Parliament, nor even the rest of the Cabinet (though this is disputed) were told of the decision. After the war, the Americans, who had organised the international scientific team which developed the bombs dropped on Hiroshima and Nagasaki, refused the British access to nuclear technology. Clement Attlee, convinced that Britain should remain a leading world power, decided that, rather than allow the Americans to go on alone, a British nuclear bomb should be developed. This required the creation of organisations to research and design the process of bomb production. It also required an industry to produce the hardware, in particular the radioactive material to be used in the explosive device. It was this decision that marked the beginning of Britain's long journey to nuclear-generated electricity.[14]

Attlee created an Official Committee on Atomic Energy to make the decision on nuclear power, which significantly brought together a range of interests whose concern extended well beyond energy production. The Committee included officials from the Chiefs of Staff Secretariat, the Foreign Office and the Ministry of Supply. Yet more interesting, a place was found for Sir John Anderson, an opposition spokesman, who while being a fierce critic of the Government, was also an expert in the field of nuclear energy.[15]

The link between the civilian and military programmes is formed by the radioactive chemical element plutonium. Unlike uranium, which occurs naturally, plutonium cannot be mined; it has to be manufactured. This is achieved by the controlled radioactive decay of uranium. The decay of uranium, the essential mechanism of the nuclear reaction, generates heat through the splitting of uranium atoms. This splitting, or fission, leads to the creation of lighter, radioactive elements and the release of minute particles – neutrons. These neutrons then hit another uranium atom, and are either absorbed or cause the atom to split, releasing more neutrons, which repeat the process. This is the chain reaction. The absorbed neutrons have a different effect: they convert uranium into a heavier radioactive element, plutonium. Why do some atoms of uranium absorb neutrons, while others are split by them? Though we need not go into detail, the answer lies in the fact that natural uranium exists in two forms or isotopes. Approximately 0.7 per cent of natural uranium is of the kind that splits and emits neutrons. The rest is relatively stable, except when struck by neutrons. The reason that the earth, or at least uranium mines, are not boiling ovens is that the 0.7 per cent of uranium that is radioactive is not a sufficient quantity to maintain a chain reaction; also, the emitted neutrons are not travelling at a speed which causes fission in all cases.

The nuclear reactor uses uranium in which the radioactive element has been increased (enrichment) or it uses a moderator (like graphite or heavy water) to slow the emitted neutrons to the correct speed. The result is the generation of a large quantity of heat and the production of plutonium. This plutonium can then be extracted through a system known as reprocessing. This is how the link between military and civilian goals is formed, and how a commitment to nuclear weapons entails the development of considerable technology, which itself has peaceful uses.[16]

The first nuclear power station, Calder Hall, was built primarily to increase the rate of plutonium production; the generation of electricity was a secondary consideration. The UKAEA, the Government and the management of the first nuclear reactors (besides Calder Hall there was also a reactor at Chapelcross in Scotland), all saw their task as being to provide a source of plutonium. The first British bomb, successfully tested in 1952, had used plutonium generated from a relatively small nuclear reactor and had no commercial application. With the expansion of the bomb programme, more plutonium was needed.[17]

Though the decision to build Calder Hall was taken in 1953, it was not opened until 1956; in the meantime, the UKAEA had been formed in 1954, and the first programme of nuclear-generated electricity had been announced. Thus when Calder Hall was opened, it was presented as part of a civilian project. Indeed the Queen declared at the opening ceremony that Calder Hall was a 'vital and timely addition to the industrial resources of our nation and to our material welfare'[18]. Calder Hall was held to represent the peaceful use of the atom.

While the building of nuclear power reactors was presented in this light, it was recognised that this initial programme was less an exercise in economic efficiency than an experiment. The CEGB had to be forcefully persuaded to take on the proposed twelve reactors, whose construction was to take ten years and whose contribution was to be 10 per cent of electricity demand.[19] The reactors were to be based on the design used at Calder Hall, and were to use a gas coolant and natural uranium. This design was inspired by technical and military considerations, rather than strictly commercial ones. Enriched uranium was effectively unavailable to the British because of its cost, so natural uranium had to be used. The Magnox reactor had the added advantage of producing plutonium rapidly. The disadvantage of its design was that it did not transform heat into electricity very efficiently – it was 20 per cent efficient, compared to the 30 per cent of conventional coal-fired generators.[20] It was only with the second generation of gas-cooled reactors that comparable levels of efficiency were to be achieved.

The technical decision to opt for the Magnox reactor had a profound effect on subsequent political decision-making. Once the UKAEA took on responsibility for the research and development of reactors, it focused its efforts on the problems of the Magnox reactor. It was less concerned to develop different models than to improve the existing one. This is not simply a case of blinkeredness or a lack of imagination, but an inevitable consequence of the initial commitment. Expertise was built up in gas-cooled reactor technology; careers were dependent, therefore, on the success of that type of reactor. Roger Williams writes of the development of the AGR by the UKAEA: 'The decision was *their* decision, its problems were *their problems*, the solution to those problems constituted *their* success' [his emphasis].[21]

Quite simply, the UKAEA acquired an interest in the Magnox reactor and the models developed from it. Since the Government was reliant on the UKAEA, it too felt pressure to persist with the design to which it had committed resources and on which it received advice. More generally, the Government, by its own decision to establish the UKAEA, created an in-built nuclear power lobby. The establishment of institutions, dependent on nuclear power, meant that energy policy came to be seen as synonymous with nuclear power policy. This is not to suggest that all was plain sailing, and that policy emerged uncontroversially from the network of bodies concerned. What happened, though, was that the question of whether Britain needed nuclear power and the opportunity for public participation were both given minimal or no consideration. The first 35 years of the nuclear power programme has been a classic example of élite decision-making, driven by technical or bureaucratic interests. The conflicts that emerged were those engendered by disputes within the nuclear fraternity, a body in which the Government was an important, but never absolutely dominant, partner, despite its role as the initiator of the project.

One such conflict was over the appropriate reactor to be used. This was a dispute that runs throughout the period from 1955 to the late 1970s. A key source of the tension is to be found in the UKAEA. Though the UKAEA was responsible for the development of the Magnox design, there were scientists attached to the UKAEA who favoured a rival American design, the Light Water Reactor. The supporters of the LWR argued that it was a technically superior design, and it was left to the head of the UKAEA, Sir Christopher Hinton, to persuade both his colleagues and the relevant politicians that the British model would be easier to service and maintain.[22] This issue, however, was to reappear at every stage of the history of Britain's nuclear industry.

One of the other sources of debate was the size of the programme and its anticipated contribution to Britain's electricity demand. The 1955 decision had been for twelve reactors contributing 1,500 Mw of electricity. But this was changed in 1957, following the Suez Crisis when worries had emerged about Britain's reliance on oil from the Middle East. It was now intended that 6,000 Mw be produced. To allow for this increase, which did not require the building of more reactors, the completion date was put back one year to 1966. However, anticipated energy needs are one thing, the satisfaction of those needs is quite another. Developing a new technology is obviously fraught with difficulties, and there is always a problem in projecting future costs when the exact shape of that future is determined by experiment rather than experience. Nuclear power is no exception. The enthusiasm of the scientists led them to be over-optimistic, and this, combined with the inexperience of the industrial consortia responsible for building the new power stations, resulted in an unexpectedly high cost for each reactor. As a result, the programme was further modified in 1960. The output was cut back to 5,000 Mw and the completion date delayed to 1968. The CEGB, in particular, was having doubts about the cost and size of the first programme.[23]

Despite these concerns, the three main participants, the electricity boards, the UKAEA, and the Government, all persisted in their commitment to nuclear power, albeit with varying degrees of enthusiasm. Even as the first programme was undergoing revision, they were all drawing up plans for the second programme.

Discussions took place from 1961–4, and again one of the central issues was the choice of reactor. The rivals were each improved versions of their predecessors. The Magnox reactor had been modified into the AGR; while in America the LWR had been changed into the PWR. The AGR, unlike the Magnox, used enriched uranium, as did the PWR, and they competed therefore on the basis of their efficiency, economy and safety. The PWR had the advantage of being easier to build, but it was thought to be less safe. Both designs were submitted to the Department of Energy for consideration. The accompanying specifications for each reactor were impressive, if not exact reflections of the truth. The AGR design was provided with claims for its efficiency which were alleged to be accurate to three decimal places, despite the fact that the design itself was in a very rudimentary form. One of the engineers involved commented: 'If we had got the first decimal place right it would have been a miracle'.[24]

The competition between the two models led to extravagant boasting on both sides. Reality became rather obscured as political manoeuvring and self-interest took over. While the UKAEA pressed the Government to advocate the AGR, the CEGB, somewhat disillusioned with the Magnox programme which had been forced upon it, was becoming increasingly self-confident about nuclear technology. The CEGB was no longer prepared to be the passive recipient of the Authority's advice and recommendations. Sir Christopher Hinton, who as head of the UKAEA's industrial group had advocated the Magnox reactor, was now Chairman of the CEGB. The change of job reflected a change of perspective. For the first time, the consumer of electricity became a factor in the course of nuclear power policy. The CEGB had obligations to its customers which did not necessarily coincide with the interests of the UKAEA. The CEGB began to make it clear to the UKAEA that it was in the market for the most economical reactor, not the most British; national loyalty was not a substitute for cheap electricity.[25] Hinton's scientific background was important. He was aware of the problems the UKAEA was having in developing the AGR and was able, therefore, to assess the technical arguments made on its behalf.

The CEGB's new-found authority did not affect the final outcome. The British AGR was the reactor chosen for the second programme. But what the Board's intervention achieved was a detailed assessment of the options and the recognition that American designs were worthy of consideration. Furthermore, economic viability and efficiency were presented as major priorities in any future developments of nuclear power.[26] The UKAEA could not afford to be complacent. In the end, the AGR was adopted largely because of its alleged economic and technical superiority. *The Sunday Times* later recalled the decision in these terms: 'The American PWR was the clear favourite but at the last moment, to almost universal amazement, the British won . . . both sides had submitted "doctored" data. The AGR men were just better at fudging the figures'.[27]

This is to over-simplify, for the decision took considerable time. In 1964, the Conservatives planned to produce a further 5,000 Mw by 1975; at this stage the type of reactor was unspecified. The basic outline of this programme was unchallenged by the new Labour Government which did, however, decide in 1965 that the AGR was to be used and that the output was to be increased to 8,000 Mw. This fitted well with Labour's promises of a British technological revolution. The Labour Minister, Fred Lee, described the AGR as 'the greatest breakthrough of all time'.[28] The CEGB denied that it was under any pressure to adopt a British design: it was simply a matter of economics. The CEGB claimed that it had considered the tenders from consortia for the AGR and the PWR, and had decided in favour of the AGR on costs alone. The CEGB also denied that it had been subjected to unreasonable influence from the UKAEA.[29] This happy coincidence of interests – much helped by some imaginative accounting and optimistic forecasts – restored harmony in the nuclear institutions. It did not last long.

The AGR proved to be an expensive and unsound design. The economist and ex-civil servant, P. D. Henderson, compared the AGR with Concorde, and described them both as major and costly errors of government policy.[30] One year after the planned completion date of the AGR programme, only a single reactor was working; the costs for each reactor had escalated from £418 million to £1,000 million; their total contribution had decreased from 8,000 Mw to 6,000 Mw; and even as late as the 1980s, some of the reactors had not come on stream and others were proving very difficult to operate.[31] The responsibility for, and cause of, these problems stemmed from a variety of sources. There were technical difficulties which were increased by the fact that a variety of AGR designs were used and each was built by a different consortium. It was therefore hard to make useful comparisons. Furthermore, the consortia proved unable to cope with the complexities of the AGR. A chairman of the CEGB described the AGR programme as 'a disaster we must not repeat'.[32]

These set-backs created considerable doubts, not so much about nuclear power, as about the means by which nuclear policy should be decided and implemented. For though enthusiasm for the AGR was considerably dampened, the years from 1970–4 saw the formulation of plans for a third programme of nuclear generators. This time to help solve the perennial problem of reactor choice, the Conservatives, through the Department of Trade and Industry, set up the Vinter Committee in 1972. This body, composed of civil servants and the Chairmen of the electricity boards and the UKAEA, was to examine the relative merits of the various reactors. As is typical of nuclear policy generally, the Committee's report was kept secret. The Committee in fact concluded that the advantages of the rival reactors were 'extremely finely balanced'.[33] The leading contenders were familiar: they were the AGR, the PWR, and the Magnox of old. There was one newcomer, the SGHWR, which the UKAEA had developed but which was relatively untried. The main suggestions of the Committee were directed towards improving the policy-making process. To this end, they recommended that a rival to the AGR be developed by the UKAEA, and that the various industrial consortia be consolidated into a single body. The latter had been suggested by a parliamentary select committee several years before, but nothing had been done.[34]

The Conservatives took notice of this advice. In 1973, the Vinter Committee was replaced by the more permanent Nuclear Power Advisory Board. This body was intended to act as an intermediary between the elected but inexpert politician and the expert but unelected technocrats. More importantly, the Government followed Vinter's advice and reduced the number of consortia to one, the National Nuclear Corporation (NNC). The NNC was led by the General Electric Company (GEC), which owned 50 per cent of the shares, the rest being distributed between the UKAEA and British Nuclear Associates.[35]

This move undoubtedly improved some aspects of decision-making on nuclear power but it also added increased force to the PWR lobby. GEC was an enthusiastic supporter of the PWR. It was the only reactor with any commercial potential. The AGR's market was limited, since at that time no other country used it; while the PWR was being used world-wide. Furthermore, the PWR had the advantage of being easier to construct, because it could be part-assembled in a factory and then transported to the site, unlike the AGR which had to be constructed *in situ*. David Fishlock of *The Financial Times* compared the problems of building an AGR to those of building 'jet engines in an aircraft hanger'.[36] But GEC was not the only supporter of the PWR. The CEGB was also looking more and more favourably on the American-designed reactor. This growing PWR lobby was further enhanced by the presence of Dr Walter Marshall as Chief Scientific Adviser at the Department of Energy. Marshall was also deputy head of the UKAEA and had been a long-time supporter of the PWR.[37]

Despite this impressive array of PWR supporters and despite the changes in the management of nuclear decisions, the Conservatives reached no conclusion about future nuclear policy before they left office in 1974. The clash with the miners had distracted attention from the long-term problems. Furthermore, the CEGB alienated their potential political allies by requesting a vast expansion of the nuclear policy, asking for eighteen PWRs over ten years.[38] In a world reeling from the economic consequences of the oil crisis of 1973, the Government was in no mood to sanction massive capital expenditure, especially when the CEGB's chosen reactor, the PWR, had not been passed as safe by the Nuclear Installations Inspectorate (NII).[39]

The caution evinced by the Conservatives was continued under the Labour administration. Eric Varley, the new Secretary of State for Energy, announced a limited four-year programme to produce 4,000 Mw of electricity. The surprising aspect of this decision was the choice of the SGHWR as the reactor. The PWR had failed once again to carry the day. The SGHWR met with a mixed response from its designers, the UKAEA. The CEGB was unenthusiastic; and GEC was so angry about the decision that it decreased its holding in the NNC from 50 per cent to 30 per cent.[40] The SGHWR had few friends. The Nuclear Power Advisory Board was ambivalent. One of the only enthusiasts appears to have been Sir Francis Tombs, Chairman of the South of Scotland Electricity Board. Otherwise, what support the SGHWR received was due to it being British and being certified as safe by the NII.[41]

The lack of support for the SGHWR presaged its lack of success. No reactor was completed. In a manner redolent of the AGR programme, the economic costs and technical problems increased with each passing day. In 1976, Tony Benn, who had replaced Varley at the Department of Energy, brought the SGHWR programme to an end. This was a great relief to the CEGB, one of whose executives reported that the reactor was proving 'more difficult than Concorde'.[42] The following year, the NII announced that the PWR was safe to be used in Britain, although its decision was hedged with qualifications.

The 1976 decision did not see the end of Britain's nuclear power programme. No one in government appeared to question the need for nuclear power. The argument continued about which reactor to use and how much electricity to generate. Once again the main rivals were the PWR and the AGR; and once again the nuclear élite broke into opposing camps, although the sides were not identical to the ones in 1974. The AGR camp was led by Tony Benn and his political advisers, with slightly hesitant support from the electricity boards. The opposition was led by GEC and the UKAEA, whose cause had been boosted by a think-tank report in favour of the PWR.[43]

The conflict between these two groups determined the resultant policy. The corridors of Whitehall echoed to the sound of axes being ground. To Tony Benn, the PWR was a deliberate attempt by the unholy alliance of big business and the Civil Service to subvert the course of democracy. Brian Sedgemore, Benn's Parliamentary Private Secretary, has written of: 'the most astonishing and deliberate attempt by Civil Servants to frustrate ministerial authority . . . over the question of the future development of nuclear power in Britain'. He saw Whitehall as intent upon persuading 'the government to throw caution to the winds' and to spend £20 billion on PWRs.[44] To the civil servants, the politicians' commitment to the AGR was an example of political ideology taking preference over technical rationality. This view was further enhanced by Tony Benn's general political isolation in Cabinet. The Prime Minister, for example, was known to favour the PWR, a view he apparently adopted following assiduous lobbying by Sir Arnold Weinstock, Chairman of GEC.[45] Of course, the dispute was not simply caused by conflicting political prejudices.

The issue that most clearly divided the sides was the safety of the PWR. Benn was doubtful whether the PWR could meet the safety standards established by the AGR. These doubts had arisen after his correspondence with the scientist, Sir Alan Cottrell, who expressed concern over the safety of the PWR vessel. Out of these differences, a compromise was found. The main architect of this was Sir Jack Rampton, Permanent Secretary at the Department of Energy. The solution involved a commitment of two AGRs and a promise of an investigation into the practical viability of the PWR. For the first time in the long history of Britain's nuclear power programme, the PWR was given government approval, albeit tacitly. Four years later, Tony Benn declared that even this small concession was wrong, and that nuclear power should be used less and less and the PWR not at all.[46]

In 1979, the year after the compromise, the AGR's fall from prominence was temporarily avenged. A PWR in the USA failed and nearly resulted in a major catastrophe. The Secretary of State ordered an immediate end to all work on the PWR in Britain. The order was ignored by civil servants who anticipated the end of the Labour Government and who recognised Tony Benn's growing political isolation.[47] The perspicacity, if not the loyalty, of the civil servants was confirmed by the Conservative victory in 1979.

Benn's successor, David Howell, was quick to affirm Conservative commitment to nuclear power in general and the PWR in particular. Indeed, the early days of the Conservatives' reign saw considerable attention devoted to the nuclear power issue. One of Mrs Thatcher's first policy announcements concerned nuclear power. The fourth nuclear power programme had begun. From 1982 onwards, one reactor per year was to be built for the following ten years. The programme was to generate 15,000 Mw and was to cost £15 billion. At the same time, the production of plants was to be organised by a single body, the NNC (the NPC was abolished). The issue of the choice of reactor was still not finally decided, indeed the NNC was divided between AGR and PWR supporters, but it was resolved that the first PWR should be built at Sizewell in Suffolk.[48]

The generation of electricity was not the only advantage the Conservatives identified in the expansion of the nuclear power industry. On the one hand, it gave work to an industry which had been in the doldrums since the early 1970s; and on the other hand it promised distinct political benefits. On the latter point, leaked Cabinet papers revealed that the Government saw nuclear power as a way 'of removing a substantial portion' of the disruptive potential, through industrial action, of coal miners and transport workers.[49]

Opposition to the Conservative proposals came from two main sources. The first of these was the Select Committee on Energy, which under its various titles has been the one forum of public debate that nuclear power has consistently received. The Committee favoured more emphasis on coal and conservation; and argued that if nuclear power was to continue, it should be based on a Canadian-designed reactor, not the PWR. The Government rejected this advice, and instead defended the PWR and the conservation of energy through the use of price mechanisms, not direct intervention.[50] The second source of opposition was the growing anti-nuclear movement. With the Sizewell decision, the Government recognised, almost for the first time, the right of public participation in the decision-making process.[51] It is obviously arguable whether the lack of opposition until the late 1970s was due to ignorance, apathy or deliberate policy. What is indisputable is that the decisions taken until very recently had been the exclusive province of the nuclear élite. With the emergence of public concern, the agenda for the first time in 30 years included the question of whether Britain needed a nuclear power programme. It was not a development with which Whitehall was altogether happy.

The leaked Cabinet papers referred to the Government's desire to engender as little opposition as possible through the judicious use of public relations exercises. Both the CEGB and the UKAEA were allocated substantial funds to produce exhibitions and information to defuse public concern and to convince people of nuclear power's benefits. In 1981, the Government set up a 'task force', under the ubiquitous Dr Walter Marshall whose job was 'to allay public fears'. Marshall saw his role as one of teacher; for him and other members of the nuclear fraternity, the PWR was safe and in the best interests of the British people. Those who believed otherwise were blinded by ignorance and political prejudice.[52] In 1982, Marshall was made head of the CEGB, following the pattern set by Hinton before him and reinforcing the club-like character of the nuclear policy community.

It is ironic that Marshall was himself to become a victim (in his own eyes, at least) of political prejudice. In 1989 he left his job as head of the CEGB in protest at the Government's handling of nuclear power and its failure to provide proper protection for the technology's future. The 1980s saw radical shifts in government policy on nuclear power and energy production in general. The original proposals had seemed to promise a revolution in nuclear policy. Hugo Young, author of a biography of Mrs Thatcher, describes the expansion of nuclear power as 'one of the Prime Minister's particular obsessions'.[53] But by the end of the decade surprisingly little had changed.

The grandiose plans for ten stations in ten years faded with the many months taken up in the Sizewell Inquiry. And although the Government was determined to short-circuit the inquiry system to cut down their political and economic costs, a subsequent investigation into a third station at Hinkley Point (another PWR) took eleven months and was finally published in 1990.

The political controversy that surrounded nuclear power policy in the late 1980s, and that led to Marshall's departure, was engendered by the privatisation of the electricity generation and supply industry. This policy was a continuation of the privatisation programme that had become a defining feature of the Thatcher Government and which previously had changed the ownership and control of British Gas, British Telecom and several other public utilities. The selling of electricity, however, proved to be more difficult than that of its predecessors. Privatisation was itself less popular, but there were particular problems associated with nuclear power.[54]

The original plan proposed by Cecil Parkinson in 1987 was to decentralise power-generation and supply. The key to this was the breakup of the CEGB and creation of regional suppliers who bought their electricity from a variety of competing sources. Walter Marshall and his colleagues at the CEGB tried to persuade the Government against such a move. They argued that without the CEGB's controlling influence insufficient energy would be generated. In particular, there would be no one prepared to bear the risks and costs of developing nuclear power.

The Government, on the other hand, had an electoral promise to keep. The privatisation of electricity had been in the 1987 manifesto. There was also an ideological point to be made. Parkinson and his Cabinet colleagues felt that the previous privatisations had simply replaced public monopolies with private ones. Electricity was to be different. The CEGB had little chance of countering this plan, but it did its cause little good by employing some inept political tactics. As a journalist observed: 'The CEGB was so out of touch that it foolishly failed to attend meetings of the Whitehall committee mapping out the new industry'.[55] More astute were the electricity boards who persuaded the Department of Energy to stick to a decentralised, competitive system. The plans for this were published in a 1988 White Paper. The CEGB's generators were to be divided between two companies, both to be sold on the stock-market, PowerGen and National Power. The latter was to have the nuclear power stations.[56]

These plans, however, proved to be immensely difficult to implement. The Department of Energy had to decide upon the contractual relations that were to exist between the various companies. The deliberations introduced considerable delays into the privatisation programme.

These problems were compounded by increasing unease within National Power over the true cost of nuclear power. In the competitive market for electricity, it mattered whether nuclear power was an economic investment; this was not a concern that really featured in its earlier history. Relations between the Department and National Power deteriorated. It was revealed that previous accounting of nuclear power had grossly underestimated its costs and exaggerated its value. This was particularly true of Sizewell B, and it led to a decision by government to abandon its grand plans for the PWR in Britain. It also precipitated Marshall's resignation.[57]

In July 1989 in response to growing concern over the real costs of nuclear power, the Magnox reactors were removed from the public sale. Their decommissioning threatened to impose too great a burden on the privatisation programme, and four months later, National Power was relieved of all responsibility for nuclear power. All the nuclear generators were hived off to a new public company, Nuclear Electric. At the same time, John Wakeman replaced Cecil Parkinson as the minister responsible for electricity privatisation.

These later twists in the tale of nuclear power decision-making, therefore, tend to replicate the pattern established in the earlier era. Despite the radical changes promised by the Thatcher Government, nuclear power has remained a protected species. What has changed, however, are the reasons for its preservation. Positive claims for its benefits have been replaced by a more negative defence. Its political importance may have diminished and the power of its supporters weakened, but this decline in the institutional force behind nuclear power has been replaced by the equally pressing idea that it is too expensive to be disposed of. And as with all previous nuclear power decisions, this is not simply an economic judgement, but one founded on political and institutional considerations as well.

CONCLUSION

There are many who criticise the nuclear power decisions for their failure to meet the standards of either democratic accountability or technical efficiency. Such critics point to the lack of parliamentary or public involvement in the decisions, to the excessive influence of the Civil Service and other institutions without popular mandate. Further, they refer to the substantial problems engendered by the AGR programme and to the total failure of the SGHWR programme. These judgements are important. No account of nuclear power policy, or any other British government policies, can make sense without some evaluation of the outcome. Description is a form of explanation, and explanation rests on claims about what might have happened had not certain groups, individuals, or interests intervened. In explaining something, we compare the actual course of events with other possible stories, and we praise or blame those involved according to how we evaluate the various outcomes. Our judgement depends on the extent to which we can attribute responsibility to the different participants, and this assessment will itself depend both on the available facts and on our understanding of human motivation. If, for example, we believe that nuclear power is an expensive and unnecessary technology, then we will evolve an explanation of the course of events which refers to political incompetence or ignorance or self-interest. If, on the other hand, we judge nuclear power to be a vital addition to Britain's energy resources, then we will be inclined to fit the various participants into a framework of rational or democratic decision-making. Ultimately, therefore, the lessons to be derived from the nuclear power decisions will depend on the judgement made of the outcome. There is neither time nor space to discover whether Britain does, in fact, need nuclear power or whether the forecasts for future energy demand are realistic or whether the calculations about the cost of nuclear energy are accurate. Such issues are enthusiastically discussed elsewhere.[58] Here it is more appropriate for us to understand, in fairly general terms, the processes and factors which came to shape the nuclear power decisions. It is best to begin with the problem itself.

Taking decisions about nuclear power involves taking decisions about a vast, expensive and sophisticated technology. This apparently simple description has important political consequences. When we talk of democratic decision-making, we tend to think of discrete issues, which involve a number of straightforward options. We tend to assume that decisions exist as isolated entities: they can be neatly described, the options can be listed, the effects calculated, and the preferred course of action implemented. In fact, very few decisions are like this, even in ordinary everyday life, let alone in government. And in the case of decisions about advanced technology, this simple picture is a serious distortion. The planning and research for nuclear power was done at a time when no comparable decision had been taken elsewhere. There was no way of knowing what problems would arise in translating theory into practice. The viability of nuclear power as a source of energy was something that could only be known once it was in operation. But the only reason for financing such a project was because of its viability as a source of energy. The launching of a nuclear power programme requires a financial commitment of considerable size over a long period, at which stage it is impossible to judge whether the money is well spent. The assessment of the project can only properly be made when it is in operation, by which time freedom of action has been drastically reduced. We might summarise the problem like this: (a) The best time to change a policy is at the beginning, before any large commitment of resources has been made. (b) The worst time to try and change policy is at the end, after considerable commitments of time and money have been made. (c) The best time to know the consequences of a policy or a decision is at the end, after the costs and benefits have been identified. (d) The worst time to assess the consequences of a policy is at the beginning when only costs, and no benefits, are known.[59]

In other words, when a decision is taken, people are in a state of ignorance about the likely outcomes, and when they come to assess the decision, they are not in a position to effect any changes. A rational decision is one which takes account of costs and benefits, and which selects the most favourable balance. Such computations are almost impossible for a technology which takes several years to develop and which provides benefits only after a long period involving costs alone. Our understanding of the nuclear power decisions has to emerge through a recognition of these general problems. The structure of the policy-making process owes much to these features of advanced technology.

The establishment of the UKAEA is one example of the way in which the Government attempted to cope with the inescapable problem of ignorance about the likely consequences of nuclear power technology. Government itself was not in a position to design and implement a nuclear power programme. The tasks of research, design and production had to be left to those with the expertise and equipment to develop nuclear technology. But while the Government had to be dependent on outside experts for the technical details, those experts were dependent on government for finance. It was only government that could pay for the years of research and development that preceded the use of nuclear power; it was only government that could coordinate such a project.[60]

Before we discuss the role and influence of the UKAEA, there is one important issue to be raised. Why should government be interested in the promotion of nuclear technology anyway? We should be wary of simply accepting that nuclear power is inevitably the responsibility of government. Just because governments are the only bodies capable of coordinating and financing such projects, it does not follow that they must coordinate and finance them. It is important to recognise that the origins of the policy lie in two particular sets of government commitments: firstly, the need, following the Labour Cabinet's 1945 decision to develop the nuclear bomb, to provide a source of weapons grade nuclear material; and secondly, the obligation to find a source of energy for Britain's industrial future. Neither of these commitments were inescapable; the government could have identified its responsibilities in quite different terms, but it chose not to. In this decision, it established the grounds for the development of nuclear power. What we must recognise is that, though government was the initiator and coordinator of the move to nuclear power, this did not mean that it was in charge. Only in the early days, before any significant expenditure, was government in command; once the policy had advanced from this initial stage, influence no longer resided with the formal institutions of government. And when we talk of government, it is as well to remember that the decisions which launched Britain's nuclear power programme emerged from a select and secretive group within the Labour Cabinet. Parliament itself had little part to play.

But while government initiated the policy, it could not make that policy. This was the task of the UKAEA. In the same way that civil servants provide information and experience, so the UKAEA acted as an adviser to government in its declared intention to develop nuclear power. But in creating such a body, the Government did more than establish a source of information and a centre of research. Just as civil servants are servile in name only, so the UKAEA, as the sole repository (at least in the early days) of expertise on nuclear power, came to be an important source of influence. Effectively, the UKAEA, together with the other bodies attached to nuclear power policy, came to act as a pressure group for nuclear power. Advisers became advocates as they recognised that their interests lay with the continuation of the policy on which they offered advice. This is not necessarily a criticism: too often it is supposed that advisers behave as complete agnostics on all matters. Such an approach is both impossible and undesirable. Governments appoint and use advisers precisely for their ability to select information and to make judgements. Thus we should not expect the UKAEA to act with complete indifference in matters of nuclear power policy; and hence the line between self-interested advocacy and responsible advice is not easily drawn. Nonetheless, the creation and financing of a body like the UKAEA did establish an interest in the continuation and development of nuclear power. The phenomenon is that of 'institutional momentum', whereby the mechanisms evolved to help advise and inform government become pressures on government.[61] This process is most eloquently demonstrated in the matter of reactor choice.

The selection of the AGR as the most appropriate reactor for most of the programmes cannot be seen simply as a matter of objective assessment. There were, of course, good technical reasons for choosing the AGR, but these were never sufficiently persuasive to discount other options. The AGR featured prominently because it was the model devised by the UKAEA. It was a variant of the Magnox reactor, itself chosen for its ability to produce plutonium from natural (unenriched) uranium. The UKAEA geared its research to the problems of the Magnox reactor. This meant that future developments were variants of old designs. In the case of the AGR and the Magnox, the most important linking feature was the use of gas as a coolant. Both the Magnox and the AGR used carbon dioxide. Effectively, the commitment of resources and expertise to gas-cooled reactors meant that there was a natural bias against the water-cooled technology used in the United States. Thus, the advice upon which government and the electricity boards relied, was coloured by the UKAEA's interest in the gas-cooled version. Alternative designs would, therefore, have to compete against an established prejudice, backed by financial commitment, in favour of the UKAEA model. The important lesson to be derived from this is to understand that the choice of reactor model, which in theory should conform to the principle of rational choice, in practice is less clear-cut. The gas-cooled reactor appears almost as a fact of nuclear power policy, and it was only with its technical failure and the growth in self-confidence of the electricity boards that alternative designs appeared on the agenda.

The UKAEA is but a specific example of a general trend. The development of advanced and complex technology creates its own political world, with pressure groups, interests, and lobbyists. The competing arguments in the choice of reactor can be understood only as part of this alternative political realm. The apparently straightforward technical question of which design of reactor to choose, became instead an issue of political debate. But it was not a political debate that simply involved politicians. Political leaders formed but one group of participants, and they joined battle with scientists, civil servants and others, in seeking a policy. This brings us to another important feature of the nuclear power decisions: the role of conventional politics.

The demands put on the political system by advanced technology appear to be in tension with the organising principles of that system. The interests of a politician competing for votes may be at odds with the interests involved in decisions about advanced technology. The size, cost and complexity of advanced technology mean that there is a long gap between the initiation and implementation of a policy. With nuclear power, this gap could be as long as ten or fifteen years. This means that the administration which takes the initial decision is not the same one that organises its implementation, or even finances it. What is significant about nuclear power is the almost complete absence of variations in attitude between the two political parties. Even if the two parties had different policies on nuclear power – and the fact that, until recently, they have not is itself significant – they would be unlikely to express these differences in practice. Governments are left to manage what already exists, rather than starting something new. This is a further example of the phenomenon of institutional momentum. The original commitment to nuclear-generated electricity has changed very little in the subsequent

30 years. Those variations that have taken place are at the margins: the number of reactors, the time of their completion and their output. Advanced technology imposes continuity on government, and thereby limits the range of alternative policies to be offered or implemented by different elected governments. To imagine that newly elected governments come to power with their desks cleared of their predecessors' decisions and policies is a fiction that is preserved only for the few weeks of an election campaign.

One final observation we might make about nuclear power decisions concerns the participation of the public. Both the public and its representatives in Parliament play a peripheral role in the story of nuclear power. Although the select committees of the House of Commons have provided one of the few public forums for discussing nuclear power policy, they have had only limited effect on the course of that policy. The information necessary to the assessment of nuclear power policy remains the property of bodies like the CEGB and the UKAEA. The need for nuclear reactors was based on the CEGB's forecast of energy demand; it is only by independent assessment of such figures that policy can be questioned. And even then, since the argument is about an unknown future rather than an identifiable present, the CEGB can only be proved wrong ten years from now, by which time it will, of course, be too late. This veil of ignorance limits the extent to which parliaments, committed by political interests to the short-term, can exercise significant control over a long-term decision like nuclear power.

The problems of ignorance also help explain the lack of public debate and participation. Nuclear power has, for the most part, remained a technical issue. John Hill, then Chairman of the UKAEA, once announced: 'The public doesn't and cannot be expected to understand the issues of nuclear power in other than the broadest terms'.[62] It has been possible to present nuclear power as a technical matter which is beyond the people and the politicians. With the Windscale and Sizewell Inquiries, we have seen the recognition of a limited right of public involvement. The practice of such Inquiries has, however, tended to provide a way of legitimating the decisions of established interests, rather than subjecting those decisions to thorough analysis.[63] Certainly, it is important for us to recognise that there is a narrow divide between the political and the technical and how this is drawn is itself the result of values and interests in competition with each other. The exercise of political power is not only observed in the outcome of public debate, it also is observed in the deliberate exclusion of some issues from debate.

7 The rise and fall of the Civil Service Department

INTRODUCTION

When we think of decision-making we tend to think of policy areas where politicians are trying to affect or control society. Yet as we saw in our general discussions, the way in which government operates and is organised can play a major role in determining the nature of decision-making. In this chapter we want to turn the spotlight inside government itself: to the dispositions which politicians have made concerning the organisation of central government itself. In particular we will concentrate on the fortunes of one department, the Civil Service Department, which became an early victim of the Thatcher Government.

Ever since the First World War administrators have been interested in the question of the 'machinery of government'. Among the areas covered by the machinery of government are: the direction of government at the centre; the number and size of government departments and the distribution of functions between them; the relationship of ministerial departments to other non-departmental organisations; and, more narrowly, the organisation of work within government offices. This whole subject is perceived to be important because of the assumption that sensible and effective policies will more readily emerge when the correct machinery of policy-making is in place. Given the stability of the general political system in Britain, the extent of the chopping and changing in the organisation of Whitehall is perhaps surprising. This reached a crescendo in the Wilson and Heath years, when Whitehall departments of state seemed to be merged, created or abolished at almost yearly intervals, and other areas of public administration, such as local government or the health or water authorities underwent massive upheaval. In the Thatcher years such change has been more sparing. In 1981 the Civil Service

Department (CSD), the subject of this case-study, was dismantled. In 1983 the Departments of Trade and Industry were merged and the Central Policy Review Staff (think-tank) was abolished, and in 1988 the Department of Health and Social Security was split.[1]

Common sense might suggest that changes in the structure of Whitehall would not be all that susceptible to purely short-term political factors, but would tend to result from broad strategy or measured analysis of the relationship of means to goals in administration. Here surely might be an area where the disinterested expert or the broadly-based commission, with its eye on the long term, could be expected to make a major impact upon policy-making. From time to time governments have indeed appointed such commissions or committees to lay down principles for the organisation of the state, of which the most celebrated is the Haldane Committee in the First World War. History suggests, however, that the rational analysis of such bodies forms only one factor, and a minor one at that, in shaping the machinery of government. Important changes also tend to be made for purposes of expediency and in a somewhat haphazard manner, with the Prime Minister of the day taking a key role. Thus Peter Hennessy has charged Harold Wilson with treating 'Whitehall as a kind of adventure playground-cum-laboratory with departments as so many pieces of Lego to be stuck together this way and that almost as the mood took him'.[2] Another factor is the general intellectual fashion. In the 1965–75 period the emphasis everywhere was on economies of scale. Thus just as large firms were held to be more efficient than small, so giant or 'mega' departments were seen as a 'good thing'. A decade later 'small is beautiful' ruled.

Our study of the fortunes of the machinery at the centre during the 1970s and 1980s reveals a surprisingly rich amalgam of factors which influenced the process. Administrative theories, general strategies, political ideologies, personality clashes, bureaucratic politics and political accident all played a part.

THE CREATION OF THE CIVIL SERVICE DEPARTMENT

Control of the Civil Service had already had a long history before 1966. In the early nineteenth century the 'public establishments' were organised in a haphazard and erratic fashion with each department virtually a law unto itself. Following the Northcote-Trevelyan Report of 1854 was a lengthy process of standardisation of recruitment procedures, grading of work, and administrative procedures. The drive to ensure economy in government played an important part here and the Treasury came to exercise a key coordinating force, controlling such matters as recruitment, pay and the organisation of the Civil Service, by virtue of its power over the purse strings. In the inter-war years the power of the Treasury increased as the Civil Service became more united and it became common for senior civil servants to move around the Whitehall departments. However, during this period the Cabinet Office also emerged as another force for coordination at the centre of government, although its concern was more with the coordination of government policy than with broader issues of the structure and organisation of the government machine.[3]

The Treasury's position at the centre rested on two foundations: its financial powers which affected all aspects of policy-making and its control over management of civil service matters. From the early part of this century it is possible to find critics who charged the Treasury with neglecting the latter at the expense of the former, for being too dominated by narrow financial concerns and too preoccupied with economic matters. This was a view consistently taken by trade unions in the Civil Service but it was also adopted by many interested in public administration and in the machinery of government questions. From 1900–61 the question as to whether civil service matters should not be hived off into a separate department was regularly considered by a whole series of committees or commissions of one kind or another: the MacDonnell Royal Commission of 1913, the Bradbury Committee of 1917, the Haldane Committee of 1918, the Tomlin Commission of 1929–31, the Commons Select Committee on Public Expenditure in 1942 and the Plowden Committee of 1961. These bodies all favoured the development within the Treasury of management or administrative questions rather than the creation of a completely new department. The Plowden Committee, a small independent committee, set up within Whitehall, recommended a reorganisation of the Treasury and in 1962 Macmillan's Government made the Finance and the Establishments side of the Treasury into separate divisions each with a permanent secretary at the head, but the option of setting up a new department was explicitly rejected.[4]

Thus by the time a Labour Government returned to power in 1964 the question of the control of the Civil Service had long been debated. One problem was that the whole issue was by its very nature somewhat intangible. It was difficult to find precise criteria by which to assess whether the Treasury or any other body was operating successfully in this field. The outputs of policy on this area are difficult to measure. It was broader political and ideological factors which gave the issue added urgency in the late 1960s.

Whereas during the 1950s British institutions, including the Civil Service, had generally been admired, by the 1960s it had become fashionable to ascribe to these institutions responsibility for the ills of British society and the failings in economic policy. As far as the Civil Service was concerned, critics concentrated their attention on the élitist nature of the mandarin class, on the privileged position of the generalist as opposed to the specialist, and on the inadequate attention which had in the past been given to in-service training and to the efficient management of resources and personnel within government departments.[5] All this reflected the more general political stance of reformers in the 1960s who wanted to create a more egalitarian system of government and to bring more professionalism (usually undefined) to the making of economic and industrial policy. The call for a reform of the Civil Service and of the machinery of government had an obvious appeal to members of Mr Wilson's Labour Government, especially to the Prime Minister who saw himself presiding over the modernisation of a Britain which had for too long been dominated by a worn-out and outmoded establishment. In February 1966 Mr Wilson announced the appointment of a departmental committee, under the chairmanship of Lord Fulton, to examine the structure, recruitment and management, including training, of the Home Civil Service. The members of this committee included three academics, four top civil servants, two MPs, two leading industrialists and a white-collar trade unionist. One of the most active was the academic, Dr Norman Hunt (later Lord Crowther-Hunt), who was close to Mr Wilson and who was sympathetic to the radical critique of the Civil Service. He devoted a year working full time for the committee. The Fulton Report of 1968 attacked the excessively generalist nature of the top Civil Service, and called for the appointment of more specialists and professionals to senior administrative positions, reforms in recruitment procedures and the setting up of a Civil Service College to further post-entry training. The committee recommended the abolition of the existing class system, its replacement with a unified grading system, and the setting up of a new department, independent of the Treasury, which should run the Civil Service.

The Fulton Committee was perceived in different ways by those concerned with it. For radical reformers like Hunt, it was essentially a manifesto of radical change. It was designed to do for the latter part of the twentieth century what the Northcote-Trevelyan Report had done for the late nineteenth century. They saw it as providing a coherent programme of reform. The generalist all-rounder was to give way to the specialist and more emphasis was to be placed on introducing management techniques into administration. Recruitment procedures, in-service training and personnel work were to be radically changed. A decade later these reformers admitted that their expectations had been unfulfilled. This they attributed to a failure of political will on the part of the Government and to the determination and skill of senior civil servants who had wished to scupper the Fulton programme.[6] For many administrators, however, the Fulton Report appeared rather differently. It was seen as but an episode in a complex and slowly evolving pattern of administrative reform. Sir James Dunnett, one of the civil servants on the Committee, although conceding that the controversial first chapter of the Report contained the views of the critics, considered that the rest of the Report 'though not without recommendations for change, was broadly conservative'. It by no means 'heralded a great new Eldorado', rather its role was to expose the Civil Service to the perspectives of outsiders.[7] Sir William (later Lord) Armstrong of the Treasury, who became head of the new CSD, saw the Fulton Report not so much as a blueprint to be followed to the letter, but more as a guideline:

> I was very, very careful, very careful indeed, to say that the appearance of the Fulton Report was a great opportunity. I called it on television an ice-breaker. What I meant was that it was a catalyst and enabled all kinds of ideas to come through.[8]

The Crossman and Castle diaries of the Wilson Cabinet clearly show how for the Prime Minister the Fulton Report had a broader political significance. Fulton and Norman Hunt were Wilson's protégés and the idea of a radical reform appealed to the Prime Minister's urge to shake up the establishment. Crossman expressed this less charitably: 'he thinks this way he can improve his image as a great moderniser'.[9] Other ministers were less ecstatic, notably Roy Jenkins, the Chancellor of the Exchequer, who objected to the setting up of a new department and argued for a period of delay. Initially Jenkins did a deal with Crossman, usually a Wilson supporter, who recounts the following exchange:

> 'If I agree with you about postponing the decision on Social Security cuts for a week will you give me your full support on Fulton?' 'Yes', I said, 'if you will support me on Lords' reform as well.' And that, roughly speaking, was the deal we came to.[10]

On 20 June Wilson found himself in a minority on the issue in the full Cabinet and according to Crossman got 'so upset he stopped the meeting' and asked that it should be resumed later.[11] In the meantime Wilson mobilised support among his colleagues. Barbara Castle, for her part, when summoned for a talk over the brandy in Wilson's No. 10 study, found the Prime Minister brooding about the conspiracies against him. Taking full advantage of the situation she said:

> I . . . was all in favour of his announcing acceptance in principle but that I wasn't going to agree to any reference to 'phasing in' the expensive parts of Fulton unless and until we had announced the phasing in of equal pay in the industrial field about which I was in touch with the Chancellor . . . Harold replied, 'Work me out a formula for this side of my statement'.[12]

At the Cabinet meeting of 26 June Wilson managed to get Cabinet endorsement for the Fulton Report. 'We gave him an easy time', noted Crossman, 'Harold needed a success for himself'.[13]

These little details are significant. They show the extent of the purely departmental interests and concerns of Cabinet members and the way in which single issues can get mixed up in extraneous deals and personal rivalries. Even an area apparently so far removed from party political concern as the machinery of government can be profoundly affected by the fortuitous day-to-day manoeuvrings of Cabinet politics.

The CSD was set in being on 1 November 1968, and its new Permanent Secretary, Sir William Armstrong, became Head of the Home Civil Service. From the start there were ambiguities concerning its purpose. For Lord Crowther-Hunt and radical reformers the new department was to play a pivotal role in the future process of the Civil Service. It was to serve 'as a sort of battering-ram of change, to make the Civil Service as a whole more professional and more efficient'. It was to be 'the main driving force for implementing the rest of the Fulton recommendations', and not merely the 'old "Pay and Management side of the Treasury" writ large'. In their view the staffing of the new department was to be critically important: in particular they called for 'a number of appointments at senior level to be made from outside the Service of people with appropriate knowledge and experience of managing large organisations both at home and abroad'. The new department was to pioneer the most modern techniques of management and to encourage the remaining Whitehall departments to follow suit, and if necessary: 'be in a position to call all departments to account for failure to use the recommended techniques and to put in its own men to investigate any departmental organization and to recommend improvements'.[14]

In short the creation of the CSD was to mark a radical transformation of the spirit of Whitehall itself.

Within Whitehall the creation of the CSD was seen in less dramatic terms. Many officials saw the new department as simply a following-through of tendencies which had been in evidence since 1940. Sir Ian Bancroft, who was the last Permanent Secretary of the CSD, certainly in retrospect saw the creation of the CSD in 1968 as being merely a continuation or development of previous trends, namely giving more weight to management issues.[15] Sir John Hunt and Sir Robert Armstrong, as Secretaries of the Cabinet, held the same perspective. In their view the new Department had been created because there was feeling that the Treasury had done the Civil Service 'on the cheap', that more resources might beneficially be allocated to personnel management and management techniques, and that there would be considerable advantages in having a Cabinet Minister other than the Chancellor of the Exchequer who could make the business of management and efficiency in the Civil Service a main charge upon his time and energies. The need to have a new department to push through the various suggestions for reform contained in the Fulton Report was seen as an additional factor and not as a prime concern.

Even when the CSD was wound up in 1981 there were some who maintained its creation 'was a destructive irrelevance, spatchcocked into the general design of reform at the specific and arbitrary stipulation of the then Prime Minister'. The accuracy or otherwise of this claim (by Peter Jay) is less important than the fact that even in 1981 it could give rise to a heated correspondence on the subject in *The Times*. All this subsequent controversy clearly reflects the degree of uncertainty which had originally surrounded the purpose of the new Department.[16]

There was therefore never any generally agreed conception of the *raison d'être* of the CSD. It is impossible to say that here was a policy or a decision which had any clear objective. Equally striking is the way in which the creation of the CSD took place without any attempt to relate it to any systematic analysis of the workings of the centre of British government. A feature of the late 1960s and early 1970s was that a series of commissions of enquiry were set up and innovations made in constitutional and machinery of government matters in isolation from each other. No attempt was made to relate the work of the CSD to these broader issues. All this reflected the more general approach of the Fulton Committee, the more radical members of which had sought to bring about a major change in the workings of the government machine – but had been precluded from considering such crucial questions as the workings of ministerial responsibility and the direction of government from the centre.

THE CSD AT WORK AFTER 1968

In Lord Crowther-Hunt's view the CSD had been 'an enormous disappointment' from the very start. It was not so much that the Department ran out of steam as that 'it never had any steam in the first instance and that is basically what has been wrong with it'.[17] His view was that the senior Civil Service élite had undermined the whole policy of Civil Service reform and that politicians had lacked the interest or the will to push reforms. Here was a failure of implementation.[18]

Most Whitehall official opinion put a rather different gloss on matters. For most the changes had in any case been incremental, verging on the cosmetic. Lord Helsby, a former Head of the Civil Service, for example, offered a low-key interpretation. The creation of the CSD was 'not a fundamental change . . . There may well be advantage in creating a new department with a brighter public image – so long as this is not expected to work wonders by itself'.[19]

Lord Croham, who as Sir Douglas Allen served as Permanent Secretary to the CSD in the 1970s, saw the subsequent history in terms of a loss of momentum. The first task had been to work through the new ideas and then subsequently:

> In . . . its day-to-day working it was not so exciting and it was not so effective, and if you want a department to have steam then you keep making changes. I do not believe it did run out of steam. I believe that the pressure on Whitehall to make the changes was relaxed.

As attention in the early 1970s was turned to other questions such as the economy, and prices and incomes so the influence of the CSD may have been diminished as its work was seen as being of less importance.[20]

Certainly 1972 marked a turning point in the fortunes of the CSD. There were a variety of factors coming into play here. In the first place, it was about this time that the political emphasis moved away from issues concerning the machinery of government towards questions such as economic management and industrial relations. Subsequently after 1975, the emphasis in Whitehall moved towards economy and especially manpower reduction.[21]

Secondly, the CSD suffered a loss of political influence. This may be traced back to 1969 when Harold Wilson was unable through pressure of work to give the attention to Civil Service reform which he would have liked.[22] Junior ministers in charge of the CSD tended either to be figures of minor political weight, or, if they were of importance, to be preoccupied with other duties. Lord Soames, when in charge of the CSD, could hardly have kept an eye on its affairs when administering the transfer of power in Zimbabwe! Just as there were problems at the ministerial level, so all did not go smoothly at the official level. The position of the Permanent Secretary of the CSD, which bore the title 'Head of the Home Civil Service', became devalued. This in some part resulted from the misfortunes of Sir William Armstrong, who was used by Mr Heath as his right hand man between 1972–4 in furthering the Government's industrial and economic policies. Sir William, thus removed from his purely CSD work, became the subject of considerable political controversy and was even dubbed 'Deputy Prime Minister' in opposition circles.[23] His successors, Sir Douglas Allen and Sir Ian Bancroft, had to live under that shadow. Neither Mr Wilson nor Mr Callaghan used them as general advisers and neither official enjoyed ease of access to the Prime Minister. The Secretary of the Cabinet instead became *de facto* leading adviser.[24] After 1979 matters in this area went from bad to worse with a clear temperamental clash between Bancroft and the new Prime Minister, Mrs Thatcher. For her Bancroft represented the epitome of the mandarin élite she so distrusted.

A third cause for disquiet among many outsiders was the way the CSD increasingly seemed to be seen as the custodian of the vested interests of the Civil Service itself. Peter Hennessy has written how Ian Bancroft, in particular, 'did a good deal of work on the Civil Service's public profile'. As a result of a review of the Civil Service image, an Image Unit was set up.

> It would meet early in the day to pluck the previous night's news bulletins and current affairs programmes off its video and tape recorders and read the morning's papers. If there was criticism and it was unfair, the permanent secretary of the affected department would be urged to write a letter putting the miscreant right; if it was justified, the permanent secretary would be asked to put his house in order.[25]

Moreover, as industrial relations in the Civil Service deteriorated, it was unfortunate that most ministers' contacts with the CSD were in its capacity as managing industrial unrest and as the advocate of Civil Service interests. With the election of a government inspired by New Right ideas after 1979 this took on new significance.

Fourthly, there were structural reasons why the division of powers between the Treasury and CSD came to be questioned. Important here was the growing recognition that the division of functions secured in 1968 presented as many disadvantages as advantages. Chief among the disadvantages was that it was neither possible, nor indeed in the long-run desirable, to separate responsibility for the control of public expenditure (Treasury) from the control of expenditure on manpower (CSD). From the very beginning some Treasury officials had been unhappy at the division. But in the early years the problem had not appeared so acute, partly because in the early years the senior staff of the CSD had largely been comprised of ex-Treasury people.

> They knew their opposite numbers in the public expenditure divisions, they were used to working with them, and they had a lot of common experience. That is, inevitably, through no one's fault, a wasting asset, and you cannot go on running a department simply on old contacts.[26]

These problems led to a renewed review of the whole organisation of the centre of British government in the late 1970s. Before continuing the narrative it will be helpful to analyse the nature of the structural dilemma.

DEMARCATION DISPUTES AT THE CENTRE

Disquiet at the performance of the CSD reflected the fact that control of central government was by its very nature something of a seamless garment. It involved four broad strands all of which were intertwined at various points:

1	2	3	4
Macro-economic Policy, Taxation and Revenue Raising	Control of Public Expenditure	Control of Manpower, Management Efficiency	Personnel Functions, Recruitment, Training etc.

The difficulty was to know where to draw the lines between the functions in organisational terms. The old Treasury of the early 1960s had controlled all four areas, although with only loose surveillance over areas of number four, especially recruitment. Between 1964 and 1967 it had contended with the short-lived Department of Economic Affairs, another product of Wilson's tinkering with the machinery of government, for dominance over areas one and two. After 1968 the lines of demarcation between the Treasury and the CSD fell between areas two and three. Any arrangement seemed to offer disadvantages.

Under the old system of Treasury dominance there had already been a problem of overload, which would, if recreated, now be rendered all the more serious given the increased economic problems and membership of the EEC. Moreover, some feared the reuniting of the Treasury and CSD would mean the subordination of the interests of areas three and four to those of one and two. Lord Armstrong, for example, recollected that during his time at the Treasury young people trained in economics had been dismayed when told: 'the time has come "to do your stint on establishments" . . . It was popularly regarded as equivalent to the salt mines or the galley, and the quality of the work, in spite of many heroic efforts, suffered accordingly'. It was important in his view to have a Cabinet Minister properly equipped to deal with Civil Service matters:

> From the Chancellor's point of view Civil Service work is inevitably a minor excrescence on his major preoccupation of framing and carrying out economic and financial policy. Time and again I saw some Civil Service crisis suddenly obtrude on the Chancellor, who was himself coping with urgent financial matters which, inevitably, seemed more insistent and more important. The result was that he turned to Civil Service matters with reluctance, scrambling through the meetings with the help of a brief, and left people feeling that his mind was on other things.[27]

The defenders of the CSD stalwartly supported this line of argument.

On the other hand, the critics maintained that the existing separation of functions two and three often meant that efficiency fell down the middle. Successive Secretaries of the Cabinet, who were in a good position to observe, took this view. Sir Robert Armstrong, reflecting on his previous experiences in a spending department (the Home Office), remembered how:

> irrespective of the political complexion of the Government in power, the Treasury was at us to control our expenditure from the one side, and the Civil Service Department was at us to control our manpower from the other, and perhaps it felt a bit like being slugged from the left by one boxer and slugged from the right by another boxer, perhaps without the co-ordination of punches that one might have expected from a single pair of hands. Perhaps it made it a little easier to dodge the punches![28]

His predecessor, Sir John Hunt, stressed how the CSD was bound to come out second best in the battle for resources and its nominal control over manpower counted for little. Departmental policies were argued with the Treasury; once the necessary resources were granted, the policy issue was seen as settled. Hence the CSD lacked clout.[29]

However, if the integrationist solution of bringing together functions two and three, entailed separating function one from two, severe problems might result for economic management. The control of public expenditure was now so intimately a part of economic policy that any such attempt at separation here might seriously affect the running of the economy. This point was forcefully argued by Lord Diamond. Equally the rationale of dividing areas three and four was not without problems. Where would the responsibility for pay fall? Although primarily in the sphere of manpower control (area three) it had repercussions for expenditure (area two) and industrial relations (area four). All this is a good illustration of how in government there are rarely easy or clear-cut solutions to organisational problems.

A Parliamentary Select Committee, chaired by Michael English, investigated all these questions in depth. A minority of Labour members, notably Brian Sedgemore and John Garrett, wanted to see the break-up of the Treasury – a 'bureau of budget' solution. However, the majority of the Committee came out in favour of transferring only those elements of management services and manpower divisions which were concerned with efficiency from the CSD to the Treasury.[30] Garrett later criticised this recommendation as 'fairly superficial and not supported by extensive evidence', relying upon 'the observations of a few witnesses' and not backed by research.[31]

Clearly the prevailing consensus both inside Whitehall and in political circles favoured some kind of closer integration of manpower and public expenditure controls. Mr Callaghan, the new Prime Minister, was not altogether averse to making changes in the structure of Whitehall departments. In September 1976 he had dismembered the Department of the Environment after warning only a handful of officials. He seriously considered a reconstruction of the centre; however, he decided that it was inopportune to embark on any major upheaval at a time of political uncertainty – the Labour Government of 1974–9 only survived as a result of a succession of deals or accommodations with various minor parties – and so the future of the CSD remained unresolved until after the general election.[32] As something of a question mark hung over the Department's continued existence, the morale of its staff suffered.[33]

MRS THATCHER AND THE CSD 1979–81

The victory of the Conservatives at the general election of 1979 indicated a profound change of emphasis in Whitehall. The incoming Government approached the whole question of economy in government in more messianic terms than its predecessors. Mrs Thatcher and her leading ministers not only were committed to a radical monetarist economic strategy, but also had an ambition to roll back the frontiers of the state – in other words reduce the amount of government as a whole. This involved both the hiving-off or privatisation of areas of the public sector and a determination to attack waste. The two ambitions were not always clearly distinguished in the Government's rhetoric; but both were accompanied by a striking hostility towards officials as a breed. The tendency of the Conservatives in opposition had been to attack the bureaucracy as being over-manned, privileged and to a large extent feather-bedded, being immune to the discipline of the market which automatically ensured a degree of accountability in the private sector. To the dismay of civil servants these attitudes persisted in government, with senior ministers being noticeably disinclined to rally to the defence of the Civil Service in the face of criticism from the press and outside sources.[34]

Mrs Thatcher and her closest associates were also temperamentally averse to any wholesale reshaping of the departmental machinery of Whitehall. They believed that such upheavals often consisted of little more than the shunting of desks or the changing of name-plates; or alternatively the immediate costs in morale or finance outweighed any long-term benefits. The Heath Government, in their view, had erred in this direction. Both Mrs Thatcher and her mentor, Sir Keith Joseph, set more store by attempting to change the frameworks of thought of their officials. Moreover, the new Government was more concerned about the sharp end of government than the Heath administration had been, that is to say the actual results of policy and in particular elimination of waste. Special emphasis was placed upon the managerial responsibility of ministers in charge of departments, and their task of monitoring services against expenditures.

The new Prime Minister was not initially particularly happy at the dispositions she found at the centre of Whitehall. Suspicious of the deeply entrenched Keynesian outlook of the Treasury, wary of the degree to which the Cabinet Office had recently influenced economic policy-making, and dissatisfied at the performance of the CSD, she felt the need for some means of injecting prime ministerial influence within Whitehall. One solution was to appoint in June 1979

Sir Derek Rayner, Joint Managing Director of Marks and Spencer, to a part-time position as her adviser on the elimination of waste within Whitehall. Sir Derek possessed considerable experience of Whitehall. He eschewed instant solutions and grand strategies. His tactic was to work from the particular to the general, to pursue some in-depth investigations with a view to producing general recommendations. Sir Derek was given a small unit housed within the Cabinet Office but seconded to No. 10 Downing Street, and proceeded to conduct a series of in-depth scrutinies into detailed aspects of work in government departments. The object of these exercises was to analyse in cooperation with departmental officials the actual operation of certain government tasks, with a view to posing fundamental questions about the necessity for and the organisation of various administrative procedures. By October it was estimated that savings of £70 million had resulted from his piecemeal scrutinies.[35]

The investigations confirmed Sir Derek in his suspicion that the whole ethos of Whitehall needed changing. Whilst recognising that questions of efficiency in public administration were more complicated than in industry, he nevertheless felt that bureaucratic attitudes tended to be antithetic to innovation and to entrepreneurial initiative: 'in Whitehall, bureaucracy can grow and stifle initiative and distract from efficiency unless positive steps are taken to counter it'.[36] This led him to consider more general proposals for what he termed 'lasting reforms' which would ensure that momentum was carried on even when the political will and initiative might have weakened. In April 1980 he presented a Cabinet paper, The Conventions of Government, in which he pinpointed certain general areas in which the conventions and the approach of Whitehall needed to be modified. In this paper he recommended among other things: better and more precise analysis of the cost of central government on a departmental basis, a shortening of the Whitehall hierarchy, more emphasis upon managerial skills in promotion procedures and direct incentives in terms of financial and career prospects for individuals who showed initiative regarding the elimination of waste.[37] In Sir Derek's view managerial skill and cost-effectiveness should be given as high a value as the traditional skills of policy-making and the delineation of policy options.

Sir Derek Rayner's work was significant in two respects. In the first place he enjoyed the wholehearted support of the Prime Minister, who not only was in sympathy with his general philosophy, but also listened with respect to his specific recommendations on governmental matters. Indeed she treated him as a kind of unofficial head of the Civil Service. Secondly, Sir Derek was outside the CSD, and this in itself was symptomatic of the Government's hostility to the CSD.

It was arguable that if any department should have been concerned with the general efficiency of the Civil Service and had a brief to stimulate creative change it was the CSD. The House of Commons Select Committee investigating the future of the CSD in 1980 clearly took this view and pushed Sir Ian Bancroft, the Permanent Secretary of the CSD and Head of the Civil Service, very much on the defensive in this respect.[38] It is significant that Sir Derek Rayner used relatively junior officials on his various scrutinies who presented their recommendations to their own ministers; thus the Rayner exercises in effect bypassed the CSD. Sir Derek soon became convinced of the need to integrate as far as possible the Treasury and the CSD:

> To my mind, the centre is in its divided state much less of a match for departments than if it were a single organisation. In its present state the centre has to coordinate itself. This takes time and blunts its strength, whereas what is needed is a strong policy for good self-management by central government with a strong and determined centre in the lead.[39]

He believed that the creation of a 'single organisation, under vigorous leadership' could make a 'very greatly increased and sustained contribution to effective management'.

Sir Derek's forceful views in favour of 'integration' received the broad backing of the Secretary of the Cabinet, Sir Robert Armstrong. Whilst recognising that there were two sides to the question, Sir Robert believed the time had come to look at the organisation of the centre again. He agreed that the separation of the control of spending on manpower from other public expenditure in government was illogical and wasteful.[40] It is significant that integrationist views had the backing of two advisers who had special access to the Prime Minister, Sir Robert by virtue of his office, and Sir Derek by virtue of his personal influence. By contrast Sir Ian Bancroft, Head of the CSD, rarely saw the Prime Minister.

During 1980 the position of the CSD came under close scrutiny. A subcommittee of the House of Commons Treasury and Civil Service Committee was set up to further investigate 'The Future of the Civil Service Department'. This all-party committee was chaired by Robert Sheldon, who had been a junior minister in both the CSD and the Treasury in the previous Labour administration.[41] The committee took evidence from the key Permanent Secretaries involved; from Sir Derek Rayner, Lord Croham, Lord Crowther-Hunt and William

Plowden, a public administration specialist. The Committee had before them the English Committee's evidence and covered much the same ground as their predecessor. Although the Prime Minister welcomed the enquiry as contributing 'to the discussion of a subject in which there was considerable parliamentary and public interest', some members of the Committee over the summer clearly felt that the real decisions were being made elsewhere.[42] They voiced the suspicion at one point that they stood in danger of being a 'stalking horse' while the decision to dismember the CSD had already been taken. They were particularly unhappy at the way in which the officials who gave evidence steered them in the direction of four options only, whereas, as both Lord Croham and Mr Plowden pointed out, the possible permutations were far more numerous and interesting.[43] Moreover, a study by two assistant secretaries (Hawtin and Moore) into technical aspects was even more limited in its terms of reference; it was formally confined to analysing the implications of integrating the CSD and the Treasury. The study team 'did not feel precluded from drawing attention to measures likely to strengthen further the coordination and cooperation between the Departments were they to remain separate'.[44] But nevertheless the study did not consider the options of dividing the functions of either the Treasury or the CSD.

While the Committee sat, a power-battle was clearly being waged within Whitehall. Within a week of the report in *The Times* of the questioning of Sir Ian Bancroft and Sir Douglas Wass by the Select Committee the correspondence columns of the paper – then known as the tom-toms of the British establishment – were publishing letters in support of the CSD from its former political and permanent heads, a sure sign that the Department was under threat. The Civil Service unions protested against any idea that the CSD should be wound up. Meanwhile behind the scenes, Sir Ian Bancroft was reported to be putting up a vigorous fight to save the department he led. A small steering group of permanent secretaries met in October to advise the Prime Minister. They had before them the Hawtin-Moore study on the integration of the two departments. The majority of opinion in the steering committee appears to have been in favour of integration, although the matter was not as simple as this.[45] For integration as the Hawtin-Moore study made clear and as the Select Committee had discovered, could mean two things. On the one hand there was 'shallow integration' which would mean essentially shifting across the CSD's pay and manpower functions to continue as a separate unit within the Treasury. This could be achieved relatively swiftly. On the other hand a 'deep integration' of all the CSD's manpower divisions with the corresponding Treasury public spending branches was likely to take at least a year to achieve.[46] But it was this latter option which was perhaps more calculated to appeal to a government anxious to see results at the sharp end rather than cosmetic changes in the machinery of government to which Mr Wilson and, to a lesser extent, Mr Heath had been so addicted.

By mid-November 1980 all the signs were that the CSD was to be merged in one form or another with the Treasury. However, as the Commons Treasury and Civil Service Subcommittee came to conclude their work, they were conscious of a change in the climate. In large part this was due to the intervention of Sir Geoffrey Howe, the Chancellor of the Exchequer, who let it be known that the pressures of running the economy at this period were such as to preclude him from undertaking any additional burdens. The Treasury was clearly more interested in getting its hands on pay and manpower control, but was less than enthusiastic about the personnel and management functions. The six members of the Subcommittee were themselves somewhat divided on the complex question of the future shape of central government, but Mr Sheldon, the Chairman, was firmly of the opinion that the CSD should survive and his views won the balance of the argument.[47]

In its report the Sheldon Committee concurred with the prevalent feeling in Whitehall that the CSD was 'not on top' of the problem of government growth. Changes were needed to allay the widespread disquiet aroused by the CSD's failure to pursue a more active role in managing the Civil Service. Past political failings were part of the cause of this, but organisational reforms would help remedy matters. Among other things the Committee called for the strengthening of staff at a senior level and improved coordination between the CSD and Treasury. The broader concerns of the CSD in such areas as training, recruitment and personnel management should not be lost sight of in the search for immediate economies and savings.[48] In calling for a 'revitalisation' of the Department the Subcommittee was in effect suggesting that it be placed on probation.

Given the reluctance of Sir Geoffrey Howe to sanction any immediate changes and the considerable hostility of the Civil Service trade unions to the idea of winding up the CSD, the Commons Subcommittee's and Sheldon Committee's report proved more influential than it might otherwise have done. On 29 January 1981, Mrs Thatcher announced that she had decided to strengthen and improve the existing organisation of the CSD rather than merge it with the Treasury:

I started off marginally in favour of merging the two Departments but came to the conclusion that if we were to do that, all concentration would go on re-organisation rather than on dealing with the true problem which . . . is effective control of public spending.[49]

A White Paper in February outlined proposals for improving the pattern of career development in the Civil Service, so that more emphasis could be placed on management experience in government, and the commitment to economy and cost-consciousness was underlined.[50]

A firm decision to keep the existing structures thus seemed to have been made, but by the end of the year it was totally reversed. On 12 November 1981 Mrs Thatcher announced the abolition of the CSD and the dismemberment of its functions. Control over pay, conditions of service, and manpower numbers was to be vested in the Treasury, as well as other various computer and catering services; on the other hand management systems and organisation (including the Rayner reviews), recruitment, training and personnel management were to be put under a new Management and Personnel Office (MPO) which was to be attached to the Cabinet Office. Lady Young, as Chancellor of the Duchy of Lancaster, was to be minister with day-to-day charge of the work of the new office under the Prime Minister. At the official level the Secretary of the Cabinet and the Permanent Secretary to the Treasury were to become joint heads of the Home Civil Service. The Prime Minister, announcing the changes in the Commons, declared that, notwithstanding a good deal of progress in controlling the cost and size of the Civil Service and in improving its efficiency, 'the time has now come when some organisational changes will help us to make sure that the progress we have already achieved is maintained'. She wished to restore to the Treasury 'unified and purposive responsibility for the management of the public sector resources'. She was careful to emphasise that she was not 'merging' the CSD with the Treasury: 'The efficiency of the Civil Service in carrying out its functions and the selection and development of civil servants are as important to the Government as the control of public expenditure'.[51]

The new arrangements clearly marked a major defeat for the more conservative approaches within Whitehall to Civil Service management. The civil servant who was, under the aegis of Sir Robert Armstrong, to have control of the new Management and Personnel Office was to be John Cassels, and he had been recently appointed second Permanent Secretary in charge of Sir Derek's unit, and had been specially chosen in September by Sir Derek as his 'progress chaser'.[52]

What had brought about such a striking change in the fortunes of the CSD which had only recently narrowly survived rigorous scrutiny? A large part of the explanation for the apparent volte face must lie in the industrial unrest in the Civil Service which lasted throughout the greater part of 1981. This took the form of a series of selective strikes in key government installations in protest against the Government's pay offer and its decision to suspend the work of the Pay Research Unit. The industrial action proved less effective than had been anticipated and after several months the unions were forced to call it off and more or less accept the Government's terms. As a result relations between the Government and the trade unions had become glacial by autumn 1981, and the decision to abolish the CSD was seen by the union leaders as 'tit for tat'. It was 'all part of the Prime Minister's personal vendetta against the Civil Service Unions'; here was an example of the ' "Marks and Spencer ethos", which might be OK for selling knickers but it is no way to run a country'.[53] Although the issue was never so simple or crude, ministers were determined to exert closer control over Civil Service pay, manpower and efficiency. The CSD, already on probation, was identified in the Government's eyes as the sponsoring department of the Civil Service. Set up to bring about radical change, it had come to be seen as the custodian of conventional practices and the defender of vested interest.

CHANGES AT THE CENTRE AFTER 1981

The winding up of the CSD certainly marked a decisive shift in the nature of the Thatcher Government's policies towards the Civil Service. Sir Ian Bancroft and his deputy were pensioned off into early retirement and for the next few years it was the MPO within the Cabinet Office which made all the running on administrative reform. A series of reforms and initiatives came from this source, all with the blessing of the Prime Minister. These included the Financial Management Initiative, the Top Persons' Training Programme, and the 'Next Steps' proposals for hiving off from central control large areas of executive government work. Consideration of the content of these reforms lies outside the scope of this chapter.[54] Suffice it to say that they do represent, when taken together, a developing efficiency strategy to instill into the Civil Service a concern for good management, a more entrepreneurial spirit and a concern to monitor the effectiveness of administrative decisions and outputs.

In contrast to the Fulton reformers the method of work of Rayner and his successors, notably Robin Ibbs, has been to concentrate on the specific and thence develop the principles for further reform. The work has thus been more incremental in character. It has also been far more intimately connected with the political concerns of the government of the day. Efficiency has been primarily redefined in terms of cost cutting and value for money which relate to the sharp end of government policy. Finally, the reformers since 1981 have concentrated very little upon the classic machinery of government and much more upon bringing about shifts in the Whitehall culture.[55]

However, once again outside political factors concentrated attention upon the machinery at the centre. The aftermath of the Westland affair of 1986, with all its revelations of leaked letters and the like, raised important questions concerning the loyalty and responsibilities of civil servants, questions which had already been raised by the Clive Ponting affair. The Treasury and Civil Service Committee of the Commons investigated the duties and responsibilities of civil servants in 1985–6. The absence of a department for the Civil Service raised two questions of relevance: had it led to an overload of work for the Secretary of the Cabinet?; did it present a possible conflict of loyalties? Most of the evidence before the Committee answered in the affirmative to both questions. The Committee believed 'as a matter of principle there should be a single Minister for the Civil Service' who should have under her or him a full Permanent Secretary as Head of the Civil Service. Such a solution 'would go a long way towards restoring Civil Service morale'. It would help to reassure civil servants that 'legitimate interests' would be protected and that 'the strengths and effectiveness of the Civil Service as an enduring institution will not be undermined by the actions of any particular government in power'.[56]

Such was not the language of Thatcherism and the Government rejected the findings of the Committee.[57] In August 1987 changes went in another direction. Mrs Thatcher and Sir Robert Armstrong commissioned a retiring Permanent Secretary, Kenneth Stowe, to advise about the control of the Civil Service. He found the existing division of responsibilities between the MPO and the Treasury to be illogical and unsatisfactory. His recommendation for the creation of a management board was not accepted. However, the MPO was abolished and its managerial functions for civil service pay and conditions of service were absorbed once more into the Treasury. Its residual functions, including the work of the efficiency unit, became the responsibility of a junior minister for the Civil Service attached to the Cabinet Office.[58] Thus the Treasury had regained the largest part of its former empire, but the Cabinet Office had also strengthened its position at the centre. Under the new dispositions the Cabinet Secretary was to be the Head of the Civil Service, an important position, especially regarding control over senior appointments in the bureaucracy.

The abolition of the CSD and the extra responsibilities and work-load borne by the Cabinet Secretary indeed had important and largely unforeseen repercussions for the ordering of Cabinet Government. Robert Armstrong devolved much more power and responsibility to his junior deputy secretaries in the Cabinet Office. The result has been for the Cabinet Office itself to become more compartmentalised. This has accentuated a tendency, apparent over the past twenty years or so, for the Cabinet Office to grow and become more complex, in turn leading to a certain degree of compartmentalism at the centre.[59]

CONCLUSION

Control of the Civil Service is important for several reasons. It directly affects the relationship of government with its employees; it is important for ensuring the efficiency of administration; and it affects the structure and organisation of government at the centre.

A rational perspective upon decision-making would suggest certain common sense conclusions might be drawn. One would not anticipate this to be an area where political issues loomed large. Secondly, sudden changes in the Whitehall structure or any periods of prolonged uncertainty would seem to be unlikely. Long-term planning and careful monitoring of performance against agreed objectives would seem more likely. Again one might expect to find any reorganisation of the control of the Civil Service to be related to a discussion of the centre of British government as a whole: namely the roles of the Cabinet Office, the Treasury and such constitutional issues as devolution and the workings of ministerial responsibility. Finally, it would be natural to assume that due weight would be given to the views both of academic experts in public administration and of Parliament, which had a constitutional responsibility for ensuring the accountability of the executive. The story of the rise and fall of the CSD shows that all these 'rational' expectations need heavy qualification.

What general conclusions may be drawn from this case-study? In the first place, it comes as little surprise to find that this was not an area which greatly concerned the general public, political parties or public opinion. The only real exception here is the Civil Service trade unions, whose power and influence was relatively weak.

Nevertheless, political factors, often of an extraneous nature, keep bursting in upon the story at different times and places. Thus deals among ministers in the Wilson Cabinet affected the fortunes of the Fulton recommendations; the Civil Service strike of 1981 and the Westland affair were important catalysts for change at the centre in the 1980s; and the difficulties of William Armstrong and his preoccupations with the miners' strike and the economic problems of the Heath Government determined some of the fortunes of the CSD in its middle period. Not to be neglected also under this category are personality clashes: Norman Hunt and William Armstrong; Ian Bancroft and Margaret Thatcher. Final decisions in this area of the machinery of government were the prerogative of politicians and the issue was always presented as one where they were exercising judgement less as party leaders than as custodians of Whitehall efficiency. The reality was very different. For politicians, and perhaps leading bureaucrats as well, the political concerns of the short-term appeared more pressing than those issues of administrative rationality and abstract analysis of policy-making that tend to be the concern of academic theorists of administration.

This brings us to a related point. The machinery for the control of the Civil Service was the subject of numerous investigations by committees, including three all-party parliamentary committees. None of these were able to achieve much directly, although their reports may have contributed to a rather nebulous climate of opinion and to have cleared the ground. Parliament here appears less as a motive force than an investigatory one, an *ex post facto* aid to the researcher or subsequent intelligent historian. Yet such impartial arenas where a great deal of evidence was collected, necessitating the expenditure of much time and money, might, according to the rational model of decision-making, be expected to have played a major role in decision-making.

Equally interesting, however, is the effect which changes in the broader ideological outlook or climate had upon the way in which the machinery of central government was viewed. As Sir Robert Armstrong stressed, the issue was 'not just a matter of pure organisation, not, I think, a matter of eternal verity; the structure has to be adapted to the priority policies of the Minister'.[60] These policies themselves, as Sir Ian Bancroft recognised, related to the overall philosophy of the government of the day: 'Every single Government that I have served has been interested in achieving both the implementation of its policies and the pursuit of efficiency'. Efficiency, however, was to be defined in different terms at differing times: 'In the early 1970s the emphasis was mainly on improving systems of management . . . Since then for wider economic reasons, the emphasis has moved very much towards economy'.[61]

Once efficiency was redefined in these terms the position of the CSD was weakened, since its role had come in some quarters to be interpreted in large part as defending the interests of the civil servants, whereas the hatchet role in government was more naturally identified with the Treasury. During the long time-span of this case-study one can see a competition between different general philosophies. In the late 1960s and early 1970s the radical Fulton reformers wanted to shake up Whitehall and to impose managerial ideas predicated upon an expansion in government. By the 1980s the battle was between the New Right-influenced reformers and the conventional views of Civil Service administration. The Civil Service was at one and the same time the target of reform and the means of steering it into workable plans.

Ideas and ideology are important in this story but these also become wrapped up with issues of mere institutional bureaucratic politics. Departments came to be associated with a particular ethos or policy line. The reformers in the 1960s felt strongly, for example, that a new department was necessary to break the pattern of Civil Service management. Similarly in 1979–81 the Treasury and the CSD were characterised by different outlooks concerning the management of the Civil Service. The permanent heads of these departments, although careful not to be overtly seen as advocating particular policies, nevertheless felt obliged behind the scenes to fight for their corners. Each had certain priorities: in the case of pay, for example, the Treasury was primarily concerned with the control of public expenditure, the CSD with labour relations within the Civil Service. So apparent were these bureaucratic identifications that Mrs Thatcher in the end felt obliged to override her strong prejudices against Whitehall restructuring, being convinced that the abolition of the CSD was necessary for the effective implementation of government policy.

The story of the machinery at the centre further illustrates the power of bureaucracies to influence the policy-making process. The key decisions concerning Whitehall restructuring were certainly taken by politicians, or more accurately by the Prime Minister of the day. However, this is a simple point of decision – should a new department be created or an existing one abolished? Far more complex is the style and operation of a government department. Thus the kind of department the CSD turned out to be was determined less by politicians than civil servants. The whole history of the implementation of the Fulton Report indicates the difficulties of political control in this complex area. Not least of the difficulties is lack of time and lack of expertise. Harold Wilson, for example attributed the disappointments following the Fulton Report to a failure on his part to see the business through due to the sheer rush and pace of Government at the time. Political direction even when it can be clearly determined is difficult to sustain. Mrs Thatcher proved to be far more adept in this respect by ensuring that the efficiency strategy had the necessary political clout and was related to the strategic concerns of her governments.

A further conclusion emerges out of this: the importance both of informal procedures and of administrative constraints in modifying the formal institutional frameworks. The position of the Permanent Secretary of the CSD is a classic case in point. Although formally Head of the Home Civil Service the experience of the 1970s showed that he was frequently unable to act as a key coordinator. Sir William Armstrong's position in 1972–4 illustrates this. If on the one hand the head was truly to become the right-hand man of the Prime Minister, he could not possibly keep in touch with the day-to-day running of the CSD in all its complexity. If, on the other hand, he immersed himself in Civil Service matters he was bound to become distanced from the concerns of the Prime Minister and the Cabinet. In neither way was the CSD able adequately to lie at the centre of Whitehall. Likewise, although the Treasury and the CSD formally had an equal status at the centre of Whitehall, the influence of the former soon outweighed the latter. In the first few years of the CSD when its senior staff were ex-Treasury officials personal contacts helped ease the relationships, but after about 1972 the CSD was very much a fifth wheel of the coach. The real influence of each department was determined by the substance of its work. The CSD was not in a position to benefit from the formal powers it held. The remarkable influence of Sir Derek Rayner after 1979 strikingly confirms the importance of informal networks. Sir Derek wielded his influence not by virtue of his formal office but because of his proximity to the Prime Minister and his identification with the dominant ethos which underlay Mrs Thatcher's Government's policies.

Lord Bancroft later reflected ruefully about what he called decades of fussiness in dealing with the government machine at the centre. He did not believe that sufficient attention had been paid to the huge inefficiencies of unnecessary structural change. Yet the incessant tinkering with the machinery controlling the Civil Service to some extent reflected the fact that there were genuine dilemmas. There was no single correct or satisfactory solution. The demands of macro-economic policy; the necessity for Treasury financial control; the problems of personnel and labour relations; the strategic needs of the Prime Minister all conflicted at various times. Real shifts in power do not always correspond to institutional changes in the machinery of government. But institutional reshaping is one of the policy options open to administrators and politicians. Such changes are often made for pragmatic reasons in the heat of pithy political struggles, but this is not to say that participants are not influenced by the Holy Grail of the ideal administrative structure.

8 Legislating for trade unions

INTRODUCTION

The 1964–70 Wilson Government tried and failed to introduce legislation to curb the power of trade unions; its successor, the 1970–4 Heath Government, was no more effective in its attempt to impose similar restrictions on organised labour. Only with the election of the Thatcher administration in 1979 has a post-war British government successfully carried through its policies for the reform of trade unions. How one government succeeded where others had failed is the subject of this chapter.

Each government sought the same end: to reduce one element among the many uncertainties with which economic policy-makers wrestle. They all saw trade unions as a potential source of disruption and a threat to the power (and public standing) of their governments. Each administration had different reasons for acting; each had different policies; each worked in different conditions; but they shared this common goal: the creation of order in their world. Without order, they felt, they could not keep their promises, they could not give the impression they were the source of legitimate authority, sanctioned by the popular vote, in the country. The reality may have been quite otherwise, but as far as the political leaders were concerned, this was their rationale for acting. Their successes and failures in their attempt to translate their intentions into effect tell us a great deal about the constraints on decision-making in a liberal democracy.

The trade union legislation of each administration demonstrates a different aspect of policy-making, but the experience of each bears directly on subsequent decisions. It seems sensible, therefore, to deal with the policies chronologically.

IN PLACE OF STRIFE

In 1969, the Labour Government's policy document for trade union reform, 'In Place of Strife', was rejected by the party itself. Under pressure from the unions, Labour MPs refused their consent. While the leadership neither wanted nor anticipated this defiance, it was always a risk, given the intimate and complex relationship between the Labour movement's industrial and political wings. Though Wilson knew that legislating for trade unionism could jeopardise the party's perpetually fragile equilibrium, he also felt that not to act threatened other, equally important, concerns, such as the re-election of a Labour government. For Wilson, 'In Place of Strife' represented a device for winning popular support for his government. For him, the prize justified the risk. Wilson told Parliament in April 1969 that the bill to reform industrial relations was:

> an essential Bill. Essential to our economic recovery. Essential to the balance of payments; essential to full employment. It is an essential component ensuring the economic success of the Government. It is on that economic success that the recovery of the nation, led by the Labour Government, depends. That is why I have to tell you that the passage of this Bill is essential to its continuance in office. There can be no going back on that.[1]

The Labour opponents of the bill saw 'In Place of Strife' as demanding an unacceptable price for an uncertain outcome. James Callaghan, one of the leading critics of the proposal, explained that his opposition was founded on three grounds, which he said he repeated *ad nauseam*: 'the legal sanctions would not stop unofficial strikes. The legal sanctions would not pass through Parliament. The proposals would create tension between government and unions at a time when morale was low, to no real effective purpose'.[2]

And yet others, most notably the architect of the bill, Barbara Castle, saw no great risks anyway: the legislation would create the framework for a socialist industrial relations policy which would satisfy the electorate and the movement. In the words of 'In Place of Strife' itself:

> Our present system of industrial relations has substantial achievements to its credit, but it also has serious defects. It has failed to prevent injustice, disruption of work and inefficient use of manpower. It perpetuates the existence of groups of employees who, as a result of the weakness of their bargaining position, fall behind in the struggle to obtain their full share of the benefits of

an advanced industrial economy'.[3]

These different beliefs were just some of the elements which compose the history of Labour's ill-fated policy.

The divergent reactions to 'In Place of Strife' are partly a reflection of its mixed character. It combined proposals to aid trade unions as well as measures to constrain them. The White Paper protected the right of employees to join unions. It promised the creation of a Commission on Industrial Relations which would help in the recognition of unions. There were to be government funds to aid union mergers, and further government help to protect against, or compensate for, unfair dismissal. On the other hand, there were proposals which would allow the Government to order a return to work in the case of an unofficial stoppage. A 28-day cooling-off period could also be imposed. The Government was to have the right to insist on union ballots before a strike.[4]

When 'In Place of Strife' was first conceived in late 1968, the Labour Party's political fortunes did not appear very bright. The Labour Cabinet was unpopular with both the electorate and its own back-benchers. Wilson was being criticised for acting with high-handed pragmatism and this led to tensions in a party that made much of its democratic structure. This feeling was exacerbated by Wilson's increasing reliance on outside advisers. For Wilson, though, the most important of his worries was the electorate. Two particular interpretations of the voters' mood were current. Firstly, there was a general concern that the Government could not govern. The years 1967–8 saw large balance-of-payment deficits. Secondly, there was a particular concern that Labour could not control its closest allies, the trade unions. There were signs of an increase in the number of days lost through strikes.

Politics, it is regularly observed, is the art of the possible. For the Wilson Government, as for any government, it was important that its attempt to win over the voters remained within the realms of the realistic. Policies had to be directed to problems that had a solution and those solutions should be ones that would work. There was little electoral advantage in attempting and failing to achieve the impossible. Furthermore, there was little to be gained in addressing a problem, among the countless ones that face any government, that stimulated little public concern. Solving such a problem would win few votes. (This is, perhaps, one reason why British – but not Irish – governments remain relatively indifferent to the problems of Northern Ireland.)

It was considerations of this kind that drew Wilson's attention to unofficial strikes. These were industrial stoppages which were not sanctioned by the national or regional leadership, and which were organised instead by local shop stewards. Unofficial strikes, the polls seemed to suggest, were a source of public concern; they were, among other things, inconvenient. Concern about strikes increased dramatically between 1966 and 1969.[5] The polls also indicated that the spread of unofficial action raised doubts about the Government's ability to maintain order. Labour had, therefore, reason to worry about wildcat strikes. But they could also take comfort. Curing the problem seemed within the Government's reach. Labour could reasonably anticipate the support of the trade union leaders who were worried by the growth of the shop stewards' power base. The legitimacy and feasibility of the policy was further enhanced by the stamp of approval given by the Royal Commission on industrial relations, headed by Lord Donovan. The Commission had been set up in 1965 by the Labour Government to examine the trade unions. The final report, published in 1968, actually rejected a legal framework for industrial relations, but it did acknowledge that present arrangements were unsatisfactory and that something needed to be done. Donovan favoured a voluntary body which would bring order to the existing chaos.[6]

While action on industrial relations made electoral-political sense, the proposed policy was neither logically nor politically inevitable. The problem and its solution were both part of a process of selection and judgement. If the problem was days lost at work, rather than the strikes themselves, then a cure for the common cold or tighter industrial safety standards would be much more effective than outlawing unofficial strikes. Sickness and accidents at work accounted for a greater loss of production than did shop steward militancy. The industrial sociologist Richard Hyman wrote of Britain's industrial relations in the 1960s:

> The evidence suggests . . . that Britain is unusual not in the dimensions of its strike record but in the attention which the latter attracts . . . In effect, the direct consequences of strikes are no more serious in Britain than in other countries; it is not so much strikes as the hue and cry which they attract which is the real 'problem'.[7]

The decision to legislate for trade union behaviour needs to be set in the context of how problems and their solutions are defined and perceived. It is easier and politically more valuable to control unions than to find a cure for colds. Not that controlling unofficial strikes turned out to be particularly easy, as Mrs Castle found.

Decisions cannot be separated from their context, and that context is established by a large range of factors. There is a long process in reaching a decision, if such a moment ever exists, and decision-makers have to take the world as they find it, not as they would like it to be. Although Barbara Castle, as Secretary of State for Employment and Productivity, is often presented as the leading actor, she was dependent on many variables. Her prominence was, for example, a consequence of the Prime Minister's decision to move her from the Ministry of Transport and to promote her. She also relied on Wilson's willingness to expedite the bill's progress through Cabinet.

Furthermore, ministers rarely, if ever, construct policy out of nothing. Precedent, party policy or dependency relationships set some of the many constraints which frame government policy. The Labour Party's 1966 election manifesto had made no mention of industrial relations. The decision to introduce reforms was taken as a result of straightforward political considerations, but also as part of a train of decision-making which had been initiated earlier in the creation of the Royal Commission. For Barbara Castle, the Donovan Commission represented one of the essential building blocks. It formed the basis of the extensive consultation which led to the White Paper. She arranged a special conference and brought together academics and unionists. The event served a dual purpose: it produced ideas for the bill and secured the support of some of the interested parties. Clive Ponting records:

> The exact nature of the government's proposal was thrashed out at an extraordinary weekend conference at the Civil Service College at Sunningdale in the middle of November [1968]. It was extraordinary because of the mixture of people involved – some from the government plus an unrepresentative sample of outside opinion.[8]

Once the proposals had been drafted as a White Paper, the task was to get agreement on it. Consent was needed from a variety of sources – industry, the trade unions, the Cabinet and the party. The plans were first examined by a small Cabinet Committee which excluded the main likely opponent, Callaghan. The Committee (MISC 230) was chaired by Wilson. It made no significant changes to 'In Place of Strife'.[9] Mrs Castle's next concern was with management and the unions. With little regard for the conventions of Cabinet government, she consulted first the employers' organisation, the CBI, and then the TUC. The industrialists were satisfied with the basic content of the bill, although they would have liked to have seen provision for the legal enforcement of pay bargains. The TUC's General Secretary, George Woodcock, was smuggled into the Minister's office. Woodcock, who wanted to see unions being encouraged to reorganise themselves, was also happy with the bill's intentions. His loyalty was further ensured when Castle offered him the chairmanship of the Commission on Industrial Relations which the bill was to establish. Mrs Castle wrote in her diary, 'Though he [Woodcock] carefully controlled his reactions, I could see his eyes light up'.[10]

It was not until the day after she had seen the representatives of the CBI and TUC that she spoke to the representatives of the people, the Cabinet. It was then that she met sterner opposition. The Cabinet meeting started at 10 a.m., continued until 1 p.m., resumed at 2.45 p.m. and finished finally at 5.45 p.m. Castle failed to get agreement from her colleagues in the morning session. Richard Crossman explains this failure: 'as it got on towards midday it became clearer and clearer that she wasn't all that conversant with the details of her scheme'.[11] Crossman also records that he thought that the Cabinet was being rail-roaded by Wilson into supporting the bill.[12] On the White Paper's content, a number of ministers were worried about how the bill would be received by the left. Their objections were directed in particular to the bill's proposed conciliation clause. There were no questions raised about the compulsory strike ballot, although this was an issue on which Castle expected trouble and over which she was prepared to make concessions. For Crossman, the Cabinet's main concern remained 'its right to argue and re-argue the whole thing'. Crossman favoured the bill being taken to a Cabinet Committee and to another full meeting of Cabinet; Wilson was reluctant to do this because of the possibility that the bill might be delayed and diluted. Crossman's plans were effectively scuppered by reports in the next day's papers which said that 'In Place of Strife' had received Cabinet backing and would be published shortly. This was despite the fact that, according to Crossman, Wilson had stressed that 'on no account must Barbara be embarrassed by any press leaks'.[13] The leaked story, whatever its source, effectively pre-empted any attempt by Cabinet to modify the proposals substantially.

Even without the judicious leaking, the Cabinet was in a difficult position. A general election could not be far off. A publicly divided Cabinet would be an unfortunate handicap, particularly when the division was over something which the electorate had fairly strong views. Although Wilson allowed for several further Cabinet meetings, the policy remained largely unaffected.

Once the Cabinet had given its reluctant consent, the next task was to get the bill onto the statute books. This required a rescheduling of the parliamentary timetable and the consequent loss of legislation proposed by other departments of state. Furthermore, the arguments in Cabinet and consultations with the TUC and CBI were in stark contrast to the treatment of the Parliamentary Labour Party (PLP) and the party nationally. When eventually Mrs Castle took her proposals to the PLP, she found considerable opposition. Labour's National Executive Committee (NEC) rejected the proposed bill with the tacit assent of Callaghan, one of Mrs Castle's Cabinet colleagues, who was a reluctant party to collective Cabinet responsibility. The vote was 16:5 for rejecting any legal interference. As these splits emerged, the TUC too began to show concern. An emergency conference was called and hectic consultations took place between ministers and trade union leaders. The PLP took more direct action. At the second reading of the bill, 58 Labour MPs voted against the bill and 40 abstained. Wilson responded by sacking the Chief Whip, John Silkin, replacing him with Bob Mellish, a trade union-sponsored, working-class MP. Wilson went so far as to hint at the dissolution of Parliament if the party failed to follow his lead.[14]

The TUC began to build support around an alternative programme. Such events served to erode the false consensus that held the Cabinet together. When the new Chief Whip explained to Cabinet that the PLP could not be guaranteed to support the bill at the next stage, the consensus seemed to collapse completely. Roy Jenkins, wrote Crossman, 'slid elegantly onto the fence'. Castle records her bitter disappointment:

> the wreckers were not interested in the merits or demerits of my proposals: all they wanted was a settlement: peace at any price. Harold, however, was extraordinarily ebullient. Quite early on he passed me a note: 'Not to worry. Leave it to me'. So I sat silent while, one after another, the vultures moved in on us.[15]

Wilson and Castle lost their battle. Their fate was further evidence of Richard Neustadt's belief that political power is about the power to persuade.[16] Castle and Wilson had failed to persuade those groups and interests who were inextricably part of their decision.

The failure was not just of the Government. For Callaghan, the trade unions too had faltered. They had not recognised the need to respond to the public concern over their practices:

In 1969 they still had the opportunity to demonstrate that autonomous self-governing institutions could respond to adverse public opinion and reform themselves. They failed to do so, and this, coupled with the excesses of some activists in the 1970s, led inexorably to the Parliamentary legislation and the intervention by the courts in their affairs.[17]

The 1971 Industrial Relations Act, introduced by Heath's Conservative Government, was just such a development.

THE INDUSTRIAL RELATIONS ACT

Labour's failure to introduce 'In Place of Strife' created an ideal political opportunity for the Conservatives. Had Labour succeeded, they might have denied their opponents the chance to make political capital out of the union problem. With no trade union legislation on the statute books, the Conservatives were able to present themselves as the party with the answers to Britain's industrial relations malaise.

While the Labour Party struggled with the difficulties of making and implementing their union policy, the Conservatives were able to enjoy the advantages of opposition: to design policies which were politically attractive rather than practically detailed. And while the Labour Party strove to get the consent and cooperation of the various interested parties, the Conservatives had only to tap current party opinion, although they did have formal and informal meetings with employers and trade unionists. As Michael Moran observes: 'the most striking feature of the whole process was the extent to which policy-making in the party was insulated from the main interest groups in industrial relations'.[18]

The Tory leadership's problems were seen largely as ideological ones. Their task was confined to resolving the tension between the conflicting pulls of market liberalism, which argues for free collective bargaining, and state authoritarianism, which requires centralised control. Otherwise, it was simply a matter of devising policies which would win elections first, and could be made workable later. Ironically, the very ease of the conditions in which the Industrial Relations Act was conceived were partly responsible for its ultimate failure.

The Act began as part of the party's pre-election programme, where it was known as 'Fair Deal at Work' and was drafted by the party's senior policy advisers, under the direction of (later Sir) Robert Carr. Their main concerns were the ideological nuances that accompanied the policy. Should society be ordered by an authoritarian state or by the free interchange of individuals in the market? In the context of industrial relations, the party had to decide what could or should be enforced in matters of management–union behaviour. How much state intervention in the operation of market forces, as represented by free collective bargaining, was legitimate?[19]

For the party, accepting the need for statutory involvement in industrial relations was a substantial change, albeit one that had been growing in acceptability since the early 1960s and was further encouraged by the party's defeat in 1964. The main problem that party policy-makers faced was the balance between the party's twin sympathies for liberalism and collectivism. In many aspects of industrial relations, these leanings pulled in different directions. Moran notes the way market sympathy for the locally-based shop stewards ran counter to the collectivist sympathy for nationally coordinated wage negotiations.[20]

Setting policy was not just a matter of deciding upon the goal – in this case, ordered industrial relations. It was also a matter of determining how the goal was to be achieved. Issuing decrees would not necessarily bring results. So Conservative policy-makers gave thought to the mechanics by which their ends were to be realised. One of the most crucial elements was the trade unions. These were required to deliver the 'order' which the policy sought. Though open defiance was possible, and could not be totally guarded against, the Conservatives thought that by requiring unions to join an official register, a mechanism would be provided which obliged unions to discipline their members. In doing so, they echoed much that had been in 'In Place of Strife'.

Like Labour's White Paper, the main aim of the Tories' industrial relations policy was to set pay and conditions negotiations within a legal framework. The main institution of this new arrangement was to be an Industrial Relations Court. Parties to disputes could be required to go to arbitration; there was to be an enforceable cooling-off period; unions were to be required to register; and ballots were to establish union legitimacy. All these proposals were the basis of the Conservatives' pre-election promise. Industrial relations was the only issue in the Tory Manifesto which had been considered in detail prior to the election and accession to power.[21] The paradox is that this very practice of advance planning was probably the cause of the policy's ultimate failure.

The Industrial Relations Act was largely a party, rather than a government, creation. Neither Whitehall nor the TUC was involved in the policy's drafting, and the CBI's contribution was to voice its suspicions of the proposals. The business community was wary of the usefulness of law in industrial relations. Part of the reason for this weakening of business support for the party's proposals was the changing character of strikes. Someone had moved the goal posts while the Tories were shooting. Brief, wildcat strikes were becoming less common; instead disputes were lasting longer. Employers' thoughts, therefore, turned to other forms of union control. The restriction of social security payments was one technique they came to favour. The CBI's general point was that they wanted the Government to adopt a position of 'flexible response', to leave specifics until after the election, and then to adapt policy to suit the circumstances. And rather than rely on the courts, the CBI favoured the use of direct government intervention.[22]

Despite these misgivings, the Conservative Government chose to implement the policy established in their 'Fair Deal at Work'. This was what they had fought the election on and this enjoyed considerable party support. The support was not quite unanimous. Senior party figures voiced their concern at the Party Conference both about the use of law to organise industrial relations and about the role allowed to the TUC in the new framework. It was felt that the proposed legislation would legitimate a power that either was already too dominant or – quite contrarily – was unable to control its member unions. These qualms were to reappear when the bill was debated in Parliament, when they led to splits on the Tory backbenches.

After the election, the Government published a consultation document which was to form the basis of their industrial relations legislation. The Government argued that their legislation was intended to establish four main principles: first, that collective bargaining would be freely and responsibly conducted; secondly, that there should be orderly procedures for the settlement of disputes; thirdly, that the unions should be representative, responsible and effective; and finally, that there should be freedom and security for workers. Not everyone saw the legislation in the same way that the Government did. On 13 October, a week after the publication of the Green Paper, Robert Carr met the TUC's Finance and General Purposes Committee. Prior to this meeting, Carr had made it clear that there were a number of principles which he would not concede. Jack Jones, leader of the Transport and General Workers' Union (TGWU) in 1970, recalled the state of relations with the Government: 'The Conservative government produced the IR Act and did not want any consultation, didn't want to talk about reforms. They laid down the . . . pillars and would not budge'.[23]

This stance was to lead to the breakdown of relations between the unions and the Government. Without Carr's willingness to negotiate on the pillars of the legislation, the TUC could see no point in talking to the Secretary of State.

The trade unionists were vehemently opposed to the introduction of law into industrial relations; this had been the focus of their opposition to Labour's proposals. They wanted relations to be conducted on a voluntary basis. Because Carr was unwilling to concede the main principle of this legislation, the TUC called a special conference to organise opposition to the bill. The breakdown of the Carr–TUC talks determined the final fate of the Act, especially when combined with the reluctance of the CBI to give their wholehearted support. Like the TUC, the employers were wary of legislation, and in February 1970 the two organisations had issued a joint statement arguing against legislative intervention in industrial relations.[24]

The Industrial Relations Bill itself was published on 3 December 1970. It was a major piece of legislation with considerable ambitions. Among other things, the Bill was intended to: a) establish a code of industrial relations practice; b) protect the rights of individuals in respect of trade union membership and unfair dismissal; c) enforce written collective agreements; d) provide new regulations for the conduct and registration of trade unions and employers associations; e) extend the jurisdiction of existing industrial tribunals; f) create a National Industrial Relations Court; g) allow for civil actions to be brought against unofficial strike leaders; h) establish a Commission on Industrial Relations; i) introduce the concept of a 'cooling-off' period. The size and sweep of the legislation, together with the lack of support of key groups, added to the Government's problems.

Having failed to win over the Government within Whitehall, the TUC organised a strong public campaign against the Act. In March 1971, before the bill became law, the TUC called a one-day strike which was supported by three million workers. After the Act reached the statute books, the TUC instructed all its member unions to refuse to register.[25] The Government responded by using the law it had just created.

Much as the CBI had predicted, the intervention of the courts served to politicise and worsen relations. The AEU's (Amalgamated Engineering Union) and the TGWU's refusal to pay the fine imposed upon them for non-registration added to the political costs involved.

Moran summarises the situation in which the Government found itself. On the one hand, 'opposition to the Act was most intense among those deeply involved in the conduct of industrial relations'. On the other hand, while there was considerable public support for the Act:

> The public at large did not have the capacity to make the legislation work. Success depended on the cooperation of union leaders, shop stewards, personnel managers and employers generally. These were precisely the people who were most suspicious of the measures.[26]

In the end, the Act became unworkable, politically and administratively. The combined effect of the Act itself and the unions' non-cooperation made it impossible for the Government to achieve its goal. In fact, it achieved quite the opposite. According to Colin Crouch, 'The Act had virtually no impact on mainstream collective bargaining; it actually led to rather than prevented strikes . . .'.[27]

One reason for the Act's failure was, no doubt, the non-cooperation of the key parties. But there is another cause that is worth considering: the inadequacies of the system of administration and those who staffed it. Such an explanation is provided by the civil servant, Antony Part:

> Although there was, of course, a great deal of contact on the 'professional front' between the Ministry of Employment and the TUC and so on, relations between the members and the government as a whole, and ministers' knowledge of unions, made it difficult to get started on an effective piece of diplomacy. That may have accounted for the fact that when something was embarked upon it was very ambitious . . . We got stuck with the idea that because the system had not worked for many years under governments of different colours, that meant somehow or other that some enforcement had got to be introduced into the proceedings, and they didn't see how that could be done, except by legislation. I think there was a degree of frustration at what had happened before, coupled with a lack of informed thinking on the part of ministers.[28]

Part's description provides telling evidence for the view that the British policy process can often fail to match ideas to evidence. But to observe this is not to claim that the system is incapable of learning from the past.

The 1974–9 Labour Government introduced several pieces of industrial relations legislation. There were the Trade Union and Labour Relations Acts of 1974 and 1976; and there was the Employment Protection Act of 1975. Between them, these measures repealed the Conservatives' Industrial Relations Act, sought to increase job security and to legitimate the closed shop. They are not discussed in detail here, not because they are unimportant, but because they do not represent any very distinctive shift in the way governments have decided upon trade union policy. The decisions of the post-1979 Thatcher Governments have, by contrast, radically altered the way in which trade unions are expected to act.

TRADE UNION LEGISLATION SINCE 1979

The most distinctive feature of the Thatcher Government's policy on trade unions was its success. Unlike its predecessors this administration was able to introduce and implement its electoral promises. For those curious about decision-making in British governments, its achievements are instructive. They demonstrate the intricate linkage between political ideology and social or economic circumstances. They show also how governments learn from the experiences (or conventional wisdom about those experiences) of their predecessors. This learning process, though, is not as simple and obvious as it might seem. Writing before Mrs Thatcher came to power, Robert Taylor reported:

> Jim Prior, the Conservative spokesman on industrial relations, emphasised in a speech at Manchester in February 1976 that a future Conservative government would not introduce any major legislation to reform trade union law. The lesson of 1971 had been learnt.[29]

As it turned out, major reforms were introduced; and Jim Prior was the minister responsible for some of them. This is not to say, however, that the lessons of 1971 were not learnt. It is just that 1971 was interpreted differently from the way that Prior had anticipated. Instead of being a warning against all trade union legislation, it became a guide as to how to implement it more effectively.

In February 1979, Prior conceded that there should be: 'a recognition that the law has a part to play in industrial relations, but there is a need to ensure widespread public support for such legislation'.[30]

This time the legislation was not to be introduced as part of a grand, all-encompassing package. Instead, it was introduced piece by piece. As Prior explains in his autobiography:

> While I could not expect the legislation to be fully accepted or be properly effective during the first period of Conservative Government, if we won a second time the trade unions would have to come to terms with it. It was therefore all the more important not to push our reforms too far in our first period of Government, for fear that one might undo everything by rekindling Labour's and the union's fighting spirit.[31]

Prior's strategy was not backed by all his Cabinet colleagues. Geoffrey Howe, for example, wanted the wholesale reform offered by the 1971 Act and spoke publicly (and without consulting Prior) about the need for tougher laws. Howe's views were shared by the Prime Minister. She added to the political tensions by improvising further nuances of the legislation at Question Time. In doing so she was responding to Tory back-bench pressure for more draconian measures. But through a combination of energetic lobbying and a low-key public campaign, Prior retained support for his approach.[32]

The first piece of trade union legislation was the 1980 Employment Act. This sought to restrict the scope of legitimate trade union action. It was to be achieved by banning secondary action. The intention was to confine trade union activity to matters of immediate concern to the relations between managers and workers, and to prevent industrial action being used in places where the original dispute did not extend. There was to be a ban on secondary picketing, preventing unions from attempting to restrict the operation of firms not explicitly involved in the dispute. There was also to be a ban on secondary industrial action. In other words, workers would not be allowed to take strike action in support of others who were in (legitimate) dispute with their employer. Although the Act sought to make these activities illegal, it required that any legal action be initiated by the employer.

The second piece of trade union legislation was introduced in 1982. This was a further attempt to restrict the legitimate extent of trade union involvement, but it also sought to bring under legal control the internal practices and form of trade unions. Both aspects of the Act were intended to limit the activity of the trade union: first, by specifying the arena in which it could operate; second, by seeking to introduce internal restraints on its actions. In particular, the Act outlawed political strikes and further limited the range of legitimate industrial actions by denying the right of strike in cases involving inter-union disputes. Furthermore, the legislation sought to make trade union funds vulnerable to fines or sequestration when unions were in breech of the law. Previously trade union funds had enjoyed legal immunity. The third piece of industrial relations legislation, introduced in 1984, was the Trade Union Act, which, as its name suggests, extended the law on the internal behaviour of unions. It required the direct election by union members of the union executive; it called for secret ballots on strike action; and it demanded that trade unions vote every ten years on whether they maintain a political fund (i.e. an account by which trade unions make donations to political parties). These pieces of legislation, together with other trade union related decisions (to ban unions at GCHQ – Government Communications Headquarters – for example), were successfully implemented and subsequently observed. Unions held ballots and voted on their political funds; employers like Rupert Murdoch and Eddie Shah used the legislation to undermine union power in the printing industry.

The intriguing question is why Mrs Thatcher succeeded where previous political leaders had failed. There are a number of factors to which we can point, and the rest of this section takes each in turn. They are: the political context; the ideology of the governing party; the strength/weakness of rival power bases; the political tactics adopted; and the popularity of the proposed measures.

The political context

The Thatcher Government came to power in 1979 with an explicit commitment to reform trade unions. It was a message that had a particular resonance following the so-called 'Winter of Discontent' of 1978–9, when many public sector workers struck in protest at the Labour Government's attempt to restrict wage increases. The Conservatives' election campaign emphasised the party's support for secret ballots within unions (financed if necessary from public funds), for a ban on secondary picketing, and for change to closed shop legislation, tipping the balance in favour of those who chose not to join. It was this which received the most attention during the run-up to the election. The party strategy, to divide union members from their leaders, met with some success: during the campaign 7 per cent of trade unionists moved to the Tories. The popular political climate encouraged the Tories to make much of the trade union problem, but theirs was not a purely pragmatic reaction.

The political ideology

The election of Mrs Thatcher to replace Edward Heath in 1975 symbolised the party's shift to the right. More importantly, the way the right was defined placed considerable emphasis on the need to control the trade unions who were deemed to wield an illegitimate and excessive power. They were seen to inhibit the democratic rights of government and to distort the 'natural' operations of the market. Andrew Gamble summarises the social market philosophy on unions:

> The union problem would be dealt with partly by legislation, to withdraw many legal privileges the unions currently enjoy, partly by administrative means to reduce the effectiveness of strikes. In addition, government avoidance of pay policies and return to responsible free collective bargaining would end the 'politicisation' of industrial relations and restore the disciplines of the market in pay determination.[33]

It was this approach which was to characterise Conservative decisions about trade unions.

Rival sources of power

Ideology alone, however, is not enough to bring about change. Nor is political will. The examples of 'In Place of Strife' and the Industrial Relations Act were proof of that. The Thatcher Government's effectiveness owed much to the changed (and changing) circumstances in which trade unions found themselves. The power that trade unions had enjoyed in the late 1960s and early 1970s had been gradually eroded by the rise in unemployment and the decline in Britain's staple industries.[34] Furthermore, significant changes were taking place in the leadership of trade unions. Between 1977 and 1978, Jack Jones retired from the TGWU, to be replaced by Moss Evans, and Hugh Scanlon was succeeded by Terry Duffy as leader of the AEU. The new leaders lacked the authority of their predecessors, but more importantly they lacked the industrial strength.

This allowed Mrs Thatcher to make one of her most radical alterations to the normal pattern of British politics: to end the practice of tripartism. The rule, according to Hugo Young, was 'that trade union leaders were to be regarded with indifference verging on contempt'. The result was that the General Secretary of the TUC entered No. 10 Downing Street only three times in the period 1979–84.[35] No longer were trade unions acknowledged as interests with a particular claim on the Government's attention. For the trade unions this meant that they were denied direct access into the administrative machine. The struggles and political infighting that characterised previous attempts to legislate for trade unions were, therefore, largely absent from the new ones. The TUC, now unable to press its cause from within the Government, had to resort to less direct methods. They organised demonstrations and they attempted to enforce a policy of non-cooperation. These efforts came to nothing, and the legislation remained in effect. As Riddell commented: 'The unions have been the dog that did not bark'.[36]

Political tactics

One of the curious features of the passage of the first Employment Acts was the appointment of Jim Prior as the responsible minister. Prior was known as a 'Wet' and a supporter of Edward Heath. To give him a job which placed him at the centre of the Prime Minister's plans might seem perverse. But there were important extenuating circumstances. First, there was the need, at least in the early days, to appease the various factions within the party. Prior could not be ignored. Secondly, for all the aggressive rhetoric about putting the trade unions in their place, the success of the policy required a degree of political subtlety and experience, both of which Prior possessed.

Mrs Thatcher's instinct, shored up by the arguments of trusted advisers like Sir Keith Joseph, was that firm action was needed to curb union power. Prior, by contrast, favoured a more gradualist approach, built upon the cooperation of employers and unionists. Indeed, it was this tactic which appeared in the 1977 Conservative policy document, 'The Right Approach to the Economy'.

With Prior in charge, Mrs Thatcher could retain her aggressive pose, letting the party know that she wished 'Jim would go faster', while knowing that Prior was the best man for these initial stages of the policy. Riddell described the Conservative's approach as 'a mixture of radical intent and cautious practice'.[37] Once the first Employment Act was in place, and Thatcher had established her political authority within the party and the country, she was able to dispense with Prior, sending him to Northern Ireland. In both jobs, Prior remained on the crucial Cabinet Committee ('E'), where he argued against the general Government line. Once in Northern Ireland, he could no longer attend regularly or speak with the same authority.[38] Prior's successor was Norman Tebbit, Mrs Thatcher's personal and political ally. He was appointed to turn the screw further on the trade unions. But even so the legislation was introduced cautiously.

In both the form of the bills and the means by which they were introduced, the tactical lessons of 1971 were most apparent. There was no attempt to devise a grand scheme to revolutionise industrial relations law. Instead, the gradualist approach was adopted. Anthony King observed that Tory trade union policy was 'notably restrained', and explains this by saying that, 'whatever her instincts', Mrs Thatcher had no intention of following Edward Heath, despite some criticism from her allies that she was not acting more forcefully.[39] In concentrating on trade union funds and the closed shop, Tebbit and Thatcher ignored many of the other suggestions coming from industry.[40]

Political popularity

The Thatcher Government's ability to legislate for trade unions also owed something to the popular support their policies seemed to enjoy. Indeed part of their strategy was to ensure public support for the measures. While it is true that Wilson's concern over unofficial strikes was shared by a majority of those polled, the Thatcher Government had yet more support for its approach. A *Sunday Times* survey revealed that 46 per cent of union members felt that trade unions had too much power, although it is noticeable that this figure dropped by 14 per cent when they were asked about their own union. In the 1983 election, the electorate was, for the most part, in favour of increasing legal restrictions upon unions. The percentage of those in each social category who supported tighter union legislation were as follows: salariat– 64; routine non-manual – 61; petty-bourgeoisie – 71; foremen and technicians – 55; working class – 46.[41] What is also worth noting about these figures is that only 34 per cent of the working class is unionised; and that 29 per cent of the salariat belongs to a union. It is important to recognise, however, that although there was considerable support for tougher measures for trade unions, industrial relations was not regarded by the electorate as a major electoral issue, whatever the attention given to it in the Conservative Party manifesto.

CONCLUSION

Just as Heath's electoral victory in 1970 capitalised on Labour's failure with 'In Place of Strife', and just as Wilson's triumph in 1974 resulted from Heath's struggle with the miners, so Mrs Thatcher's success in

1979 owed a great deal to the 'Winter of Discontent'. Callaghan's misjudgement over public sector pay increases provided a convincing setting for Mrs Thatcher to argue the case for trade union reform.

But the legislation itself may be less important than other factors in explaining the Thatcher Government's ability to control trade unions. Unemployment had considerably weakened unions, not only by reducing their membership but also by creating a strong sense of caution among those still in work (who have done relatively well since 1979, at least in the private sector). The defeat of the miners owed little to the legislation itself, and much to powers which the Government already had at its disposal – or which it acquired in the course of the dispute. The Government's disavowal of corporatism of the kind adopted by Wilson, Heath and Callaghan also played its part. The Thatcher Government's avoidance of direct involvement in pay bargaining, and its attempt to distance itself from public sector pay disputes, had decreased, like these other factors, the incidence of industrial disruption. In this sense, the problem of trade union power had itself diminished, quite independently of the legislation itself. Nonetheless, we cannot ignore the fact that legislation was developed and enacted. Mrs Thatcher emerges as a key actor in this process. It is entirely conceivable that had someone other than Mrs Thatcher led the Conservative party in 1979, the trade union legislation might not have been pushed so far so determinedly. At the same time, it might also be argued that Thatcherite ideology was tempered by a good dose of pragmatism. Kavanagh, for example, argues that the Thatcher Government: 'did not push its reforms as far as some supporters wished; it did not, for example, place the onus on union members to contract in rather than out of paying the political levy'.[42]

Whatever our judgement, there seems to be an argument for studying the interests and actions of individual political actors if we want to understand fully the way in which decisions are made in British government. But such an analysis must be fitted into a wider political context.

9 Trident

INTRODUCTION

> Parliament's role in the decision to procure a successor system to Polaris has been limited to endorsing a decision already taken. Decisions on defence, and on Britain's strategic nuclear deterrent have historically been taken by a small élite of very senior Cabinet Ministers, Civil Servants and Service Chiefs, and this present decision was certainly no exception.[1]

This quotation may seem, in many respects, to be unremarkable: it is a statement about British defence policy that is typical of many left-wing critiques of the ways in which that policy is made. The surprise is, though, that it comes from the minority report of the House of Commons Defence Committee, dated 20 May 1981. This chapter is concerned with the process leading up to the decisions of 15 July 1980 and 11 March 1982 by which the British Government agreed to develop the Trident missile as the successor to the Polaris strategic nuclear deterrent.

Before setting out to trace the history of the decisions on Trident it is important to make two qualifications to what follows: the first concerns the notion of a 'Trident decision'; although it is convenient to use this as shorthand, it is essential to note that there was never any one Trident decision. Even the relatively straightforward question of whether to buy the Trident system was itself, in fact, a series of questions, concerning, for example, issues such as: how many missiles? How many warheads? Whether to buy the current (C4) or the future (D5) missile? What percentage of research costs to pay? When to phase in the missiles? How many missiles per submarine? How many submarines? This indicates that in looking at the decision to buy Trident we are actually concerned with a whole host of interrelated decisions, and, as has been argued in chapter two, one of the key features of decision-making analysis is how agendas for making decisions affect the outcomes. Thus, this case-study is particularly illuminating precisely because it deals with a highly complex, although politically straightforward, issue; examining it should indicate the dynamics of decision-making and show how the making of one decision affects the policy environment in such a way as to make subsequent decisions seem 'logical', or even merely 'technical'.

The second qualification is an obvious one. The Trident issue has led to a considerable debate in British politics, but this chapter is not concerned with most of the public aspects of that debate. Since the decision to buy Trident was announced, that decision has led to enormous political controversy, much of which focused on its strategic, political, economic and moral implications. Although the programme had become then entrenched, all main opposition parties said they would cancel it were they to have been elected in 1987. A Labour victory at a subsequent election would certainly bring the programme's completion into doubt. Our concern, though, is not with these aspects, important as they are. Our interest in the Trident decision stems from what it tells us about decision-making in British government. We, therefore, will concentrate on how that decision was made, since doing so enables us to look at an area of decision-making, defence, that is usually shrouded in secrecy, and about which detailed case-studies are rare. The debates over cost, political and strategic effects, and morality are clearly important to the debate today, and there are many useful sources on these aspects.[2] The subsequent analysis will largely exclude these considerations, preferring an explanatory to a normative analysis of the issue.

This case-study will be analysed in the following way: first we will set the Trident decision in its context, by briefly summarising the history of the British nuclear deterrent. Then we will turn to analyse the chronology of the decisions to replace Polaris with Trident. The next section will look at the involvement of Parliament in the decision. Finally, we will conclude by noting the gap between the formal view of British politics and the actual outcome in this case: it is this gap that makes the theories of decision-making we outlined in chapter two so important.

HISTORICAL BACKGROUND

The original decision that Britain would acquire nuclear weapons was in one sense hardly a decision at all; it was, in effect, a non-decision in that it was taken by a subcommittee of the Cabinet and was not even discussed in full Cabinet, let alone Parliament. It was a situation that, as will become clear, mirrored Mrs Thatcher's, when she assumed power in 1979:

> When Mr Churchill returned to No. 10 Downing Street [in October 1951], he was surprised and impressed by the size of the atomic energy project built up by the Labour government. He found with a mixture of admiration, envy and shock of a good parliamentarian that his predecessor had spent nearly £100 million on it without informing Parliament.[3]

The decision for Britain was a 'natural' one, since Britain was still considered to be a great power, and, like the other two great powers, the USA and the USSR, building nuclear weapons was simply the logical extension of the research into that area that all three had been engaged in. The strategic and political justifications were accepted without question. Essentially, all British governments since the 1940s have accepted that Britain should have a nuclear deterrent, and, despite the Labour Party's statements in opposition, the development of this deterrent continued without major revision from 1945 onwards.

By 1956 Britain had an operational nuclear capability, based on the use of bombers as nuclear weapons carriers.[4] However, by then, the planned British deterrent force of V Bombers, which came into operation in 1958, looked rather outmoded in the light of the American and Soviet development of missiles as delivery systems. Thus, in 1957 the British Government decided to build an intermediate range ballistic missile, Blue Streak. As this soon looked as if it would be obsolete by the time it was deployed (because it was liquid-fuelled and vulnerable to surprise attack, being land-based), it was in turn cancelled, at a cost of £65 million, and the British Government opted instead for the US air-launched ballistic missile, Skybolt. Skybolt could have been fitted to the V bombers, thus prolonging their life until the mid-1970s. But, to continue this sorry story of cancellation, the US Government decided, on 7 November 1962, that because Skybolt had the disadvantages of both missiles and bombers, it would be cancelled. This led to a major upset in UK–US relations, since the British felt that they had been encouraged by the availability of the Skybolt option to cancel Blue Streak.[5] This led to a meeting between the British Prime Minister, Harold Macmillan, and the US President, John Kennedy, at Nassau in December 1962. At their meeting the US offered the British the option of buying the new US submarine-launched ballistic missile (SLBM) Polaris.

Interestingly, Britain could have obtained Polaris instead of Skybolt in 1960, but this had been refused because the RAF was the part of the armed services responsible for the nuclear deterrent and buying Polaris would have involved the transfer of at least the major part of that responsibility to the Royal Navy. Not only would this have upset the RAF, but it was resisted by the Royal Navy as it would have meant diverting funds from the surface fleet to the building of a submarine fleet to carry the missile. Skybolt was a bureaucratically neat solution.

Nevertheless, with Skybolt cancelled, Britain opted for Polaris, and agreed to buy the missile from the US, with Britain building the warheads and the submarines to carry it. Polaris was obtained on very favourable terms, with Britain paying only about 5 per cent of the research and development costs of the missile, whereas the accurate pro rata figure would have been about 12 per cent. The Polaris fleet consisted of four boats: *Resolution* (commissioned in 1967), *Renown* (1968), *Repulse* (1968) and *Revenge* (1969). This four-boat force guaranteed one boat on station at any time, although the average has worked out to be around 1.4 boats. Each submarine carried sixteen A-3 missiles, fitted initially with three MRV (multiple re-entry vehicle) warheads each with an explosive power of 200 kt (kilotons). These three warheads cannot hit separate targets, but instead land in a triangular pattern around a target so as to maximise blast (three MRVs of 200 kt will do far more damage than one warhead of 600 kt). The length of the sides of this triangle are highly classified, but are unofficially estimated to be about 10–12 miles. These warheads have subsequently been replaced under the Chevaline modernisation programme, with the new figure being either two or three warheads per missile.

By the early 1970s there was a concern in British defence circles that Polaris was no longer able to hit one of its primary targets – Moscow – because of the Soviet development of a small Anti-Ballistic Missile (ABM) system. This ABM system – known as Galosh – comprised 64 launchers around Moscow. However effective it might have proven in practice, it made less credible the British deterrent capability to hit Moscow, bearing in mind that only one submarine could be guaranteed to be on station at any point in time. The Conservative Government of 1970–4 considered replacing Polaris with the follow-on US system Poseidon since this missile carried 10 MIRV (multiple independently targetable re-entry vehicle) warheads, each of which could hit a separate target. Clearly, replacing Polaris with Poseidon would mean that instead of a guarantee of only sixteen targetable warheads being on station at any time, there would be 160, and this would make the British deterrent more credible. The alternative option for Britain was to modify Polaris so as to make it more likely to penetrate Soviet ABM defences; this option, known eventually as Chevaline, involved improvements to the front end of Polaris, so as to make the re-entry vehicles more manoeuvrable, to accommodate decoys, and to harden the warheads. The Conservative Government had already inherited a research programme from the 1964–70 Labour Government on how to extend Polaris's penetrability of Soviet defences – a project known as Antelope, and started in 1967. When the Government looked more closely at the issue, they found that the Poseidon option suffered three major drawbacks. First was cost: the estimated cost of buying Poseidon missiles and fitting them in the existing Polaris-carrying submarines was in the £500 million range. By contrast, estimates of Chevaline's costs were in the order of £100–150 million; more importantly, the cost of Poseidon would come when the defence budget would be under considerable strain because of the Tornado multi-role combat aircraft programme. The second drawback was that the US Government had already decided to develop a follow-on to Poseidon, the programme that eventually became known as the Trident SLBM (submarine-launched ballistic missile); there were important benefits to be obtained from waiting until the newer of the technologies was developed (and Poseidon had already been deployed in US submarines since 1971). The third reason was the simple political one that buying Poseidon would be a very public decision, one which, because of the increased targeting capabilities of Poseidon, would open up the whole issue of the nature of the British deterrent. Whilst there was strong bipartisan support for the Polaris programme, the Commons Expenditure Committee and the Labour Party had spoken against the purchase of Poseidon. Chevaline looked like a way of overcoming the penetration problem of the British deterrent without leading to a major debate over the rights and wrongs of possessing nuclear weapons: it would be less costly and much less visible.

It was the Labour Government of 1974–9 that actually implemented this decision, since the first test associated with Chevaline was scheduled for only three months after the Government came to power. As Lawrence Freedman makes clear in his excellent analysis of this period, the decision to proceed with Chevaline was taken by a very small group of senior ministers (the Prime Minister, the Chancellor of the Exchequer, and the Home, Foreign and Defence Secretaries).[6] This group was told that a major decision was required on the project, which had, after all, been initiated by the 1964–70

Labour Government. They decided to go ahead and merely reported to the Cabinet that 'a Polaris improvement programme was under way at a cost of some £250 million. There was only slight objection'.[7] This programme was reappraised in 1977 because of a severe cost-escalation – the estimate was then that it would cost £800 million – and it was decided to continue with Chevaline for the simple reasons that cancelling would mean losing previous investment and would involve a clear (and public) choice between scrapping the strategic nuclear deterrent or replacing it with a new system. As Freedman comments: 'The tradition of secret and bipartisan policy-making, with its emphasis on continuity, was one reason why the Conservatives chose Chevaline in 1973 and why the programme survived in 1977'.[8]

On 24 January 1980, the Conservative Defence Secretary, Mr Francis Pym, announced to the House of Commons that the Chevaline programme would cost about £1,000 million. As John Simpson writes, referring to the Gowing quote cited above: 'If Mr Churchill was impressed in October 1951, one wonders what were the reactions of Mrs Thatcher and Mr Pym in May 1979 when they were "shown the books" after the Conservative Party victory at the polls'.[9]

The key point is that the expenditure had been hidden in the annual Defence Estimates. Parliament had not been informed of this programme, and there had been no public debate, despite four changes of government during the life of the programme.

THE TRIDENT DECISION

If the Chevaline programme was seen as a way of prolonging the credibility of the Polaris force it could not preserve the life of the submarines themselves. Thus, by the end of the 1970s, the question of whether to replace the Polaris force began to occupy the attention of government ministers. This section will look at the record of these deliberations so as to trace the process by which Britain opted to replace Polaris with Trident. The question of Polaris replacement was first brought to the attention of élite opinion in a report written by Ian Smart on behalf of the Royal Institute of International Affairs in 1977.[10] According to Smart, a very definite time-scale was emerging for considering the replacement of the Polaris force. The life of the Polaris submarines was estimated by the Ministry of Defence in 1971 as being 'at least 20 years', which meant that they could continue in operation until at least 1988, and, more probably until the mid-1990s.[11] But the US was scheduled to phase out its Polaris submarines by the early 1980s, so there would be increasing costs in maintaining the British fleet as time went by and as the US supplies of replacement parts became exhausted. Smart commented that: 'All the available evidence converges, therefore, to suggest that, by some time in the early 1990s, both Britain's submarines and their missiles will reach the end of the road'.[12] In the full version of his report he concluded that:

> The planning assumption must be that the existing British force will cease to constitute a reliable deterrent at a date which, for technical reasons, is likely to occur in about 1993. It may seem that 1993 is far away. From the point of view of the British deterrent, however, it is very close indeed . . . Britain, if it were to develop and produce a new deterrent force itself, would need up to 13 years to complete the process. When it comes to deciding whether or not to prepare a replacement for the Polaris force, therefore, 1993 is no further away than 1980.[13]

The Labour Government had come to power in 1974 with a clear statement about Trident in its manifesto: 'We have renounced any intention of moving to a new generation of strategic nuclear weapons'.[14] Indeed, according to the 1975 Statement on the Defence Estimates the Government stated that:

> The Polaris force . . . provides a unique European contribution to NATO's strategic nuclear capability out of all proportion to the small fraction of our defence budget which it costs to maintain. We shall maintain its effectiveness. We do not intend to move to a new generation of strategic weapons.[15]

As late as March 1978 the Secretary of State for Defence, Fred Mulley, said to the House of Commons that:

> We have no plans to develop a cruise missile or a successor to Polaris . . . In our view the existing Polaris fleet will be effective for many years and, that being the case, there is no need to take a decision on whether any other arrangements would have to be made.[16]

Also in March 1978, a Ministry of Defence official said to the Defence and External Affairs Subcommittee of the Expenditure Committee that: 'The early 1990's is 12 years away and more. I would have thought that that would have given ample opportunity for any studies that ministers might in the future think necessary.'[17] It was only in January 1979 that the Prime Minister mentioned to the House of

Commons that the decision on Polaris replacement 'will need to be taken in the next two years'.[18] The Expenditure Committee of the House of Commons began an enquiry into future strategic nuclear weapons policy, but this was interrupted by the dissolution of Parliament in April 1979 with no conclusions as to the questions of when a decision to acquire a successor to Polaris had to take place and what the options for a replacement were.

However, this official version of events under the Labour Government from 1974–9 is at considerable variance with what was going on behind the scenes. Not only was the Labour Government continuing with the Chevaline project, but it had also begun work on the question of replacing the Polaris force. In mid-1977 the Ministry of Defence suggested that the question of a successor to the Polaris force should be considered. According to Peter Hennessy:

> In Mr Callaghan's judgement the matter was too delicate to put before the Cabinet's Defence and Overseas Policy Committee (DOP), upon which sat one or two sticklers who might have reminded him of the party's manifesto commitment in the October 1974 general election.[19]

Instead, the Prime Minister convened a small *ad hoc* committee which was so secret that it did not even carry a Cabinet Office 'Gen' number (the numbering system used for Cabinet subcommittees). The Committee was chaired by the Prime Minister and comprised the Chancellor of the Exchequer (Denis Healey), the Foreign Secretary (David Owen), and the Defence Secretary (Fred Mulley). The committee asked the Ministry of Defence and the Foreign and Commonwealth Office to undertake two studies on the issue of Polaris replacement. One dealt with the military and international implications of a successor system, and was chaired by an FCO (Foreign and Commonwealth Office) Deputy Under-Secretary, Antony Duff; the other was concerned with the question of possible delivery systems and was chaired by Professor Ronald Mason, Chief Scientific Adviser to the MOD.[20] The work of these two groups was coordinated by a group of leading civil servants, chaired by the Secretary to the Cabinet, Sir John Hunt. The two working parties reported to the *ad hoc* Cabinet Committee in November 1978, and it was at this time that 1980 emerged as the optimum date for a decision. Beyond this the Government took no ministerial decisions, but because of the impending decision date, the Prime Minister informally raised the issue with President Carter during the Guadeloupe summit in January 1979. By the time of the election in 1979 the Committee had agreed that there would be a new submarine-based strategic force; they disagreed over whether it would be Cruise or Trident on board the submarine.

When the Conservatives came to power in May 1979 little had been decided regarding the question of a successor to Polaris, but it is important to note that a consensus had emerged in the MOD and the FCO, one which, Peter Hennessy claims, was shared by the *ad hoc* Cabinet Committee. This was that there should be a successor to the Polaris force and that this successor should be submarine-based (although there had been no conclusions reached as to whether the delivery systems should be ballistic or cruise missiles). Although the new Government was not formally informed of the existence of the Callaghan *ad hoc* Committee, the amount of work that had already been undertaken on the Polaris replacement issue 'cannot have escaped Mrs Thatcher's attention'.[21] One of the first Cabinet Committees established by the new Government was one to examine the nuclear deterrent; this Committee was known as MISC 7 and consisted of the Prime Minister (Margaret Thatcher), the Chancellor of the Exchequer (Geoffrey Howe), the Home Secretary (William Whitelaw), the Foreign Secretary (Lord Carrington) and the Defence Secretary (Francis Pym). This Committee received the Duff and Mason reports with new tops and tails so as to distinguish them from the original reports presented to the Callaghan *ad hoc* Committee. They then consulted the Chiefs of Staff, who favoured a successor force, and began informal discussions with the US on their attitude towards a British request to purchase a successor system. On 26 October the Defence Secretary stated publicly that the Government was considering a replacement for Polaris.[22]

The Prime Minister, following up on initial discussions between the Defence Secretaries of the two countries (Francis Pym and Harold Brown) that had taken place in July 1979, travelled to Washington and raised the issue of Polaris replacement with President Carter. The communiqué issued at the end of that meeting said that the two:

> agreed on the importance of maintaining a credible British strategic deterrent force and US–UK strategic co-operation. The leaders agreed that their Governments should continue their discussions of the most appropriate means of achieving these objectives for the future.[23]

Within Whitehall the debate then concentrated on the nature of the system Britain would replace Polaris with.[24] The debate was not a public one. Given the existing consensus on a submarine-based replacement, it concerned two major issues: whether to fit cruise or ballistic missiles, and, when this was resolved, which type of ballistic missile to go for. By early 1980 it became clear that the choice was to be for a ballistic missile replacement. Speaking in the House of Commons on 24 January 1980, in the first parliamentary debate on nuclear weapons in fifteen years, the Defence Secretary announced that the Government had decided to develop a successor to Polaris. He did not state what the choice was, but he did give an estimate of the cost – £4–5 billion. This estimate, and the comments of other Government spokespersons, made it clear that cruise had been rejected.

The working group chaired by Professor Ronald Mason had reported to the Callaghan *ad hoc* Committee that the successor system should be submarine-based; this defeated an attempt by the RAF to reclaim control over the deterrent after Polaris. The reasons for this help us understand why cruise missiles were later rejected for the submarine-based force: although there were many factors related to the operational problems of bombers as cruise launch-vehicles, and a question over the vulnerability of such a force to surprise attack, cruise missiles *per se* were also seen as problematic. Not only were they as yet untried, and therefore liable to cancellation (remember the Skybolt incident), there were also problems over their ability to penetrate Soviet air defences. A small submarine-launched cruise missile (SLCM) force, such as would be likely in any British deterrent, would be critically affected by improvements in Soviet air defence. Cruise missiles, after all, are relatively slow (500 mph), air-breathing systems that fly at a low height to avoid radar detection; ballistic missiles (such as Polaris or Trident) travel much faster (up to 15,000 mph) and do so on a trajectory which involves them leaving the atmosphere. Put simply, it is far harder to defend against ballistic missiles than it is to defend against cruise missiles. Further, there was the cost consideration; whilst cruise missiles are only one-sixth the cost of ballistic missiles on a unit-by-unit comparison, there are additional costs for cruise (such as obtaining the contour maps that are used to guide the missile) that made the cost of a cruise force seem quite large.[25] In addition, in order to be able to hit the same number of targets one would require three times as many submarines to carry cruise missiles as would be required to carry submarine ballistic missiles; submarines are the most expensive part of the deterrent force (and there are massive costs associated with having more crews, base facilities and the like). In short, the doubts about the cruise option, in the air-launched (ALCM) version, that had led the Mason group to prefer a submarine force, became central when the choice had to be made between SLCMs and SLBMs. SLCMs were expensive, because of the larger submarine fleet required to carry them, and were susceptible to being made obsolete by Soviet advances in air defence.

Attention then turned to what kind of SLBM. There were six options discussed, but of these a number were rejected because they involved a British development outside the pattern of US development.[26] The cost overruns of Chevaline had convinced Ministers that it was dangerous to follow a national route; it would be far cheaper to stay in line with what the US was developing. The options of British-made SLBMs, or of British modifications to American-made SLBMs were rejected, as much because the cost was an unknown as because estimates of that cost were too high. Buying Poseidon from the US was discussed, but was rejected because it has a very limited range due to its MIRVed warheads (which restrict the distance the missile can travel, and thus the operational radius of the submarine). For a small national deterrent – with only one submarine guaranteed to be on station at any time – Poseidon would not be a good choice. It would also be a system that would no longer be in US Navy service by the time the British submarines were commissioned, thus leading to high maintenance costs. Finally, why buy an old missile and face the prospect of having to modify it in mid-life (as with Polaris and Chevaline) if there was a more modern US missile available?

The real choice then came down to whether or not to buy the existing Trident version, C4, or to wait until the US agreed to produce the newer version, D5, upon which much research was being undertaken. Trident I (C4) was already operational with the US Navy, and had eight MIRVed warheads and a range of 4,000 nautical miles; but it was probably going to be replaced in the late 1980s by Trident II (D5), which would carry up to fourteen warheads and have a range of 6,000 nautical miles. Just as this increased range of Trident I was important in deciding between it and Poseidon so the operational range of Trident II became an argument for that missile over Trident I. Critically, the Chevaline factor was important, in that buying Trident I might leave the British having to modify a US system and keep it in service when, at the time the British force went to sea, the US had already replaced it. But there was another lesson from the past – Skybolt: Trident II had not yet been given the production go-ahead by the US Government.

The Thatcher Government announced, on 15 July 1980, that it intended to build four (or possibly five) new submarines, each carrying sixteen Trident I missiles as a successor system to Polaris.

The five-boat option was a complex one: on the one hand a fifth boat would make it easier to maintain more than one boat on station at any given time; on the other, the increased targeting coverage of Trident I over Polaris (128 as against 16 targets) made a fifth boat an expensive luxury. The cost of the deterrent force was estimated at about £5,000 million (for a four-boat fleet). The negotiations started by Pym and Thatcher in 1979 with their US counterparts had proceeded smoothly, and had led to an arrangement whereby the British only had to pay 5 per cent of the research and development costs whereas the pro rata per cent would have been nearer 11 per cent. Of the £5,000 million, 70 per cent would be spent in the UK, and the total expenditure would equal no more than 3–4 per cent of the defence budget over the fifteen-year period of the procurement of the force. The years of peak spending would be 1985–91 (although this was later to change).

This announcement of the decision to replace Polaris with Trident was made on 15 July 1980; Parliament debated the decision on 3 March 1981 and approved it by 316 to 248. But this 'decision' was really only a decision in principle, because the Government had decided on neither the number of boats nor the missile to be bought. As to the former, Mr Pym stated on 15 July 1980 that a decision over a fifth boat could wait for three years; as to the latter, the largest area of uncertainty in cost estimates for the force concerned the size of the submarines, and this, in turn, reflected a lack of clarity on which Trident missile to buy. Thus, although the 15 July statement seems, on the surface, to be clear in that it refers to the Trident I, it is evident that ministers had by no means agreed on which missile to buy. In October 1980 the MOD, in evidence to the Defence Committee, commented that no firm decisions had been taken with regards to submarine and missile design.[27] By mid-1981 the indications were that in designing the submarines, provisions were being made for fitting the larger Trident II missiles. Essentially, during this period the Thatcher Government was waiting to see what the US Government decided to do over Trident II. For precisely the same reason as had applied over Poseidon versus Trident I it was seen to be imprudent to make an irrevocable commitment to go for Trident I, when that missile might be out of date by the time the British force was commissioned. Yet, it was equally problematic to opt for a system (D5) that had not yet been given the go-ahead. So, from 15 July 1980 onwards, having established the principle that Britain would purchase a replacement for Polaris, the Government left the issue until the US resolved its position on Trident II. This it did in October 1981, when President Reagan gave the go-ahead to the development of D5.

This led to a busy period of bilateral negotiations between the US and the UK. These negotiations resulted in the US treating the UK even more favourably financially, agreeing to a fixed sum of $116 million for research and development contributions from the UK despite the fact that this would not be known for some time (the 5 per cent surcharge for Trident I amounted to about $100 million, and D5 would be much more expensive to develop). On 11 March 1982, the Defence Secretary John Nott announced the Government's decision to the House of Commons. The cost was now estimated to be some £7,500 million, at September 1981 exchange rates and prices; the increase over the July 1980 estimates was partly for inflation (£700 million) and the D5's extra cost (£390 million) but also for changes in the pound–dollar exchange rate (£800 million), extra costs following from the need to build larger submarines to house the D5, and more advanced sonars and nuclear propulsion plants. The Government stated that this would be a four-submarine fleet, with each submarine carrying sixteen missiles. The decision was justified on simple cost-effectiveness grounds, with the new missile using the same warhead as had already been under development for Trident I; this meant that it was likely that the UK would not deploy the submarines with the full complement of fourteen warheads per missile; it also allowed the submarines to use the full range of the warheads. As the Government explained in the 1982 'Statement on the Defence Estimates':

> Like our predecessors, we do not comment on the number of missiles and warheads carried by our SSBNs at any given time. But it is right to make clear that the move to Trident D5 will not involve any significant change in the planned total number of warheads associated with our strategic deterrent force, compared to the original intention for a force based on the C4.[28]

The probable plan, then, was to install ten to twelve warheads per missile, for, as the same statement commented:

> The D5 missile . . . will be significantly larger than the C4 missile and will be able either to carry the same payload a much greater distance and with greater accuracy or to carry its maximum payload over approximately the same range as Trident C4.[29]

Subsequent to this, the opposition parties announced their intention to cancel Trident; at the same time estimates of its costs increased rapidly: by mid-1985 it was estimated that the cost would, at 1985 prices, be £10,008 million. This was clearly going to have a massive impact on other areas of the defence budget. Thus much opposition to Trident was based, not simply on moral or political grounds, but also on the effects that a continuing, and escalating, expenditure on Trident was likely to have on conventional forces.

PARLIAMENT'S ROLE

Having examined how the Trident decision was made by the Government, it is now appropriate to look at the role Parliament played in the decision. The picture that emerges is that the decisions over Trident were taken in a very secretive manner. The pattern is one of government, and only a small part of government at that, undertaking secretive case-studies and evaluations, and then negotiating face to face with US leaders. In a very important way, the key decisions were taken by a very small group of individuals (four in the Labour Government, five in the Conservative).

Yet Parliament is, of course, the body that has constitutional responsibility to accept, or not, expenditure on this scale, and naturally, this relates to a central debate about the role of representative government. But, when we look at the control that Parliament exercised over this decision, it is clear that it was unable to have any significant impact on the decisions. According to the minority report of the Defence Committee's 1981 report on 'Strategic Nuclear Weapons Policy', the role of the House of Commons in the decision to procure a successor system to Polaris was as follows:

(a) January 1979 – Defence and External Affairs Subcommittee begins an investigation into the future of the United Kingdom's nuclear weapons policy; 270 pages of both written and oral evidence are taken on 'the strategic, financial, technical and other implications associated with the choice of nuclear delivery systems, and their associated warheads, as possible successors to the present Polaris forces'; Subcommittee unable to complete their investigation due to general election of May 1979; Expenditure Committee publishes evidence gathered and hopes it 'will be of use to both Members and the public and be available for consideration by a committee of the new Parliament'; evidence is not debated by the House nor formally considered by Defence Committee of new Parliament.

(b) July 1979 – Secretary of State for Defence has 'an initial exchange of views with the United States Secretary of

Defence' on Britain's deterrent.

(c) 18 December 1979 – communiqué following Washington meeting of the Prime Minister and President says the two 'agreed on the importance of maintaining a credible British strategic deterrent force and US–UK strategic cooperation. The leaders agreed that their Governments should continue their discussions of the most appropriate means of achieving these objectives for the future'.

(d) 18 December 1979 – Consolidated Fund Bill debate on Polaris missiles, first such debate of new Parliament.

(e) 24 January 1980 – five-and-a-half-hour debate on nuclear weapons on Motion to Adjourn; first such major debate on nuclear weapons policy for 15 years.

(f) April 1980 – Early Day Motion tabled calling on Government to publish a Green Paper (consultative document) setting out the choices available to Great Britain were the Polaris force to be replaced; Secretary of State says he does not accept that the idea of a Green Paper is either 'sensible or appropriate'; says the correct constitutional procedure is for the Government to take its decision and then 'explain it and defend it before Parliament'.

(g) June 1980 – Defence Committee begins its inquiry; takes initial oral evidence on 25 June and 9 July.

(h) 15 July 1980 – Secretary of State for Defence announces Government's decision to procure a new strategic nuclear deterrent system based on the US Trident I-SLBM.

(i) 4 August 1980 – Consolidated Fund Bill debate on Polaris replacement.

(j) February 1981 – Defence Committee publishes evidence it has gathered to date.

(k) 3 March 1981 – Debate on Motion by Secretary of State for Defence 'that this House endorses the Government's decision to maintain a strategic nuclear deterrent and the choice of the Trident missile system as the successor to the Polaris force'; Motion approved 316 to 248.[30]

As this indicates, the Defence and External Affairs Subcommittee of the Expenditure Committee commenced a study of the future of the UK strategic deterrent in January 1979, but this was interrupted by the general election of May 1979. Although this Subcommittee took a sizeable amount of evidence, it was never debated in the House of Commons. What the Subcommittee was told about plans to replace

Polaris was, as we have seen, rather at odds with the work that was in progress within the Callaghan *ad hoc* Committee. The MOD memorandum to that Committee presented on 16 January 1979 stated that:

> The Government has made it clear that there are no plans for any successor system to the present Polaris force . . . The timescale for development and production of any successor system . . . would depend on the nature and scale of the chosen system . . . As there are no plans for any such system, details of a timetable for procurement and on costs cannot be provided.[31]

Fred Mulley, the Defence Secretary, said before the Committee on the same day that: 'As to what should happen when the Polaris force is eventually phased out of service, the time has not come yet when matters have to be settled. No decision is yet necessary.'[32] Under questioning, he noted that: 'The time-scale would depend on whether a decision were to be taken to replace it and if so on what it was to be replaced with. It is quite impossible to give an arbitrary time.'[33]

Fortunately, or not, the Prime Minister said at Question Time the same day that a decision would need to be taken in the next two years. Mr Mulley's answer was: 'indeed the question is whether or not at this moment we need to decide'.[34] The point is that although it was literally correct to say that no decisions had been made, Mr Mulley's evidence made no reference at all to the work of Callaghan and his committee, nor of the Duff and Mason working groups, both of which had reported in November 1978. Whilst the Committee was not told a lie, it was hardly told the whole story, for, as we have seen, by the time the Defence Secretary gave his evidence, there was consensus that a successor system should be developed.

The next involvement of Parliament came on 18 December 1979, when Bruce George initiated a Consolidated Fund Bill debate on the question of Polaris replacement, in which he accused the Government of ignoring Parliament and the public over this issue. Mr Pym, replying for the Government, denied this and said that he had tried to 'lead the argument from the front'. He added that he had 'some regret in having been so forthcoming and frank about the consideration that we are giving to the matter'.[35] On 24 January 1980 the Government opened a five-and-a-half-hour debate on nuclear weapons, and it was in his speech that Francis Pym gave the first indication that a successor was to be developed, but again it was said no decision had been made. By this time, of course, UK–US negotiations were well under way and President Carter had agreed with Prime Minister Thatcher that the US would sell Trident to the UK; but officially, there had been no decision! On 28 and 29 April, the House debated the Defence White Paper; the Labour Party argued that the Government should publish a Green Paper on the question of Polaris replacement, but Mr Pym replied that he did not feel this to be either 'sensible or appropriate'. Rather, he said the Government should take its decision and then 'explain it and defend it before Parliament'. He said that he intended to publish a 'substantial document giving the fullest possible account of all the considerations involved' once the decision had been taken.[36]

The Defence Committee began its hearings into the future of the British Strategic Nuclear Force on 25 June 1980; its terms of reference did not include whether Britain should have a deterrent, but rather only the issues of which type of deterrent and the impact of spending on the deterrent on employment and the defence budget. But on 15 July, the Government announced its decision. In replying to Mr Pym's statement about the purchase of Trident the Opposition Spokesman, William Rodgers, commented that Mr Pym had shown contempt for the House by making the announcement before the Defence Committee had completed their investigation on the deterrent.[37] Explaining how the decision had been taken, Mr Pym said that: 'what I have announced is the continuation of an existing capability. It would be a much more significant announcement if I said that we were not going to continue (with the deterrent)'.[38]

On 4 August there was a two-hour debate on Trident, during which David Steel spoke of 'the conspiracy of silence between the two Front Benches' over the issue.[39] His Liberal colleague Alan Beith commented that it was: 'a reflection on the strange procedures of this place that this is the only opportunity that we have to debate such a major decision before the House rises for a recess of several months'.[40]

The main debate on Trident took place on 3 March 1981, with the decision being endorsed by 316 to 248. In this debate, the opposition spokesman on defence, Brynmor John, said that he deplored the fact that the Government was seeking the approval of the House before the Defence Committee published its evidence, a point reiterated by John Gilbert (a Labour member of that Committee).[41] The Committee's report was published on 20 May 1981, but the Committee was unable to agree on a unanimous version. The major (Government) version supported the Government's decision, but it did criticise the MOD for not providing the Committee with sufficient information on the opportunity costs of Trident. As the final report of the Committee stated:

> We must record that it has been a matter of great regret to us that we have found the Ministry unwilling to discuss in any detail the opportunity costs of purchasing the Trident system . . . we cannot believe that the Secretary of State for Defence and his predecessor did not ask for an assessment of the likely projects to come under pressure during the period of Trident procurement. We would have welcomed an indication of what these assessments were.[42]

The report also noted that, with regards to the effect of the Trident purchase on the rest of the defence budget: 'the Ministry of Defence has not been prepared to take the Committee fully into its confidence'.[43] Finally, the Committee pointed out that: 'There has been considerable evidence that there was a lack of consultation with British industry before the 15 July 1980 announcement'.[44]

The minority report (Labour and SDP) was much more critical of the way the Committee had been treated. In the words cited at the very start of this chapter, it declared that: 'Parliament's role had been limited to endorsing a decision already taken'.[45] With reference to the timing of the 15 July 1980 decision, the report stated that:

> The Government came to the House and invited it to endorse the Trident decision when the Committee was still deliberating. We saw no reason for action by the House before the Committee reported, and consider the Government's actions in this respect to be less than courteous to both the House and its Committee.[46]

In connection with the evidence presented to the Committee, the report concluded that:

> We deeply regret the Ministry's refusal to furnish adequate information relating to the likely consequences for the remainder of the defence budget should it proceed with Trident . . . We regret the Ministry's inability to inform us which version of the US Trident C4 and D5 missiles could be available for purchase by Britain.[47]

Fundamentally they regretted:

> the Ministry's refusal to provide adequate information on . . . costs. The Ministry's case for spending £5,000 million to £6,000 million . . . on a single system has not been made . . . we feel the Ministry has not adequately justified its choice of Trident, and we could not recommend that any future Government continue the programme.[48]

The only other role Parliament had in the decision was to listen to the statement of the Secretary of State for Defence, John Nott, on 11 March 1982. The expenditure for this programme was voted on in the Defence Estimates, and, given the strict party line on such votes, the money was provided without further debate.

TRIDENT AND BRITISH POLITICS

From our analysis of the decision-making process that resulted in the choice of Trident D5 SLBMs as the replacement of the Polaris force, we can discern ten features that relate this case-study to the more general concerns of this book.

Secrecy

One of the most noticeable features of the decision-making process over the Trident replacement was the extent to which much of it took place behind very firmly closed doors. As McLean points out, this is common in all nuclear weapons decisions in Britain.[49] The 15 July 1980 and the 11 March 1982 statements were the first formal disclosures to Parliament of the work related to the replacement issue that had been going on since 1978. Not only was there no public presentation of this work, but also Parliament was kept in the dark as to what work was in progress. Even the Defence Committee was presented with a bland 'no decision has yet been taken' argument, despite the existence of a governmental consensus on the outcome of the process. This secrecy prevented Parliament from having the kind of information needed to evaluate the eventual decision. In the case of the Defence Committee, a careful analysis of the evidence they were given by the Government and the Civil Service indicates the lack of detail they were provided with. As cited above, the minority report suggested that the MOD felt that the Committee could not be trusted with this information. Thus, at all levels, outside of the very small group who made the decisions, the debate, if that is even the correct term, was marked by government provision of very limited amounts of information, justified, usually, on the grounds that national security prohibited the transmission of certain aspects of the information. Although much evidence was not presented in the published version of the hearings of the Defence Committee, it is clear that, even in confidential sessions, the kind of information presented was considerably restricted. Of course, there is a good case for withholding certain very sensitive information (such as target coverage, reliability of systems etc.), but even basic evidence relating to costs and to the existence of working groups on the replacement decision, as well as the timing of the decision, was withheld. Not only was public debate stifled by this, but Parliament was also not presented with the information necessary to evaluate the Government's decision. After all, the fact that the Government wished to replace Polaris is one thing; the choice of system to replace it is another. Secrecy pervaded the discussion and the evaluation of both aspects, and one must question the extent to which Parliament was in a position to evaluate the choice given the information it was provided with. It is interesting to compare this process with that of the US, where congressional committees are provided with much more information, and are able, therefore, to come to much better informed judgements as to the Executive's proposals.

Size of the decision-making group

A striking feature of the process was the very small size of the groups who made the decisions – four in the Callaghan Government, five in the Conservative. In the former, it will be recalled, the *ad hoc* Committee was so secret that it had no Cabinet Office number. Small groups, of course, are very efficient in making decisions, but a striking feature of the decisions in both the Callaghan and Thatcher Governments was that the key choices were taken outside of the Cabinet structure. In the case of the Labour Government it is doubtful that these were ever taken to the full Cabinet. As for the Thatcher Cabinet, the first time they heard of the 'decision' to buy Trident was when it appeared on a Cabinet agenda on 15 July 1980, just hours before Defence Secretary Pym announced it to the Commons.[50] *The Times* had broken the story on 4 December 1979, yet it was still not discussed at Cabinet until the following summer. So, to talk even of a Government decision is a misnomer, as the decisions were really those of a subgroup of the Cabinet. In the same way as Parliament's role was limited to reacting to an already-made decision, so, it would appear, was the Cabinet confined to a rubber-stamping role.

Agenda setting

What the groups that made the decisions were able to do most effectively was to determine the timing of the announcement of the decisions. There was no necessary reason for the announcement to be on 15 July 1980 or for the debate to approve this decision to be on 3 March 1981, especially since the Defence Committee was to report on this issue. In both cases, the Government was able to pre-empt the work of the Committee, and, thereby, significantly reduce the impact of its findings. There was certainly no reason why the decision had to be announced in view of the link with the US; after all, in July 1980 it was not at all clear whether or not the US would proceed with D5. Similarly the D5 announcement of 11 March 1982 was made despite the fact that the Government had decided to go for that option long before. It has been suggested that the Government chose the date of the release of the Defence Committee report (25 June 1981) to announce a major Defence Review, thereby diverting public and parliamentary attention from the criticisms contained in the minority report of the Defence Committee. Additionally, by virtue of its ability to control the announcement of decisions, the Government was able to set the political agenda for Parliamentary discussion: this was certainly the case with the 3 March 1981 debate, which took place before the publication of the Defence Committee report. Whilst the publication of this report might not have altered the vote in the Commons, it is clear that the Government was able to limit the kinds of questions that could be raised in the debate. Finally, the Government was able to set the agenda in a more long-term political manner, since its announcement of the decisions involved time-scales for the expenditure of money: by planning the procurement over the period it did, the Government could ensure that it was able to spend money on the project before the next election. It also initially offered the prospect of a fifth boat, saying that a decision would have to be taken in three or four years; this was widely interpreted as offering a sacrificial lamb for a future Labour Government that came to power committed to trimming expenditure on the nuclear deterrent. The choice of D5 had a rather different effect, in that it delayed major capital expenditure until the late 1980s, thus putting both the 1979–83 and the subsequent Conservative Governments in the position of being able to proceed with procurement without spending the vast sums of money associated with the peak years of expenditure. Similarly, although it was said that nothing would be sacrosanct when Defence Secretary Nott undertook a defence review in 1981, it was considered politically impossible to cancel or curtail the Trident programme, which had, after all, only been decided on a year earlier.[51]

Parliament's role

Parliament was effectively only ever able to approve a decision taken elsewhere. It had neither the opportunity nor the information to participate in decision-making. The fact that it approved the July 1980 decision may be of formal constitutional interest, but, in behavioural terms, Parliament was completely unable to initiate action on this issue. Even the organs of parliamentary government (such as the Cabinet and Select Committees) were unable to give Parliament any say in the decision, other than either rejecting or approving it. Again, while constitutionally rejection was an option, the behavioural patterns of British parliamentary government made this irrelevant. This was not a decision over which Parliament had either the expertise or the ability to subject the decision to the kind of analysis consistent with the constitutional role of that body. For the procedures of Parliament, such as question time and debates, produced very little in the way of detailed information, and, again, the Government's ability to set the agenda of the questions posed, reduced the options of Parliament to voting one way or the other. What this indicates is the vast gulf between the official picture of the role of Parliament and the reality. As Cox and Kirby show, the Trident case is not exceptional; it mirrors other cases of arms procurement.[52] McLean does not even list Parliament as a major influence on policy-making for nuclear weapons.[53]

The role of the Defence Committee

Whilst it is understandable that detailed information may not be revealed in public parliamentary debates, it is surprising just how limited was the ability of the Defence Committee to exercise scrutiny over the decisions; this results from three factors. First, the Committee's terms of reference were very narrow, and did not include the question of whether there should be a successor system to Polaris. Second, the Committee had very limited resources to undertake any independent analysis of the Government's case (it had three part-time staff). Third, even this Committee had severe problems in obtaining information; on many occasions, civil servants and ministers referred to 'national security' as a reason for not providing answers to detailed questions. The Committee did not have statutory power to summon ministers to appear before it. More saliently, the absence of expert full-time advisers meant that the members of the Committee were always questioning from a position of relative ignorance: they did not know which questions to ask, and civil servants, under the 'Osmotherly Rules' (which guide them as to their conduct) are instructed not to discuss policy questions or 'who gave what advice to whom' type questions. These factors meant that the Defence Committee was always at a significant disadvantage in questioning ministers and civil servants. But even then, the Government was able to pre-empt the publication of the Committee's report by having the vote on the initial decision three months before the report was sent to the Commons.

The role of civil servants

This case-study sheds light on the age-old question of whether civil servants make policy. Whilst it is evident that the decisions were taken by the Government, it is equally clear that the overwhelming consensus within the higher echelons of the Civil Service as to the advisability of replacing Polaris with Trident significantly shaped the policy debate in government. It was the MOD that originally requested that the replacement question be considered by the Labour Government in January 1978, and the Duff and Mason working groups soon established the existence of a consensus within the relevant policy community. As it happened, the Conservative Government was committed to replacing Polaris, but it is instructive to note just how important this consensus could have been to a Labour Government publicly committed not to renew the deterrent. The Chevaline case also indicates the importance of policy community consensus, and the activities of the Labour Government over both the Chevaline and the Trident issues emphasise how critical a factor this can be. Not only this, but also the flow of information to Ministers was, given the sensitive nature of the issue, exclusively from the MOD and Service Chiefs; this flow of information naturally defined certain issues as central, and the decisions on these foreclosed options later on (especially in the case of SLBMs versus SLCMs).

Bipartisanship and continuity

The Trident decisions also show the importance of continuity in decision-making, and the prevalence of a bipartisan approach. That there has been a bipartisan approach at the governmental level is indicated by the behaviour of the Labour Party from 1974–9 over both Chevaline and Trident (although the NATO Cruise-Pershing II deployment is another very clear case in point). But more saliently, the importance of continuity was also very marked: in a quite central way, the decisions over Blue Streak, Skybolt, Polaris, Chevaline and Trident all follow on from one another. Just as the Blue Streak fiasco led to the Skybolt fiasco, so the Polaris decision created a clear pattern of behaviour that made Trident seem the 'logical' choice. Choosing Trident was, in this way, the 'obvious' or 'natural' solution to the problem created by the original Polaris decision, and the choice of Trident D5 over Trident C4 had its roots in the unease caused by the costly Chevaline modification to Polaris. This is not to argue that these were 'wrong' choices, only that the logic that made them 'obvious' choices was a logic created by past policy choices. As was quoted above, Francis Pym actually made this point when he commented on the fact that the decision was simply one of continuing an existing policy. In short, the importance of continuity set the parameters of the analysis of the options and it created, in government, a norm or a status quo, the alteration of which would have required considerable justification.

Public debate

Despite Ian Smart's 1977 paper on the timetable and possible choices facing the Government, there was little public debate of the issue. On the one hand there was considerable opposition to prolonging the life of the independent British strategic deterrent, but it is worth noting that at exactly the time that Trident was announced much more public attention was focused on the NATO Cruise-Pershing decision, taken on 12 December 1979. It has been suggested that the Government was happy to see public attention concentrated on that issue. On the other hand, there was very little discussion of the precise choices facing Britain with regard to the replacement of Polaris. There were very few discussions in the media of the range of choices despite the fact that very considerable discussions were going on in government about the options available (for example SLBMs or SLCMs). Again the contrast with policy-making in the US is considerable. Nor, apparently, was there much consultation with the industries involved, as the Defence Committee Final Report pointed out; certainly British Aerospace, a proponent of an ALCM (air-launched cruise missile) replacement force, was not consulted. These features merely reinforce the earlier conclusion that this was very much a decision made within a very restricted policy-making group. Because it did not know the range of options, the public was unable to make any input into governmental deliberations; but, then, nor was Parliament.

Opposition-government behaviour

It is also rather surprising to note the behaviour of the Callaghan Government in this decision. Not only had they continued the Chevaline programme, at a (hidden) cost of £1,000 million, against the manifesto commitment, but the *ad hoc* committee formed by Callaghan did seem to be undertaking activities inconsistent with the manifesto. As Peter Hennessy wrote in 1979, when the Government announced its decision:

> The people to watch . . . will be on the opposition front bench, particularly Mr James Callaghan, Mr Denis Healey and Dr David Owen. If they baulk at the cost in an era of expenditure cuts, or suggest a cheaper (and less effective) land-based or airborne system, it will represent one of those operations in hypocrisy that oppositions can so easily mount when their private intentions in Government remain concealed under thick layers of Whitehall secrecy.[54]

What this does indicate is the rather differing pressures on individuals in opposition and in government, and it thereby reminds us of the limitations of relying on manifesto commitments, and statements made in opposition, in predicting the behaviour of governments. Indeed when Francis Pym announced the existence of the Chevaline project in 1980, he was attacked by ex-Labour ministers for disrupting continuity and bipartisanship. As one commented: 'It is one of the most outrageous, disgusting, most damaging examples of breaking the continuity of nuclear decision-making there has ever been'.[55]

Public control

What the bulk of the points just made reiterate is the severe restriction on public control over government decision-making. To a degree, this is an atypical case, in that it involves a very sensitive and secret area of decision-making, but in another sense it indicates the ability of governments to present electorates with *fait accomplis*. The dominant theme running through these concluding remarks is the inability of the public or Parliament to alter or even influence governmental decision-making in the area of nuclear force policy. There are many reasons for this, but it does lead us to ask where democracy fits in to this picture. Of course, governments can reply that they can be removed from office at elections, but precisely because elections are both fought on a multiplicity of issues and are determined overwhelmingly by domestic ones, it does mean that behaviourally, if not constitutionally, governments possess enormous autonomy in the area of defence policy; and, the more secret the area the more they can restrict information, thereby precluding informed evaluation of their decisions, on the one hand, and appealing on the other to notions of national interest to legitimise their decisions and render criticisms of them illegitimate.

TRIDENT AND THEORIES OF DECISION-MAKING

We can now comment briefly on what this case-study tells us about the theories of decision-making we discussed in chapter two; a more formal summary will be found in the next chapter. The first conclusion we can make relates to the very notion of a decision. Not only was there no one decision on Trident, but it is also important to question what we mean when we say that we are explaining a decision. In the case of Polaris replacement, it is revealing to note just how often government spokespersons said that no decision had been taken. Whilst this was literally correct, it ignores the important processes by which decisions emerge. The House and the Defence Committee were constantly told that no decision had been taken; in fact many decisions had been taken. So, when Ministers referred to no decision having been taken they really meant that no announcement of a final decision had occurred. The analysis of policy-making over Trident would not proceed very far if we accepted the Government's definition of what the decision was and when it took place. The case-study also shows the importance of continuity and non-decisions in government. Precisely because the Government was able to set the agenda and create a policy-community consensus, the eventual July 1980 and March 1982 announcements were essentially exercises in non-decision-making. The treatment of the Defence Committee is a classic example of non-decision-making, in that the control of its resources, the inability of the Committee to hire or fire its own staff, its restricted terms of reference, and the limits on what it could be told, all acted so as to prevent it from affecting the smooth process of governmental dominance over the issue.

Another theoretical implication of the case-study concerns the importance of bureaucratic forces in governmental decision-making. The exact nature of the decisions reflects a very precise set of bureaucratic interests: one of these was the consensus within the MOD for the replacement of Polaris, and this apparently convinced

Fred Mulley, against his personal predisposition, to support such a policy. A second was the rivalry between the RAF and the Royal Navy as to which of them would possess the strategic nuclear deterrent.

The Trident decisions also illustrate the limitations of the synoptic view of decision-making. At no time was there a once-and-for-all decision on what to replace Polaris with, if anything. Rather, policy emerged incrementally, with each decision defining the parameters of the debate over the next one.

The salience of the belief-system of decision-makers is also a prominent feature of the Polaris replacement decisions. There are three ways in which we can see belief-systems having a significant impact on how the decisions were made. First, there was the importance of the shared belief, among both Conservative and Labour Ministers involved in the replacement decision, of the fact that Britain was a nuclear power. This meant that the decision to scrap the British deterrent force could never simply be a question of what was the most appropriate force structure for the country, but was, instead, related to major questions about Britain's role in the world. Second, there was very evidently a shared set of assumptions and beliefs in the MOD, and at the mandarin level of the Civil Service generally, about the need to replace Polaris. There seems to have been little doubt that replacing Polaris was simply the natural thing to do. This perception seems to have been shared by the small group of Government Ministers involved in making the decision. Third, there was the psychological impact of the 'lessons of the past'. There were three of these: (a) The experience with Chevaline, especially its cost, indicated that it was unwise to buy a US system that would be out of date halfway during its British service thus necessitating modifications. This was crucial in the choice of D5 rather than C4. (b) The Skybolt incident created a disinclination to choose a system that had not yet been given the go-ahead in the US. This explains the hedging over C4 and D5 from July 1980 until March 1982. (c) The perception of a special relationship predisposed Ministers to think of a British purchase of a US system as the natural choice. This belief militated against other options, notably collaboration with the French.

CONCLUSION

Finally, one must comment on the glaring disparity between the way in which the policy-making process operated and the way in which it is officially, or constitutionally, described as operating. Models of the process that concentrate either upon the statements of Ministers or on the constitutional framework of policy-making would be unable to explain (as distinct from describe) the decisions to replace Polaris. In this instance, the power of governments to set agendas, provide information, and determine the timing of discussions was crucial to the outcome.

The decisions to purchase Trident as a replacement for the Polaris force emerged out of a kaleidoscope of factors. The most important of these were the appeal of a policy that stressed continuity; a shared set of beliefs at senior Civil Service and ministerial levels as to the effects of opting out of the strategic nuclear business; bureaucratic pressure for a replacement, and bureaucratic pressure for a particular kind of replacement; the lack of parliamentary control, especially in an area of technical complexity; the long lead-time for procurement, which necessitated a decision some thirteen years before the force would begin operations; cost considerations; and the weight of lessons of past procurement decisions. These factors lie outside an official or constitutional view of policy-making in British government, and the overwhelming conclusion of this case-study is that governments have enormous autonomy in defence matters. Despite the fact that Trident was a controversial decision, despite its enormous cost, despite the kind of escalation of weapons capabilities that the D5 option represented, Parliament was still unable to affect the decision at all. Its role was simply that of accepting a decision made elsewhere; one must note that the rejection of this decision was never really a behavioural option given the nature of party discipline. Even the Defence Committee was unable to evaluate the options fully, and any possibility of its exercising an independent role was curtailed by limitations on its resources, terms of reference, and, above all, by the ability of the Government to gain ratification of the decision before it could publish its report. This gap between the official view of policy-making and the actual process is precisely why policy-making models are so important in the explanation of decision-making in British government.

10 Conclusion

We started this book by commenting that we live in a democracy, and we will conclude by reflecting on this theme. What, then, can we learn from our six case-studies about the way in which democracy influences the policy-making process? It would indeed be strange if we found no evidence of the democratic process at work in the case-studies we have been looking at; this would certainly be at odds with the 'official' picture of policy-making that politicians and the media paint. However, anyone who has read the six case-studies must be aware that the way in which policies were made (if calling them policies is not an exaggeration in the first place) did not accord with the institutional view which was outlined in the first chapter.

Before we return to the question of democracy, we will consider four other issues raised by the case-studies. The first and most important question, to which we will devote most attention in this chapter, is what do the case-studies reveal about the utility of the various decision-making theories we examined in chapter two. Secondly, does the evidence of the case-studies support or undermine any of the portrayals of the British decision-making process outlined in chapter three? Thirdly, what are the main factors changing the context of the British policy-making environment? Finally, what do the case-studies tell us about British politics and about the nature of British democracy?

Our chief reason for adopting a case-study approach, set within the context of theories of decision-making and models of the British decision-making process, was that the detailed examination of specific cases would allow us to introduce theories and models that are not commonly found in discussions of British politics. Too often, in our view, the subject is discussed in terms of either formal processes or ideologies; and this, we feel, biases the account in favour of the way that politicians like to see it. After all, if the bureaucratic politics view is taken to its extreme there is no point in having elections since whoever is elected will merely face the same set of bureaucratic forces, and policy will continue to be decided by the interplay of these forces. No one who is a politician or is politically active, likes to see politics in this way (except when blaming the bureaucracy proves a useful excuse, or reason, for failure). Such a portrayal also has enormous normative consequences, specifically with regard to what being a democracy entails. Of course, we do not wish to maintain so stark a view of British politics, but we do want to suggest that the picture that politicians and activists paint is equally extreme. The consideration of the use of policy-making theories and alternative models of the British political process in combination with a series of case-studies should allow us to get beyond the view created by the media. It may appear less exciting to focus on the implementation of a policy than on a general election campaign or a Conservative Party leadership clash, but our belief is that such an approach may well be far more useful in explaining the British decision-making process.

Are there weaknesses in our method? As we said in chapter one, there certainly are, and it would be misleading to hide them. There are three main ones. In the first place we have only looked at six case-studies, and, although we think that they are not unrepresentative, it would be foolhardy to move from six cases to general statements about the British political system. We will, therefore, simply say that our case-studies *suggest* certain conclusions about British politics. Secondly, and more problematic, there is the worry that our case-studies are not typical, that they are, in some sense, a set of extreme examples giving a misleading picture of how decisions get made in Britain. We are well aware of this problem, and this worry guided our choice of case-studies. There are important areas that we have not covered, such as social policy and economic policy, but this merely represents our own areas of expertise. Our judgement is that although our case-studies do not include examples from all areas of the political agenda, they are representative in terms of the *types* of policies and the *forms* of decision-making found in British politics. Finally, there is always the danger of setting up a straw figure to knock down with ease. You should think closely about whether the account we have given of the institutional version of British politics is simplistic. Of course, no politician would accept that he or she believed so naive a version without qualification. Our concern, though, is that the formal version of the political process is precisely the one that gets accepted as the common-sense one; allowances for other factors are made, but always as deviations from the parliamentary model.

Let us give just one example: the role of the 1974–9 Labour Government in modernising the British Polaris nuclear system is completely at odds both with the parliamentary model of how decisions get taken and with the account of how policies get made within the Labour Party. Not only was Parliament omitted from the decisions over the Chevaline programme, but so was the full Cabinet; similarly, the Trident purchase, which was in direct contradiction to the party's election manifesto commitment, was effectively decided upon outside the formal process. Not only this, but the Chevaline programme's cost, over £1 billion, was hidden from Parliament. Many Labour activists have been appalled, if not surprised, by these events; however it is worth noting that there are many other examples in the nuclear weapons field of a similar character: enough to suggest that this is a clear pattern. The point is that such examples get explained away, either as being exceptional or as representing the corruption or the failings of specific individuals. Our suggestion is that the Trident and Chevaline cases are far more representative than is usually suggested. In summary, although we accept that no one believes the simple institutional model of British politics to be accurate, its presence in the media, and in many elementary textbooks, gives it pride of place in the interpretation of British politics. To repeat, everything else is seen as a deviation from this model. The danger here is that the popular perception of decision-making comes to bear little, if any, relationship to reality.

What do the case-studies tell us about the theories we outlined in chapter two? The most obvious conclusion is that some of the theories are more useful in some cases than in others. In fact, no one theory of decision-making has been shown to be the best in each case-study. We need to pause at this point and note that to some extent this is because each theory defines the issue and, critically, the evidence in a distinct way. Those who stress bureaucratic politics do not see issues in the same way as those who adopt an implementation perspective. The issue simply looks different, and, accordingly, there is no neutral body of evidence that can serve to arbitrate between rival theories. It is not as if we can use the evidence to tell us which theory is best because each theory picks on certain relationships within the decision-making process rather than others; accordingly, different pieces of evidence are more or less relevant. An implementation view, for example, sees the decision-making process in a completely different way from a bounded rationality view. For implementation theorists, the emphasis on decisions is mistaken, since what matters is not so much what policy-makers decide but rather what gets implemented; focusing on decisions ignores the fact that many decisions are 'taken' precisely because it is known that their implementation is unlikely.

Does this mean that we cannot choose between rival theories? Our view is that there are grounds for choice because of the existence of what philosophers of science call a meta-theory. Basically all this means is that there are criteria for choice that are not internal to each theory. The most obvious of these are the 'three Cs': coherence, consistency and comprehensiveness. By coherence we simply mean whether the account of decision-making contained in the theory provides a clearly argued and reasoned narrative. Consistency refers to the internal logic of a theory and the linkage between the theory and the external facts that it purports to explain. Comprehensiveness concerns the degree to which a theory can account for all the available evidence, and the issue of how much evidence it leaves unexplained. To these we might add the further criterion of parsimony, which simply refers to the economical nature of the explanation offered; for example all things being equal you would prefer a theory if it could explain all the things that other theories could explain, and more.

This last point brings us to the central issue in comparing the utility of the various theories we outlined in chapter two. Mentioning parsimony automatically makes us aware that the task in evaluating theories is relative rather than absolute. That is to say, we are not concerned with arguing that a specific theory is wrong or right; rather we are interested in how much a theory explains in comparison to the other theories. It is a question of more or less rather than yes or no. In the discussion that follows, we will base our judgements of what the case-studies tell us about the theories on the four criteria mentioned above. We do not have the space to go through each criterion in the case of each theory, but it is important that the reader has an idea of how we have come to the conclusions that follow. Our concern, in other words, is with evaluating how well the theories explain the behaviour we analyse in each case-study. It would be interesting for readers to retrace our steps, as it were, and see if they come to the same conclusions. The vital point to remember is that the task is not one of saying that such-and-such a theory has no utility, or complete utility, but rather that on grounds of coherence, consistency, comprehensiveness and parsimony, this theory has more explanatory utility than that theory.

Finally what of the tempting view that the way out is to combine the theories? This is very appealing, in that if bureaucratic politics explains this bit of a case-study, and the rational actor theory explains that part of the same case-study, then surely they simply need to be combined to get an overall account. But, like every simple solution, this one is fraught with serious difficulties. We do not have the space to go into this in great detail, particularly since the debate soon gets very deep and complex, but the three most obvious problems can at least be summarised. In the first place the theories focus on different aspects of the decision-making process, so that combining two accounts means combining two different starting points, and, accordingly, two different sets of criteria for what counts as evidence. Secondly, how does the observer know which of the theories accounts for which piece of behaviour? The observer would need to be omniscient, and it is surely possible to disagree over which theories explain which parts of behaviour. Finally, and most fundamentally, the different theories have mutually exclusive views of power and of the nature of social action and agency. This sounds complex, and it is, but suffice it to say that some of the theories see individual decision-makers as being able to make choices, whereas others see their behaviour as caused by the structures within which they have to operate. For example, a bureaucratic politics account cannot be combined with a rational actor account, even although Allison thought that they could, because the former sees actors as having their perceptions caused by their position within a bureaucracy, whereas the latter has no way of explaining the agenda within which actors have to operate. In the end, this comes down to a debate about power, and whether individuals are free to choose or whether they are conditioned. We disagree amongst ourselves as to where we line up on this debate, but we agree that combining accounts is usually done at the price of sacrificing coherence and consistency. If you are tempted to combine theories to obtain an overall account, be careful that you are not combining incompatible notions of action, power and the source of preferences within the same account. With these provisos, we can now look at the theories we discussed in chapter two. What do the case-studies tell us about the explanatory utility of each of them?

THE RATIONAL ACTOR MODEL

The central idea behind this theory is that actors make decisions on the basis of clear preferences, and after assessing the costs and benefits of the various alternatives for achieving these preferred outcomes. It is a means-end account, and one that is very popular with politicians when they describe or justify their actions. Our case-studies indicate that, virtually without exception, this theory is far removed from the actual practice of decision-making. Although any theory includes assumptions, and is, in part, an analytical device (saying, in effect, think of policy-making as if it was rational), the gap between the assumptions and reality is so vast here as to call the theory's coherence and consistency into question. The case-studies show that the synoptic ideal of rational choice was never the basis of policy. Decision-makers rarely had complete information, had conflicting preferences, and no clear idea of what results were likely to follow from any given policy option. In this light the rational actor theory bears little resemblance to the actual processes of decision-making.

At first glance AIDS would seem to provide an example of a policy area where the rational actor theory might be on fertile ground. Here was a 'problem' to which decision-makers consciously addressed themselves to seek 'solutions'. It was, furthermore, a 'new' problem unencumbered by the debris of past policies or constrained by existing commitments. Apart from the financial costs of any programme, it could be isolated from other policy concerns. However, our case-study reveals the shortcomings of the rational actor explanation. The clearest example is the AIDS case-study. Decision-makers never had enough information on the nature of the disease, on the likely means of transmission, or on the possible pattern of the disease's spread, to make any rational choice. Furthermore, the lack of information seemed not to be confined to the early stages of the problem; information, or rather the lack or ambiguity of it, has never been available to decision-makers in the way that the theory requires. More fundamentally, what exactly was the AIDS problem? Was it AIDS, HIV, the production of a vaccine, prevention of the spread of the disease – and if so, which was the most important group to target? Finally, there was no single AIDS policy, since various parts of the Government were involved in so many different bodies and organisations, hence coordinating the policies was a major problem. On detailed examination the AIDS case is as clear a case of the limitations of the rational actor account as it is possible to find. Reflect on the criteria for rational decision-making outlined by Arrow and Downs, cited in chapter two, and compare them to the decision-making process over AIDS. There was no one policy, no one goal, no consensus on the costs and benefits of the alternatives, and no one body making the decisions. But, critically, the information that the rational actor account deems essential was never unambiguous and was often contradictory. The adoption of one bit of information tended to reflect previous normative considerations about the nature of the disease and the culpability of those with it. In short, information was the problem, rather than the basis for the solution.

A similar pattern may be found in the other case-studies. Of course, there are examples of rational analysis in each case-study, and of attempts to link ends and means to costs and benefits. There are good examples in the case of the Falklands, since this was an issue that could be separated from the rest of the policy agenda. The policy options were indeed periodically examined by the FCO in the way suggested by the model. But the policy-making took place against the background of great uncertainties of information. The FCO never had the information to justify sending a naval group to forestall the invasion. Such were the departmental and other political constraints that the whole issue of the Falklands could not get onto the Cabinet's agenda after January 1982 until the very eve of the invasion. This shows the difficulty not only of defining problems but of getting things to a setting in which rational analysis is even possible. After invasion the goal was certainly relatively clear cut. However, even when the Task Force was sent it was by no means clear that the actual outcome (i.e. invading the islands and forcing the Argentinians to withdraw) was what the policy-makers had in mind. That linkage and logic was very much *ex post facto* rationalisation.

In all other areas, the theory is of little help. The case of the CSD again looks on the surface to favour the theory. This, after all, was an issue that was relatively uncontentious, politically; it was a case of reorganising within the government, thereby involving a very small set of actors; and it seemed to involve both a clear goal and clear preferences. The fact that the model does badly here is particularly interesting. Specifically, it proved very difficult to distinguish between and decide precisely what were the policy goals and, even more problematically, how to measure the outcomes. The Fulton Report appears to be a clear case of rational analysis, but much of its background research was skimped and its fate shows how rational plans run into trouble as soon as they have to be implemented. Essentially the CSD case shows that deciding what the goals are can be very complicated; goals, moreover, may involve clear contradictions and have a nasty tendency to change over time. It is one thing to want to reform the Civil Service in order to make it more efficient, but it is quite another to specify what that means in practice. Efficiency will be defined in terms of broader political outlooks or values.

Similarly, in the case of nuclear power, the evidence vividly illustrates the difficulties of obtaining the kind of information that the theory requires. It was impossible to ascertain reliable indicators of the costs and benefits of various reactor designs or even of various sources of energy. Similarly, even knowing what future energy requirements were, or what the decommissioning of reactors would cost, was more a statement of political faith and orientation than a matter of rational judgement. Rational choices were made over how to build the bomb and how to develop nuclear energy production, but in a manner much more consistent with the theory of bounded rationality than with this one.

Neither the Trident nor the trade union case-study shows much evidence of the use of the rational actor model. Again, of course, there are elements of rational choice (over, for example, the missile to replace Polaris, and the Thatcher Government's choice of policies for dealing with union power), but these fit much more within a bounded rationality perspective than a rational actor one. In each case, there was rarely one decision, never a single goal, and always a trade-off between competing pressures from distinct policy areas.

Is all of this too hard on the rational actor model? Surely you would have to be naïve to think that decisions get made in the sterile and precise way in which rational choice theorists suggest? Surely they know that in practice it is never this simple? Finally, is it possible to make decisions in any way other than by relying on some form of rational, means-end, choice? Suffice to say that we realise that rational choice theorists would never accept our stark version, and they would certainly want to deal with our objections. But two problems remain. First, this model is very popular in much contemporary political theory, and largely dominates economic theories of choice. Our version may be a simplification but it is not simplistic. More importantly, the second reason is that *in every case, politicians used the rational model to explain and justify their actions*. They presented their choices as ways of achieving clear goals, as based on 'the facts', often ones that we, the public, could not know or comprehend, and as being almost a matter of technical assessment rather than politics (that is to say, values). In each case, politicians justified their actions very much along the lines of 'we've considered the options, weighed up the costs and benefits of each, and the only way to proceed is as follows'. Our case-studies show that this was never the way in which it worked, and yet this is the picture you would get from watching the *Nine O'Clock News* or *News at Ten*.

We must stress that to abandon the rational actor account is not to dismiss the existence of any rational input into decision-making. Our conclusion is simply that the choices and procedures adopted by actors were very much less technical and rational than they like to imply. The choice of information considered was crucially affected by the values of the decision-makers, a notion that lies at the heart of the next theory we shall consider, that of bounded rationality.

BOUNDED RATIONALITY

Key elements of this theory were the notion of 'satisficing' and the difficulties of obtaining information. In this respect bounded rationality seems to us to be a considerable improvement on the rational actor model. In terms of our criteria for choice, it is more coherent, more consistent, more comprehensive, and more parsimonious.

In each case, the rationality of decision-makers was limited in precisely the way suggested by Herbert Simon. There was always more than one goal, information was never complete and unambiguous, and the balance between goals changed during the period under analysis. Since we have already outlined examples of bounded rationality in showing the limitations of the rational actor model, we need only to make general summary comments. Nuclear power shows perfectly how the choices that were made were based upon restricted information. Decisions about the type of reactors to be built were taken on the basis of little knowledge about the costs, and were circumscribed by very little information about alternatives. Critically, choices about nuclear power were always linked to at least two other policy issues, namely finance and the military nuclear programme. This was a perfect case of decision-makers satisficing.

In the case of the Falklands, there were severe problems of obtaining and filtering information. Galtieri was assumed to be behaving in much the same way as 'Western' leaders behaved; this ruled out a series of policy perceptions. The misinterpretation of signals coming from Argentina is a classic case of busy decision-makers satisficing a variety of policies in a situation of overloaded information. Finally, after the invasion, certain options were ruled out of the question because of the mind-sets and political convictions of decision-makers. There could be no rational review of all the alternatives.

A similar review of alternatives was also ruled out in the case of the CSD. Because of the nature of the British political system certain alternatives were simply non-starters. Specifically the doctrine of ministerial responsibility precluded several rational options for reform. Policy alternatives were always ranked in terms of their ability to contribute to the solving of other, often conflicting, policy goals.

The AIDS case has already been discussed in some detail; suffice it to say that limitations of knowledge and the intrusion of a variety of policy goals into what became AIDS policy represents a crystal-clear case of satisficing. In the two remaining cases, there are strong indications of the existence of bounded rationality. In the trade union study, we argued that legislation was always based on a specific, and very restricted, view of trade union–employer–government relations. Similarly, beliefs about the importance of unofficial strikes were central to the Wilson Government's attempts to reform unions, despite the fact that they represented a small proportion of the number of days lost. As we noted, if the problem really was the number of days lost, then research on the cause of the common cold would have been a better course of action. Finally in the case of Trident, the whole issue was based on a very restricted notion of Britain's place in the world. Having and modernising nuclear weapons was hardly an issue for those who made the decisions, whatever they had said in opposition. In short, the dominance of the view that Britain had to have nuclear weapons left the choice as one merely of which type Britain should have. Again, there was no question of a search amongst alternatives, nor was there ever a single policy or one decision. To repeat, rationality guided decisions, but the area within which that rationality was exercised was very restricted indeed.

DISJOINTED INCREMENTALISM

As we remarked in chapter two, disjointed incrementalism follows on logically from bounded rationality. The very notion of satisficing leads to the kind of switching between policies, and the type of incremental change, that we outlined in chapter two. The clearest example is in the chapter on Trident, where each decision in Britain's nuclear programme set the parameters for the next one. This was true throughout the post-war period, but was especially pronounced in the way in which Chevaline and Trident were dealt with. The rationale for Chevaline arose out of earlier policy failures, and these same problems were crucial in the way Trident was chosen.

In the case of trade unions, the way in which 'In Place of Strife' collapsed is a good example of disjointed incrementalism, whilst the history of attempts to reform the unions is a history of yesterday's failures leading to today's need for a decision. Policy lurched around with each attempt having more to do with a desire to get away from current social ills than with an idea of where policy should end up. Failures of policy resulted from the interaction between industrial relations policy and other, mainly economic, policies. This is a paradigmatic case of disjointed incrementalism.

The case of AIDS is similar. The earliest decisions, not surprisingly perhaps, were marked by policies of trial and error with no clear idea of where they were leading. The lack of information, combined with a conflicting set of goals, meant that early attempts to combat the spread of the disease were soon at odds with the Government's view of what information the public would accept. The case history is replete with examples of AIDS policy being affected by a variety of other policy considerations. The various stages of the publicity campaign revealed a very disjointed pattern especially as far as the choice of target groups was concerned. The sheer lack of information meant that the Government was often concerned to be seen as doing something, even if it was impossible to have a clear or consistent view of what to do. The rise of a worry that the disease was spreading into the heterosexual population resulted in a particularly disjointed shift in policy.

The nuclear power study also offers some good examples of policy being made in a disjointed incremental way. Perhaps the clearest is the way in which nuclear power policy was very responsive to changes in forecasts about future energy costs and needs. These fluctuated so greatly that they affected nuclear power policy in literally fundamental ways; two good examples are the impact of the oil-price rise in the aftermath of the 1973 Arab-Israeli War, which followed on from a very different set of estimated costs in the 1960s, and the impact of the Three-Mile Island incident of 1979. A similar pattern may be discerned in the way that privatisation of the electricity industry dealt with the issue of nuclear power stations. Finally, the selection of the AGR is another excellent example, both of how decisions get made and of how a decision once made affects subsequent decisions.

The Civil Service Department study indicates both the strength and the weakness of the model. On the one hand, the history of reforming the Civil Service is a history of other policy areas intruding to change that policy. Think of the impact of the 1981 Civil Service strike, the machinations within the Wilson Cabinet, or the effect of the miners' strike. In each case, policy over the Civil Service was altered because of outside events. However, the CSD example also shows that the model may well underplay the importance of ideas; the strategy of the Fulton Report, the reforms of the 1980s, and, especially, the Rayner reforms, were all part of a perceived view of the world, one which required policies to be justified in rationalistic terms, even if in practice they had elements of the random, short-term and political. Finally, the way in which the CSD was treated in 1981 is a strong example of disjointed incrementalism; in January 1981 Thatcher decided to keep the CSD, in November she abolished it because of her concern to end industrial unrest (especially in the Civil Service). In this way, reforming the Civil Service was never a discrete policy area, and was always affected by the interplay with other policy goals. These impacted in a very haphazard manner, with a consequent effect on the fate of the CSD and Civil Service reform.

There are few examples of disjointed incrementalism in the short period dealt with in our study of the Falklands issue. In essence this is simply because there was no real consideration of the issue, so that policy went on regardless of the signals that it was not working. After the invasion, there are interesting examples of how other areas affected policy over the Falklands. These include the effect of Carrington's relations with the Conservative back-benchers following the Rhodesia episode, the debate over defence cuts, and the implications of the Falklands issue on other British nationality debates. Note also that the goals involved in sending the Task Force were developed as the conflict developed; it was not a synoptic decision. Finally, the way in which options were foreclosed after 1965 both created a set of parameters within which policy-makers had to act, and led to the violent switch in policy that the invasion occasioned. There was no logical, rationally-deliberated policy; rather it was hostage to a variety of outside events.

ORGANISATIONAL PROCESS

There is significant overlap between this perspective and that dealing with implementation; indeed, Allison, whose work we summarised in chapter two as a way of introducing this approach, merged this model with his other alternative, bureaucratic politics, a year after his book on the Cuban Missile Crisis appeared. The organisational process model became the implementation half of the bureaucratic politics alternative to the rational actor model, with Allison's original bureaucratic politics model dealing with the decision-making half. Accordingly we will leave discussion of issues concerning implementation issues until the section specifically on that topic. All we will include here is a brief set of comments about what can be called organisational style, or the impact of the standard operating procedures by which organisations work.

It must be conceded that Allison clearly makes a major point when he argues that what the rational account calls policy is more accurately described as the uncoordinated output of different organisations, each working according to the book, or, in other words, following routines.

That neatly captures the way in which the FCO dealt with the Falklands issue until the point of invasion. They had a way of seeing it which gave it a specific priority, and which caused officials to discount warnings that an invasion was forthcoming. Events were fitted into the preconceived view of the problem. Having said which, this was not a view solely to be found in the FCO: politicians shared this view.

Similar comments are relevant in the case of the CSD. Here, the fact that Civil Service matters were the responsibility of both the Treasury and the CSD meant that, as we quote Sir Robert Armstrong as saying, it was easier to dodge the punches than if one department had oversight. Efficiency fell between the middle of two departments each with its specific routines. By 1979 the CSD had come to be seen as 'the department of the Civil Service'; it was therefore difficult for a government intent on radically shaking up the Civil Service to use the CSD as its instrument. It was easier by far to bypass it by developing the efficiency strategy from within the Cabinet Office. The other four case-studies offer glimpses of organisational routines, but in no case were these routines critical to the outcome of policy. Certainly, AIDS policy-making was affected by the routines and procedures of the organisations involved, and the history of the nuclear power programme involved distinct Department of Energy and UKAEA procedures. But on grounds of parsimony, this perspective is not particularly powerful in aiding our explanation of how decisions get made.

BUREAUCRATIC POLITICS

This theory, neatly summed up by the aphorism 'where you stand depends on where you sit' is, in our view, one of the most powerful explanations of decision-making. The case-studies are literally full of examples of where decisions resulted from the bargaining between bureaucracies, with the Cabinet often the political setting where these battles were fought out.

In the case of nuclear power, the various organisations were essentially advocates for different policies, or reactor types. Policy emerged out of compromises between a number of involved ministries, with the key determinant being the relative power of the bureaucracies involved. The case-study also nicely captures the way in which the views of individuals are determined by their bureaucratic position, and how these change when individuals change position. Above all, the choice of the AGR was a perfect illustration of the impact of bureaucratic politics.

In the Falklands example, bureaucratic politics was clearly at work in the reasons why the Navy advocated the dispatch of a full Task Force; it was a way of demonstrating the need for a larger Navy than had been envisaged in the 1981 defence review. Moreover, the different ministries had different interests in the Falklands, with the effect that Falklands policy, especially before the invasion, was not the sole responsibility of the FCO. Rather the Ministry of Defence, the Overseas Development Agency, the Home Office and the Treasury all had an input into policy. In this sense it is important to note that sending the Task Force was in part a compromise between competing bureaucratic interests; its *ex post facto* rationalisation, that it was to fight the Argentinians in order to regain control of the islands, was only one of the reasons for sending it.

The CSD case shows clearly that one of the key problems facing the CSD was the battle between it and the Treasury over who ran the Civil Service. The fact that this came to a head during 1980, notably in the letters column of *The Times*, just when the future of the CSD was being decided, was crucial to the eventual fate of the Department. That it was not merged with the Treasury was largely because of the reluctance of Treasury officials and Ministers to deal with Civil Service issues other than pay. The earlier fate of the Fulton Report shows a similar tendency, especially amongst ministers, for their views on Civil Service reform to be directly determined by their other bureaucratic interests. Finally, the study clearly indicated the extent of the bureaucratic struggle between the Rayner efficiency unit and the CSD; its head was said to be fighting for his department.

In the AIDS case, the power of the medical profession and its associated bureaucratic sponsors meant that treatment was the first response to the emergence of the disease. Throughout the case-study, the medical profession is the dominant source of expertise in decision-making; this resulted in the exclusion of gay groups from the policy process. The case-study also shows how bureaucratic wrangles between the Home Office and the DHSS and between the DHSS and the DES determined the direction of policy in critical ways. Note as well how clinicians, not health educationalists, were the main actors in the policy process. Finally, there is the surprising revelation that the DHSS deliberately concentrated on the threat to the heterosexual population in order to get the Government to act; this was a clear case of a bureaucracy pushing a specific line so as to alter the rational consensus.

The clearest example in the study on trade unions was how Barbara Castle used the consultation process to build bureaucratic support for her proposals. In the case of Trident, bureaucratic battles were very heated when it came to whether the successor to Polaris should be sea- or air-based. Making it air-based would have involved removing from the Royal Navy one of the most prestigious roles, and was therefore fought against very strongly.

BELIEF-SYSTEMS

The idea that the impact of information is determined by the relationship between that information and the values that make up the core beliefs of decision-makers is amply supported in the case-studies. We have already commented that there was an FCO way of dealing with the Falklands, and the existence of a shared belief-system is the best explanation of both why that existed and what its effects were. Not only did the shared belief-system lead to the ignoring of what in hindsight seemed obvious signals that an invasion was being planned, but it also explains why the withdrawal of HMS *Endurance* was not seen in the same way as it was in Buenos Aires. Note also how the FCO view was responsible for the low-key response to the landing on South Georgia; if you believed that the Argentinian plan was to increase pressure gradually so as to culminate in a solution before the 150th anniversary of the British occupation of the islands (January 1983), then you did not expect an invasion before this pressure had built up. A slow escalatory process was what was expected, and was therefore what FCO officials and ministers saw right up to the invasion.

Decisions over nuclear power show the central role of belief-systems. In each decision examined, the issue was not whether Britain should develop nuclear power, but rather what type of, and how many, reactors should be built. The insiders shared the view that nuclear power plants were necessary, so that discussions of an energy gap and of the detailed costings were all interpreted in this light. This is a graphic illustration of how beliefs about what should be the case determine the effect of evidence about what is the case. Similarly, in the case of the Trident decision, all those involved shared the fundamental belief that Britain was, and should remain, a nuclear power. The need for a nuclear deterrent was never discussed, and indeed was not included in the terms of reference of the House of Commons Defence Committee enquiry. Replacing Polaris was simply the 'natural' thing to do, as was developing it in cooperation with the US. Finally, note how there were powerful lessons from past policy failures, and the effect of these on the belief-systems of decision-makers determined both the original choice of Trident and the subsequent choice of D5 rather than C4.

The AIDS case-study has some excellent examples of the impact of belief-systems on decision-making. Beliefs about morality influenced both initial policy responses and what it was thought government should do in the way of the dissemination of information. The problem of AIDS was defined in a way that reflected strong views about the role of the family and of the acceptability of homosexual behaviour. The original view was that this was a self-inflicted disease, and this view changed only very slowly. The lack of sympathy for the first group of sufferers was important in determining the nature of the Government's response, and it is noticeable that the major change in the direction of policy only comes after there is a proven threat to the heterosexual community. As long as AIDS could be seen as a 'gay plague' the continuation of a policy stressing cure rather than prevention was possible. Mentioning condoms, or the dangers of sharing needles, that is to say a concern with prevention, only occurs when the established beliefs about the risk groups are shattered.

There is less evidence to support the belief-systems theory about decision-making from the CSD study, probably because it was much less overtly political. Nonetheless, decision-makers shared a set of assumptions about the role of the Civil Service in the political system, and most protagonists in the policy debates used a common set of terms. These ruled out a whole host of possibilities for reform; they were not part of the agenda because of a prior perception of the role, functions and problems of the Civil Service. The 'Whitehall Village' kept outsiders at a distance, although the years after 1979 show the impact of new outside ideas breaking through.

The chapter on trades unions shows nicely how belief-systems define a problem; remember how Wilson saw the number of wild-cat strikes as the cause of his Government's low standing in the opinion polls. Throughout the period dealt with in the chapter, the problem is always defined as 'the unions'. The evidence about the relative strike rate of Britain was simply not important. Thatcher came to power, in the aftermath of the 'Winter of Discontent', promising to do something to reduce the power of the unions, and this belief that something had to be done coloured her Government's perception of the evidence. The whole issue of trade union reform is a perfect example of beliefs about a problem acting as a powerful filter on the receipt of information.

SMALL GROUP DECISION-MAKING

We discussed this in chapter two mainly in regard to Irving Janis's concept of groupthink, that is the tendency of small groups to make decisions uncritically and in the belief of unanimity because of a desire to maintain amiability and ultimately membership of the group. Our case-studies reveal few examples of this, probably because most decisions were not made by small groups. Groupthink seems best suited to explaining the behaviour of very small groups dealing with a crisis. As such the best example comes from the Falklands study, where the degree of unanimity amongst the key Cabinet members was almost certainly the result of groupthink. The meeting of the group addressed by Admiral Leach on 31 March 1982 seems to have been particularly affected by group dynamics. Although not discussed in detail in the case-study, the decision to sink the *General Belgrano* seems to have been a classic groupthink decision, based on a clear sense of moral superiority, and without outward dissent.

The only other examples occur in the case of nuclear power, with the decision to build the first atomic bomb, and, more obviously still, in the decision-making groups involved in the modernisation of the British nuclear deterrent. In the latter case it is particularly noticeable that some of the participants have now admitted that they had doubts. No one is more interesting in this regard than Denis Healey, who was involved in the original 1964–70 Labour Government decision-making group on Polaris, and was then involved in both the Chevaline and the Trident decisions. To go by his later accounts, he did not want to go along with the decisions, but felt that he was the only dissenter; this is exactly the picture of groupthink that Janis paints. In fact, the AIDS and trades unions case-studies also illustrate the way in which Prime Ministers set up small committees to deal with awkward policy issues, and then rely on the *esprit de corps* of these groups to form a united policy stance that the full Cabinet can only challenge with difficulty.

IMPLEMENTATION

The contribution that this approach can make to the study of decision-making in British politics is, on the basis of these case-studies, quite considerable. By looking not at what decision-makers intended but at what behaviour actually gets implemented, the perspective reverses our view of the policy process, thereby forcing us to ask a rather different set of questions.

The clearest example where implementation mattered is that of the CSD. The problem was that the idea of a CSD was never simply one thing to all groups involved. It looked a relatively simple and unambiguous proposal, but, critically, it relied on affected groups for its implementation. Not surprisingly, the role of the CSD looked very different to its creators (who were concerned with reform) than it did to those in the Civil Service responsible for its implementation (who saw it as more to do with image). The history of the CSD is in essence one of the difficulty of ensuring political control over administrative reform. Mrs Thatcher succeeded where Wilson failed primarily because she sited the efficiency unit in the Cabinet Office and not within the Civil Service itself. Indeed, one might argue that the failure of the Fulton Report to deal with issues such as ministerial responsibility was itself an attempt to link the implementation process to a specific outcome. As long as these areas were excluded, the report could not fundamentally reform the Civil Service.

Implementing AIDS policy was also problematic. This was primarily because it was difficult to coordinate policy in the face of so many uncertainties and areas of ignorance. Furthermore, the central problem of a policy stressing prevention was that the success of implementation was outside governmental control. In essence AIDS policy was all about implementation. The success of the policy depended on what individuals did with regard to sexual and drug-related behaviour, and so implementation was carried out by actors outside the governmental arena.

Trade union reform was similarly thwarted, at least in the Wilson and Heath administrations, by difficulties in implementation. The revolt of the unions was enough to prevent implementation, whereas, in the Thatcher case, the unions had been weakened to such an extent that they could not act as a barrier to implementation. From 1966–79, then, the picture is of governments deciding what to do, but being unable to implement their decisions. The fate of the 1971 Industrial Relations Act is the clearest example of this general feature.

Nuclear power is an interesting case because implementing decisions required agencies other than the Department of Energy. Moreover, the fact that the lead-time in constructing nuclear plants is about fifteen years meant that very different sets of people took and implemented decisions. Furthermore, as implementation proceeded the escalation of costs was so great that many plans had to be halted. The entire process of implementation was based on powerful consortia who oversaw projects from design to decommissioning.

In the Falklands, the original 1965 decision to negotiate a settlement ran into severe problems of implementation, and the 'policy of seduction' ran into similar problems. Government was never able to control the implementation process, a feature that became even more problematic after the invasion, when implementing decisions had to be carried out in an Economic Community and a US framework. In both cases successful implementation depended on resources outside the control of the FCO.

Finally, the Trident decision had few problems of implementation, although this had not been the case with earlier nuclear weapons decisions. In the cases of Blue Streak, Skybolt and Chevaline, implementation proved problematic, and in two cases impossible. It is interesting to note that Trident survived the 1981 defence cuts because it would have been impossible to scale back something so significant when it had only been decided on a year previously. Nonetheless, the recent history of British nuclear weapons decisions is one of very successful implementation. Cost overruns, however, have made the original estimates of costs seem unduly optimistic. One is left wondering whether Chevaline would have been developed had the true cost of its implementation been known.

THE SABATIER MODEL

We will only make general comments on the applicability of Sabatier's model of decision-making to the British context, because it is a complex attempt to integrate several of the perspectives discussed previously. But broadly speaking, the model seems to be of little use in the case of the Falklands, where there was really no advocacy coalition to speak of. In the other cases it has more relevance. In the CSD case there are never really competing advocacy coalitions, nor are the belief-systems as tight as they are in Sabatier's examples. Although Civil Service issues are related to broader ideological concerns, it is not clear that they correspond to Sabatier's categories of rival explanations of a causal connection in the way that applied in his case-study of clean air. The Rayner reforms seem a good example of the impact of an advocacy coalition getting its beliefs adopted as policy.

His approach seems appropriate to examining the ways in which decisions got made in the cases of nuclear power, AIDS, and trade unions. There were clear advocacy coalitions in each case, and in the case of trade unions, there were, as Sabatier suggests, relatively stable groupings over time. Identifying policy-brokers is more difficult, with maybe the Department of Energy serving as a good example in the nuclear power case, and the DHSS or the Cabinet group in the AIDS case. The Trident case seems less amenable to his model, since there were never really advocacy coalitions nor power brokers.

The evidence suggests that Sabatier's model is worth further detailed examination. However, our case-studies suggest that it may be more applicable to the US than to the British system of government. We will simply note our main reservations. Firstly, the approach is too much based on a US view of the policy-making process. The British system is not as fluid nor as pluralistic as is the American system. Secondly, the approach seems to face problems when it comes to explaining change, and change was a vital ingredient in the Falklands, AIDS and CSD cases. Thirdly, the model is based on a US system in which there is considerable interchange between individuals in different institutions. Such a pattern is not found in Britain to the same extent. Fourthly, there is a tendency to underestimate the theory-dependency of knowledge; it may not be able to play as neutral a role as Sabatier suggests. Finally, and most importantly, the model cannot account either for why certain advocacy coalitions have the views they do, or for why some views come to prominence rather than others. Linking belief-systems to knowledge by the concept of rationality may well explain why certain policies are rational within a given belief-system, but it does not explain where this linking rationality and the belief-systems come from.

MODELS OF THE BRITISH POLITICAL SYSTEM

Having spent some time discussing how far the case-studies support or undermine the various theories of decision-making we outlined in chapter two we will now turn our attention to the contents of chapter three, albeit far more briefly. What do the case-studies tell us about the various models of the British political system?

Democratic sovereignty seems to do rather badly as a model of the system. It was not an explanation of policy in the case of CSD, whilst in the AIDS case its influence was limited to cross-party pressures on government. The Trident case is an excellent example of the limitations of democratic sovereignty in Britain. The case-study shows clearly just how little Parliament could influence the policy. Similarly, the nuclear power case shows how parliamentary control was limited by the secrecy of policy-making. Public Inquiries were never more than legitimising devices; after all, the objectors could only prove the CEGB and the UKAEA wrong ten years later! The model does a little better in the case of the Falklands, where the attention paid to public opinion made it an important factor as the crisis developed. Similarly, the role of Parliament as a pressure on government was important, certainly in foreclosing certain options. Finally, the trade union case shows how public opinion can be used to justify policy; Wilson, and especially Thatcher, used the public's worry over the 'union problem' to justify their policies. Note also how Heath claimed a mandate for reform following the collapse of 'In Place of Strife'. Nevertheless, the overall picture is one of public control being very limited indeed. Of course, we must stress that our version of the democratic sovereignty argument is one that practitioners would see as naïve, but our point is simply that the official view of how policy gets made in Britain bears no relationship to the actual dynamics of the process.

Neither the party government nor the adversarial politics models are very helpful in explaining the policies covered in the case-studies. The models are of some use in the trade union case, with the Conservative Party's concern for legislation being an important pressure on both the Heath and Thatcher Governments. There were clear signs of adversarial politics at work with Wilson's desire to pre-empt Heath over union legislation, and with both Heath's response to the failure of 'In Place of Strife' and Thatcher's reaction to the 'Winter of Discontent'. In the Trident example, adversarial politics was at work with the Labour leadership's desire to keep nuclear decision-making secret, because public knowledge of its activities would have split the party. The same example, though, offers a superb study of the ineffectiveness of the party government model; policies over nuclear weapons were never altered significantly by a change of government, even when this was in complete contradiction to election manifesto commitments. The 1964–70 and 1974–9 Labour Governments are as good examples of this as you could hope to find. In the case of AIDS, although there is some evidence that rising public concerns could have led to government policy initiatives prior to the 1987 election, the overwhelming picture is that this was an area that did not really split the parties. There was no real political capital attached to the issue, and so neither model applies. In the CSD example, although there was a change of emphasis over how to reform the Civil Service between the 1964 and 1979 administrations, the overriding concern with improving efficiency was shared by both parties. This was never an issue that was important in the party government or adversarial politics senses. In the Falklands case, the models were similarly unimportant, with the important proviso that adversarial politics may explain why the Labour Party reacted as it did, thereby foreclosing government options. This reaction made it impossible politically for Thatcher not to act decisively. Similar events sank both the 1968 Stewart and the 1980 Ridley initiatives. The party government model does especially badly here, since the issues remained unchanged despite three changes of government. Finally, our case-study of nuclear power suggests that neither model can explain policy in this area. Both Labour and Conservative Governments did essentially the same things when in government, again despite their election commitments.

Our case-studies suggest that there is no easy generalisation to be made concerning the value of the Cabinet government model. The Falklands, after the invasion, showed the Cabinet working in almost classic manner as a coordinating force with all the key decisions devolved to subordinate subcommittees. AIDS policy also provides evidence of the ways in which diverse ministerial and departmental interests were brought together to forge a common policy. However, in both cases coordination emerged as a response to what participants saw as crisis conditions, where there was an element of emergency involving unknown factors. The story of the Falklands before the invasion is one of a failure of Cabinet government. The Defence and Oversea Committee of the Cabinet was the forum in which final policy decisions on the Falklands were made, but in the months up to April 1982 there was insufficient information or political will to get the issue on to the political agenda. The Trident case-study shows the way in which the Cabinet and other governmental committees can be manipulated to exclude full consideration of an issue at the Cabinet level. The Cabinet had scarcely more input into the policy process than Parliament on the governing party; its role being rather to legitimate decisions which were made elsewhere. Similarly the story of nuclear power demonstrates the primacy of departmental (and agency) interests. The early history of trade union legislation shows how difficult it was for a Prime Minister to get his way against the wishes of party and interest groups, but clearly the political salience of the issues raised by trade union reform meant that the Cabinet and its committees played an important role. The CSD shows little evidence to support the theory of Cabinet government, although it does reveal the power of the Prime Minister to initiate reforms, although their implementation is quite a different matter.

Theories which stress the departmentalised nature of Whitehall and of bureaucratic dispersion make a good deal of sense in connection with our case-studies. Such theories go well with the general model of bureaucratic politics and we have already noted some of the numerous examples of competing departmental interests fighting each other. Nuclear power and nuclear weapons show one clear instance of individual departments having primacy in the decision-making process. The Falklands, AIDS and the CSD case-studies all lend some credence to the segmented decision model in so far as they display examples of policy swiftly being elevated from the routine and bureaucratic arena to the special segment where the Prime Minister's initiative and say was important. In the case of the CSD it was Mrs Thatcher's own concern with Civil Service matters and efficiency reforms which resulted in the Rayner efficiency unit being located in the Cabinet Office and thus susceptible to her close direction and support.

The policy network or policy community model does well in explaining policies in our case-studies. Although different in certain respects, as we outlined in chapter three, these are broadly similar models. They are of much less use in two examples, the CSD and the Falklands. The CSD was never more than an essentially internal matter, so there could be no extensive policy network. Academics were kept out of any say in policy-making, and the unions involved were really only consulted. The individuals who were involved in the Fulton Report were clearly part of a wider policy community, but there is no real sense in which there was an extensive network or effective community. In the Falklands case, the only policy community was the Falkland Islands' lobby. This exercised a negative effect upon policy-making, being resistant to the policy lines of the Foreign Office. The difficulty experienced by the Foreign Office in pursuing an economic development policy in the islands illustrates the difficulties of pursuing initiatives in the absence of a policy community that was cooperative. When it came to the crisis itself, the decision-making process was closed to outside influences.

The other four examples show the importance of policy communities. In the cases of AIDS and nuclear power the model is particularly useful. AIDS policy was significantly influenced by the make-up of the policy community, with the overlapping communities based on the DHSS and the Home Office forming the pressure groups within the decision-making process. The dominance of the medical policy network was critical in determining the way in which the problem was defined and how it was to be dealt with. Nuclear power is probably the strongest example of this model at work. In effect, the policy network made policy. Disputes were resolved within that community, with the UKAEA being the centre of a major pressure group for a specific nuclear policy and a particular type of reactor. The policy network comprised people who all assumed that nuclear power was needed, and since it was this group which determined policy, then the entire policy community was one large pressure group for nuclear power. The Trident example also shows how a small policy network made policy. The network was very small indeed, with few involved outside government circles. But note the role played by Ian Smart of the Royal Institute of International Affairs in publicising the need for a decision, and in outlining the options. This was a clear case of a small policy network being in the forefront of preparing élite opinion for a decision. Finally, the trade union example shows the important role played by the policy community, although in this case the Sabatier notion of advocacy coalitions is probably more useful, since the Labour and Conservative Parties had their distinct communities. Critical to any Labour attempt to reform the unions was the power within the Labour Party of the union movement, and the need for some consensus within that policy community, hence the nature of the consultations for 'In Place of Strife'; the absence of this link enabled the Conservatives to act with much freer hands.

Pirie's model seems very useful in one case, CSD, of a little use in one other example, trade unions, but wholly inapplicable to the other four. The activities of small groups determined to end the closed shop, and to make unions more democratic is a good example of the Pirie view of decision-making. The best example is that of the Rayner scrutinies and the subsequent development of the efficiency strategy. Here the model could not fit better.

Finally, we should say something about the New Right and Marxist accounts. These are such general theories, dealing more with the direction of the political system than with the decision-making process over individual policies, that neither illuminates the actual processes we have been examining. They would both say little about the CSD case, although they would share a conviction that the Civil Service is too autonomous and too little under public control. In the nuclear power case, both would agree that only the state can promote nuclear power, but whereas the New Right would stress the importance of market considerations, Marxists would point to the role of nuclear power in supporting specific economic interests; they would also note that one aim of nuclear power policy was to undermine the industrial power of electricity workers and miners. With regards to AIDS, the New Right was concerned primarily about the degree to which the Government should be involved in what were properly individual choices about life-style, whilst Marxist writers point to the influence of the medical establishment and the pharmaceutical companies in determining AIDS policy. The Falklands was seen by Marxists in terms of Britain's imperial past, the prospects of resources in the Antarctic and the ability of the ruling classes to mobilise popular support on national rather than class issues. Trident was interpreted by the New Right as a necessary symbol of British power, although some questioned whether the money could not be better spent and whether the ties to the US might not reduce British autonomy. From a Marxist perspective, the issue merely showed how the military industrial complex operated, and how important it was for Britain to retain the semblance of great power status; they, too, worried about the link to the US. The best case-study for both arguments is the trade union case. For the New Right, the failure of the Heath and Wilson initiatives was due to the corporate power of the unions. A central concern for the New Right was that union power had to be broken if the British economy was to be regenerated. Not surprisingly, Marxists saw the problem very differently; their point was that capitalism required the weakening of the union movement in a period of technical transformation and decreasing profits.

Dunleavy's development of these structuralist and materialist accounts of British politics can be supported by a number of the case-studies. At the general level, they confirm his point that no one interpretation or theory will capture what really happened. Equally, his claims about the way in which interests and relations are structures within the state are also given credence. In the case of AIDS, for example, we noticed how certain types of patient were identified (haemophiliacs being separated from homosexuals) in order to produce different types of solution. We saw, too, how in each case-study knowledge and expertise were defined in ways which allowed them to fit the dominant interests within the policy process. Finally, each case-study demonstrated that the relations between government and other institutions was not fixed – either across policy areas or within them.

The great strength of these arguments is that they force us to shift our attention from the details of specific decisions to the general direction of policy within the political system. Moreover, they make us aware of the need to widen our definition of policy-making; in particular they challenge our definition of the boundary of politics in Britain. This is because structuralist and materialist accounts see politics as more closely linked to economics than the detailed models of the policy process suggest. In so doing, they force us to rethink our notion of power in society. Put simply, an examination of decision-making models may be interesting but maybe the shared beliefs of decision-makers and the bureaucratic structure of the decision-making process merely enable certain economic considerations to remain outside politics, and immune to the kind of analysis that we have been dealing with in this book. We will return to this concern presently, but we now need to say something about the changing context of the British policy-making process.

The major change that we wish to point to is that represented by the increasing integration of Britain within the EC and OECD (Organisation for Economic Cooperation and Development) context. The British economy is now structurally interdependent with the other OECD economies, and the EC is often the dominant setting for many areas of policy-making and implementation. This means that throughout the 1990s the picture of the British decision-making process that we have painted will change in the following ways.

First, the distinction between domestic and foreign policy is becoming increasingly blurred. Much British policy now involves the EC and this will increase after 1992 and with any economic and monetary union. One important consequence of this trend is that the FCO will cease to be the main actor in external policy-making. Moreover, the very fact of having to make policy within an EC context will mean that other ministries will increasingly develop linkages with their counterparts in other EC member states. Alliances will build up, so that British officials in, say, the Ministry of Agriculture may see their friends as their German or French counterparts and their enemies as their own colleagues in the Treasury. By the end of the decade, it is likely that the notion of national policy-making will be fast becoming outmoded in many areas of British politics.

Second, the distinction between economics and politics is becoming increasingly less clear cut, although Marxist writers would argue that it never was clear cut at all. The point is that there is no longer a set of high political issues concerning questions such as defence, foreign policy, law and order, and education, and a set of low issues dealing with economics and social policy. Economic issues are increasingly central, and are inevitably political and controversial. This exacerbates the blurring of the distinction between foreign and domestic policy, and makes the EC setting even more important.

Third, the decision-making setting is becoming increasingly more complex, specifically with regards to the number of actors involved within governmental structures. More bodies are involved in decision-making than before, with the EC being the clearest example of the cross-national and international nature of these bodies. Moreover, pressure groups are becoming more transnational, so that the entire policy community for a given policy area now involves a wider variety of groups located in an increasing number of national settings. Policy communities, in short, are becoming more international, with Brussels and Strasborg being as much their focal points as London.

Fourth, the widening of the policy community and the expansion of actors involved in the policy process means that it is becoming more and more difficult for governments to coordinate policy. There are twin pressures of centralisation and specialisation, and the Cabinet system certainly seems unable to cope with the conflict between these. The British political system has always been well suited to muddling through, because the Whitehall system is particularly good at ensuring bureaucratic compromises. Coordinating policy, especially in new areas, is becoming more difficult precisely because the policy community, and even the policy-making process itself, has widened, often outside the boundaries of the British state. This is, in part, a matter of the style of government, and the obvious contrast is between the British style of public administration and that of most of Britain's partners in the EC. This clash is particularly well illustrated by the differing British and Continental viewpoints on what 1992 means and how to legislate for it.

Fifth, and as a consequence of the preceeding points, it is becoming increasingly difficult for the British Government to monitor and ensure the implementation of policy. Implementation is now, more than ever, spread amongst a number of channels and actors, at a set of international, transnational, national and subnational levels; furthermore, the tools for implementing policy have broadened. The result is that it may be impossible for decision-makers in London to follow up effectively on implementation, especially since much of that policy has to be implemented in Brussels or in other EC countries.

Sixth, the result is that Britain seems to be losing effective control over many policy areas, since both policy-making and implementation are not strictly national in character. Meanwhile, of course, the domestic political debate continues to take place in terms of national sovereignty, which creates the picture of a much more national process than is the case. This gap has already been indicated by the failure of Mrs Thatcher to get her way in EC matters in the same way as she did in Britain. The problem is that the language of debate, which suggests that sovereignty is indivisible, is massively at variance with the reality, in which the key is no longer notional sovereignty, but effective sovereignty.

This relatively new phenomenon of structural interdependence within the EC–OECD setting looks likely to make rational policy-making even more difficult; to increase the explanatory power of bureaucratic politics and implementation approaches; to weaken still further the democratic sovereignty argument; and to increase considerably the importance of EC-wide policy networks in a wide range of policy areas. The fluidity of the new European political structures and the decentralised nature of the policy process may also offer more scope for Sabatier's theory of advocacy coalitions than does the post-war British political system. This is not to deny the importance of the other theories and models that we have discussed in some areas of decision-making, merely to try and indicate how the trends in the context of British decision-making seem likely to affect the relative explanatory utility of the theories and models dealt with in chapters two and three.

What do the findings of our case-studies and the changing context of British decision-making tell us about democracy? Not surprisingly, given the main findings of our case-studies, we feel that the democratic sovereignty, party government and adversarial politics models of the British political system are too simplistic to explain decision-making in the areas we looked at. Other models of the British system, specifically policy communities and policy networks were more parsimonious. Similarly, rational accounts were less parsimonious than bureaucratic politics, implementation and belief-systems accounts. Astute readers will have already noted that there is a clear connection between these two sets of findings; policy communities and networks are precisely the models of a political system that are implied by bureaucratic politics, implementation and belief-systems approaches. Conversely, but instructively, democratic sovereignty accounts of a political system link well with rational theories of decision-making. Interestingly, this conclusion seems to make further study of the applicability of Sabatier's model to be worthwhile, since the linkage we have noted between the most parsimonious decision-making theories and the most parsimonious models of the British political process are similar to the linkage that he sees as applicable to the US case.

As far as democracy is concerned, the most important lesson from the case-studies is that the formal political system was rarely of any importance in the decision-making process; the only possible exception is trade union reform, but even there Parliament played a very minor role. Another of our findings is that the factors which did influence policy were rarely subject to public control. This paints a picture of a heavily constrained British government, with policies emerging out of the interplay of policy communities and bureaucratic forces. When decisions are taken, our studies indicate that implementation is particularly difficult. This is no minor point, despite the fact that most accounts of the British political system treat implementation as an afterthought, the failure of which is then seen as somewhat surprising. Problems of implementation are exactly what a policy community model and bureaucratic politics theories imply. Implementation is not a less important stage in the policy-making process than the taking of decisions itself; rather it is of equal importance in the policy process. Finally, it is just as political as is making decisions.

Our main conclusion is simple. The popular official picture of decision-making in British politics is a very poor guide to how decisions get made in practice. Once made decisions have to be implemented, and we have shown that this is neither automatic nor does it always occur in the way those that made the decisions intended. The emphasis placed on the role of Parliament in many institutional, media and academic accounts seems particularly unrealistic. The adversarial style of Parliament seems far removed from the way in which decisions get taken within government, so that the view of political life that most citizens receive rarely deals with the realities, as distinct from the atmospherics, of decision-making. To repeat a critical qualifier: we know that the official institutional view we have presented would not be the one that most practitioners would accept. They would accuse us of setting up a straw figure in order to be able easily to demolish it. Our point is that the emphasis on Parliament, especially with regard to notions such as representation and accountability, tells us very little about decision-making; the strength of party discipline reduces still further any role that it could have. Explaining policy in the areas we have looked at seems barely to involve Parliament at all. Yet this is supposedly the centrepiece of our democratic system of government.

Finally, we do not want to suggest that the picture we have painted is unconnected to the world of ideas and power. We do not think that the constraints on government are neutral, nor do we see bureaucratic forces as fixed. Ideas matter. Very often these ideas are themselves the justification of particular sets of interests. Politics is about the clash of competing interests. Parties win power because they are voted into office, and winning power gives them some kind of mandate for bringing in certain policies rather than others. The decision-making process may well be similar whatever the government in power, and there may well be a bipartisan consensus over major policy areas, but we should stress in conclusion that decision-making models are essentially to do with questions of *how* policies get made. The question of *what* policies get made is where ideas and power combine. To explain decision-making in British politics you need both to account for how decisions get made and for the direction in which policies are moving. This book has hopefully helped with the first of these concerns, but in the final analysis we are only too aware that politics is about interests, ideas and power as much as it is about the details of policy communities and bureaucratic structures. In short, our study of decision-making ends by raising the question of what it means to say that Britain is a democracy.

Notes

1 INTRODUCTION

1 C. Hughes, *The Times*, 25 March 1985.
2 W. Bagehot, *The English Constitution*, with introduction by R.H.S. Crossman, London, Collins, 1963, p. 59.
3 Compare S.H. Beer, *Modern British Politics: A Study of Parties and Pressure Groups*, London, Faber & Faber, 1965 with S.H. Beer, *Britain Against Itself*, London, Faber & Faber, 1982.
4 Sir G. Vickers, *The Art of Judgement*, London, Chapman and Hall, 1965, p. 173.

2 THEORIES OF DECISION-MAKING

1 A. Downs, *An Economic Theory of Democracy*, New York, Harper & Row, 1957, p. 6.
2 W. Bagehot, *The English Constitution*, London, Collins, 1963, p. 67.
3 P. Self, *Administrative Theories and Policies. An Enquiry into the Structure and Process of Modern Government*, London, Allen & Unwin, 1972, p. 212.
4 Friends of the Earth, *Capital Schemes. The Department of Transport and Road Schemes in London*, London, Friends of the Earth, 1987, p. 43.
5 H. Simon, *Administrative Behavior*, 2nd edn, New York, Free Press, 1958.
6 M. Oakeshott, *Rationalism in Politics*, London, Methuen, 1962, pp. 81–3, 95–7.
7 Simon, op. cit., p. 241.
8 Sir G. Vickers, *The Art of Judgement*, London, Chapman and Hall, 1965, p. 36, *et seq.*
9 D. Braybrooke and C. Lindblom, *A Strategy of Decision*, New York, Free Press, 1963, p. 71.
10 Ibid., p. 67.
11 See also C. Lindblom, *The Policy Making Process*, Englewood Cliffs, Prentice-Hall, 1968.
12 Braybrooke and Lindblom, op. cit., p. 71.
13 C. Lindblom, 'The science of muddling through', *Public Administration Review*, 1959, vol. 19, pp. 79–88.

14 C. Lindblom, 'Still muddling, not yet through', *Public Administration Review*, 1979, vol. 39, pp. 516, 523.
15 Y. Dror, 'Muddling through – science or inertia', *Public Administration Review*, 1964, vol. 24, p. 155.
16 G. Allison, *Essence of Decision*, Boston, Little Brown, 1971.
17 E. Bridges, *Portrait of a Profession*, Cambridge, Cambridge University Press, 1951.
18 *The Times*, 15 November 1976.
19 R. Crossman, *The Diaries of a Cabinet Minister*, London, Hamish Hamilton and Jonathan Cape, 1975, vol. 1, pp. 24–5.
20 B. Castle, *The Castle Diaries 1964–70*, London, Weidenfeld & Nicholson, 1984.
21 For a survey of the criticisms of Allison's work, see S. Smith, 'Allison and the Cuban missile crisis', *Millennium*, 1981, vol. 9, no. 1, pp. 21–40.
22 B. Jenkins and A. Gray, 'Bureaucratic politics and power: developments in the study of bureaucracy', *Political Studies*, 1983, vol. 31, no. 2, pp. 177–93.
23 K. Boulding, *The Image*, Ann Arbor, University of Michigan Press, 1956.
24 R. Jervis, 'Hypotheses on misperception', *World Politics*, 1968, vol. 20, pp. 454–79.
25 I. Janis, *Victims of Groupthink*, Boston, Houghton-Mifflin, 1972.
26 J. Pressman and A. Wildavsky, *Implementation*, Berkeley, University of California Press, 1973.
27 R. Dahl, *Who Governs?* New Haven, Yale University Press, 1961.
28 P. Bachrach and M.S. Baratz, 'The two faces of power', *American Political Science Review*, 1962, vol. 56, pp. 947–52; P. Bachrach and M.S. Baratz, 'Decisions and non-decisions: an analytical framework', *American Political Science Review*, 1963, vol. 57, pp. 641–51.
29 S. Lukes, *Power: A Radical View*, London, Macmillan, 1974.
30 P. Sabatier, 'Knowledge, policy-orientated learning and policy change. An advocacy coalition framework', *Knowledge, Diffusion, Utilization*, 1987, vol. 8, no. 4, pp. 649–92; P. Sabatier, 'An adversary coalition framework of policy change and the role of policy-orientated learning therein', *Policy Sciences*, 1988, vol. 2, pp. 129–68.
31 Sabatier, 1987, op.cit., pp. 681–2.
32 Ibid., pp. 658–9.
33 Ibid., pp. 661.
34 H. Heclo, *Modern Social Politics in Britain and Sweden: From Relief to Income Maintenance*, New Haven, Yale, 1974.
35 C.H. Weiss and M.J. Bucuvalas, 'Truth tests and utility tests: decision-makers' frames of reference for social science research', *American Sociological Review*, 1980, vol. 45, no. 2, pp. 302–13. See also Weiss and Bucuvalas, *Social Science Research and Decision Making*, New York, Columbia University Press, 1980.
36 Sabatier, 1987, op. cit., p. 675.
37 Ibid., p. 678.
38 Ibid., p. 662.
39 Ibid., p. 663.
40 Ibid., p. 688.

3 MODELS OF BRITISH POLITICS

1 For analyses of British politics based upon general models see P. Dunleavy, A. Gamble, G. Peele, *Developments in British Politics 3*, Basingstoke and London, Macmillan, 1990; P. Dunleavy and R.A.W. Rhodes, 'Core executive studies in Britain', *Public Administration*, 1990, vol. 68, pp. 3–28; P. Norton, *The Constitution in Flux*, London, Robertson, 1982; A. Gamble, 'Theories of British politics', *Political Studies*, 1990, vol. 38, pp. 404–20; and at a more theoretical level P. Dunleavy and B. O'Leary, *Theories of the State*, London, Macmillan, 1987.

2 A.V. Dicey, *Introduction to the Study of the Law and the Constitution*, London, Macmillan, 1885.

3 A.H. Birch, *Representative and Responsible Government*, London, Allen & Unwin, 1964; see also S.H. Beer, *Modern British Politics*, London, Faber, 1965.

4 Beer, op.cit., pp. 54–61

5 J.A. Schumpeter, *Capitalism, Socialism and Democracy*, London, Allen & Unwin, 1954.

6 F.N. Forman, *Mastering British Politics*, London, Macmillan, 1985.

7 S.E. Finer, (ed.) *Adversary Politics and Electoral Reform*, Wigram, London, 1975; S.E. Finer, *The Changing British Party System 1945–1979*, Washington, American Enterprise Institute for Public Policy Research, 1980.

8 See especially D. Owen, *Face the Future*, London, Cape, 1981; S. Williams, *Politics is for People*, Harmondsworth, Allen Lane, 1981.

9 A. Gamble, and S.A. Walkland, *The British Party System and Economic Policy, 1945–83: Studies in Adversary Politics*, Oxford, Oxford University Press, 1984.

10 A. King, 'Overload. Problems of governing in the 1970s', *Political Studies*, 1975, vol. 23, pp. 284–96.

11 S.H. Beer, *Britain Against Itself*, London, Faber & Faber, 1982.

12 S. Brittan, *The Economic Consequences of Democracy*, London, Temple Smith, 1977.

13 M. Olson, *The Rise and Decline of Nations: Economic Growth, Stagflation and Social Rigidities*, New Haven, Yale University Press, 1982.

14 B. Hogwood and B.G. Peters, *Policy Dynamics*, Brighton, Harvester, 1983.

15 L.S. Amery, *Thoughts on the Constitution*, Oxford, Oxford University Press, 1947.

16 M. Burch, 'The British Cabinet: a residual executive', *Parliamentary Affairs*, 1988, vol. 41, pp. 34–48; M. Burch, 'Cabinet government', *Contemporary Record*, 1990, pp. 5–8.

17 For the classic arguments in this debate see R.H.S. Crossman and G.W. Jones's articles in A. King, (ed.) *The British Prime Minister*, 2nd edn, London, Macmillan, 1985, pp. 175–220.

18 B. Trend 'Machinery under pressure', *Times Literary Supplement*, 26 September 1986, p. 1076.

19 D. Wass, *Government and the Governed*, London, Routledge & Kegan

Paul, 1984, pp. 23–40.
20 See especially Dunleavy and Rhodes, op. cit., pp. 13–15.
21 J.J. Richardson and A.G. Jordan, *Governing under Pressure. The Policy Process in a Post-Parliamentary Democracy*, Oxford, Martin Robertson, 1979.
22 Ibid., p. 43.
23 Ibid., pp. 190–1.
24 D. Ashford, *Policy and Politics in Britain. The Limits of Consensus*, Oxford, Basil Blackwell, 1981; Beer, op. cit.
25 A.G. Jordan and J.J. Richardson, *British Politics and the Policy Process. An Arena Approach*, London, Allen & Unwin, 1987, p. x.
26 Ibid., pp. 29–30.
27 Ibid., p. 186.
28 Ibid., p. 32.
29 J.J. Richardson, *Government and Groups in Britain. Changing Styles*, Strathclyde Papers on Government and Politics, no. 69, Glasgow, University of Strathclyde, 1990.
30 R.A.W. Rhodes, *Beyond Westminster and Whitehall. The Sub Central Governments of Britain*, Unwin Hyman, London, 1988, pp. 2–5.
31 Ibid., p. 58.
32 Ibid., pp. 78–80.
33 B. Hogwood, *From Crisis to Complacency? Shaping Public Policy in Britain*, Oxford, Oxford University Press, 1987, pp. 22–3; J.G. March and J.P. Olsen, *Ambiguity and Choice in Organizations*, Bergen, Universitetsforlaget, 1976.
34 Hogwood, op. cit., pp. 82–9.
35 J.A. Chandler, *Public Policy Making for Local Government*, London, Croom Helm, 1988, p. 186.
36 M. Pirie, *Micropolitics*, Aldershot, Wildwood House, 1988.
37 W.A. Niskanen, *Bureaucracy - Servant or Master? Lessons from America*, London, I.E.A., 1973.
38 Pirie, op. cit., pp. 53–60.
39 Ibid., pp. 61–5.
40 Ibid., pp. 117–200.
41 D. Coates, *The Context of British Politics*, London, Hutchinson, 1984.
42 A. Cawson, *Corporatism and Welfare: State Intervention and Social Policy in Britain*, London, Heinemann, 1982; K. Middlemas, *Politics in Industrial Society. The Experience of the British System Since 1911*, London, Deutsch, 1979.
43 A. Gamble, *Britain in Decline. Economic Policy, Political Strategy and the British State*, 3rd edn, London, Macmillan, 1990.
44 P. Dunleavy, 'Group identities and individual influence: reconstructing the theory of interest groups', *British Journal of Political Science*, 1988, vol. 18, pp. 21–49; P. Dunleavy, 'The political implications of sectoral cleavages and the growth of state employment', *Political Studies*, 1980, vol. 28, pp. 364–84, pp. 527–49.
45 P. Dunleavy, 'Reinterpreting the Westland Affair', *Public Administration*, 1990, vol. 68, pp. 29–60.
46 Ibid., p. 56.

4 THE RESPONSE TO AIDS

1 *HC Debs.* (*House of Commons Debates*), 13 January 1989, col. 100.
2 Health Education Authority (HEA), *AIDS Programme: First Annual Report*, AIDS Programme Papers, 1989, no. 4.
3 Department of Health monthly press bulletins include these details. One attempt to estimate the spread is the Cox Report on *Short-term predictions of HIV infections and AIDS in England and Wales*, London, HMSO, 1988.
4 Social Services Select Committee (SSSC), *Problems Associated with AIDS*, London, HMSO, 1987, vol. i (182-I) and vol. ii (182-II).
5 Quoted in J. Lewis, 'AIDS Policy', *The Lancet*, 14 May, 1988, p. 10.
6 The Government has made money available (£29 million) to help haemophiliacs, although it refuses to describe the payment as 'compensation' (which would be to accept blame for its part in the transmission of HIV).
7 Subsequent investigation has discovered a sailor from Liverpool who died in 1959 of an AIDS-like disease.
8 HEA, *Annual Report*, 1990, p. 39.
9 The *Guardian*, 22 November 1986; The *Guardian*, 17 November 1986.
10 The *Guardian*, 12 November 1986.
11 J.E. Campbell and W.E. Waters, 'Public knowledge about AIDS increasing', *British Medical Journal*, 1987, vol. 294, 4 April, p. 893.
12 The *Observer*, 19 June 1988.
13 Media *Week*, 21 November 1986.
14 DHSS, *AIDS: Monitoring Response to the Public Education Campaign*, London, HMSO, 1987.
15 K. Alcorn, 'AIDS in the public sphere', in E. Carter and S. Watney (eds), *Taking Liberties: AIDS and Cultural Politics*, London, Serpent's Tail, 1989, pp. 193–212.
16 SSSC, *The Problems with AIDS*, vol. ii, p. 53; S. Connor and S. Kingman, *The Search for the Virus*, London, Penguin, 1988.
17 The *Guardian*, 31 January 1987.
18 H. Young, *One of Us*, London, Pan, 1990, p. 548.
19 *HC Debs.*, 24 February 1986, col. 411; *Department of Health Briefing*, 88/347, 21, October 1988; *Parliamentary AIDS Digest*, no. 3, Summer 1989, p. 3.
20 *HC Debs.*, 13 January 1989, col. 1109.
21 *New Scientist*, 2 June 1988, p. 22; 3 December 1988, p. 24.
22 Department of Health, *AIDS: Response by the Government to the 7th Report from the Social Services Committee Session*, Cm 925, London, HMSO, 1989, pp. 8–9.
23 *DHSS Circular*, HC(88) 26 March 1988.
24 The *Guardian*, 13 December 1986.
25 *Department of Health Briefing*, 83/166, 1 September 1983; *WHO Press Release*, WHO/15, 25 November 1983.
26 See Cox Report, op. cit., and Day Report, *AIDS in England and Wales to End 1993*, Public Health Laboratory Service, 1990.
27 D. Campbell, 'AIDS: the race against time', *New Statesman & Society*, 8 January, 1989.
28 See DHSS, 1987, op. cit.

29 *HC Debs.*, 30 April 1986, col. 992.
30 D. Altman, *AIDS and the New Puritanism*, London, Pluto Press, 1986, p. 1.
31 In December 1989, 2288 of the 2830 people with AIDS were homosexual or bisexual.
32 R. Klein, 'Between nihilism and utopia in health care', unpublished paper, University of Bath.
33 W.H. McNeill, *Plagues and People*, Harmondsworth, Penguin, 1979, p. 249.
34 Ibid, p. 262.
35 Quoted in J. Lewis, op. cit.
36 R. Garland, 'AIDS – the British context', *Health Education Journal*, vol. 46, no. 2, pp. 50–2.
37 A. Brandt, *No Magic Bullet*, Oxford, Oxford University Press, 1985, pp. 5–6.
38 Quoted in P. Strong and V. Berridge, 'No one knew anything: some issues in British AIDS policy', in P. Aggleton, P. Davies and G. Hart (eds), *AIDS: Individual, Cultural and Policy Dimensions*, Basingstoke, Falmer Press, 1990, p. 242.
39 M. Kapila, 'AIDS prevention through public education: the work of the Health Education Authority', *Royal Society of Medicine: The AIDS Letter*, London, October/November 1989, no. 15, pp. 3–4.
40 *HC Debs.*, 13 January 1989, col. 100.
41 Altman, op. cit., p. 33.
42 SSSC, op. cit., vol. i, p. lxii; vol. ii, pp. 139, 174.
43 Brandt, op. cit., pp. 5–6.

5 THE FALKLANDS WAR

1 T. Dalyell, *One Man's Falklands . . .*, London, Cecil Woolf, 1982, p. 101.
2 For the fullest accounts of the pre-invasion crisis and of the war see: L. Freedman and V. Gamba-Stonehouse, *Signals of War: The Falklands Conflict of 1982*, London, Faber & Faber, 1990; G.M. Dillon, *The Falklands: Politics and War*, Basingstoke and London, Macmillan, 1989. For a useful shorter assessment see L. Freedman, *Britain and the Falklands War*, Oxford, Blackwell, 1988.
3 *Falkland Islands Review*, report of a committee of Privy Counsellors, Chairman the Rt. Hon. Lord Franks, Cmnd. 8787, London, HMSO, 1983, pp. 5–7. (Hereafter cited as the *Franks Report*). For journalists' accounts see The Sunday Times Insight Team, *The Falklands War: The Full Story*, London, Sphere Books, 1982; M. Hastings and S. Jenkins, *The Battle for the Falklands*, London, Pan Books, 1983.
4 Freedman and Gamba-Stonehouse, op. cit., pp. 3–13.
5 For a full account see Dillon, op. cit., pp. 55–89.
6 P. Hennessy, 'Throwing light on secret world of intelligence', The *Independent*, 8 October 1990.
7 *Franks Report*, op. cit., para. 61, p. 17.
8 Ibid., paras 22–5, pp. 5–7.
9 Ibid., para. 30, p. 8.

10 Ibid., para. 48, p. 13.
11 Ibid., paras 59–61, pp. 15–17.
12 Ibid., para. 71, p. 20.
13 M. Hastings and S. Jenkins, op. cit. pp. 53–4.
14 *Franks Report*, op. cit., paras 86–93, p. 24–6.
15 Ibid., paras 91–9, pp. 25–8; Freedman and Gamba-Stonehouse, op. cit., p. 17.
16 *H.C. Debs* (*House of Commons Debates*), 26 March 1968, col. 1464; 28 March 1968, col. 1871; 1 April 1968, col. 4.
17 Hastings and Jenkins, op. cit., p. 49.
18 Sunday Times Insight Team, op. cit., p. 53.
19 *Franks Report*, op. cit., para. 96, p. 27.
20 Ibid., para. 99, p. 28.
21 Dillon, op. cit., pp. 26–8; P. Cosgrave, *Carrington: A Life and Policy*, London, Dent, 1985, pp. 16–41.
22 Dillon, op. cit., p. 32.
23 S. Jenkins, *Sunday Times*, 22 March 1987, quoted Freedman and Gamba-Stonehouse, op. cit., p. 16.
24 *Franks Report*, op. cit., para. 116, pp. 33–4.
25 Hastings and Jenkins, op. cit., pp. 59–60.
26 *Franks Report*, op. cit., paras 151–3, 329, pp. 45, 87–8.
27 Hastings and Jenkins, op. cit., pp. 69–70.
28 *Franks Report*, op. cit., para. 291, p. 79.
29 Ibid., para. 292, p. 79.
30 Ibid., para. 282, p. 77.
31 Ibid., para. 61, p. 17.
32 Ibid., para. 289, p. 79.
33 Freedman and Gamba-Stonehouse, op. cit., pp. 26–7.
34 Ibid, pp. 71–9.
35 Dillon, op. cit., pp. 17–18.
36 Cosgrave, op. cit., p. 19.
37 *Franks Report*, op. cit., para. 306, p. 83.
38 Sunday Times Insight Team, op. cit., p. 54; *Franks Report*, op. cit. paras 94–5, pp. 26–7.
39 Freedman and Gamba-Stonehouse, op. cit., p. 23.
40 *Franks Report*, op. cit., paras 149–51, pp. 43–5.
41 Freedman and Gamba-Stonehouse, op. cit., pp. 40–67 gives a full account.
42 Ibid., pp. 67–71.
43 Hastings and Jenkins, op. cit., pp. 75–6; Lord Carrington, *Reflect on Things Past*, London, Collins, 1988, p. 361.
44 Sunday Times Insight Team, op. cit., p. 81.
45 C. Seymour-Ure, 'British "war cabinets" in limited wars: Korea, Suez and the Falklands', *Public Administration*, 1984, vol. 62, pp. 181–200.
46 Sir Nicholas Henderson, 'America and the Falklands: case study in the behaviour of an ally', *The Economist*, 12 November 1983, p. 54.
47 For analysis of public opinion during the crisis see Freedman, op. cit., pp. 92–104.
48 A. Barnett, *Iron Brittania: Why Parliament Waged its Falklands War*, London, Allison & Busby, 1982, p. 20.
49 Hastings and Jenkins, op. cit., pp. 85–7.
50 M. Charlton, *The Little Platoon*, London, Blackwell, 1989, pp. 193–4.

51 C. Ponting, *The Right to Know*, London, Sphere, 1985, pp. 71–2.
52 Hastings and Jenkins, op. cit., pp. 89–90.
53 Ibid., pp. 96–7.
54 Henderson, *The Economist*, 12 November 1983, p. 53.
55 Dillon, op. cit., pp. 104–7.

6 NUCLEAR POWER DECISIONS

1 The *Sunday Times*, 16 December 1979; The *Independent*, 13 March 1987. The best sources for an account of British nuclear power decisions are: R. Williams, *The Nuclear Power Decisions*, London, Croom Helm, 1980; T. Hall, *Nuclear Politics*, Harmondsworth, Penguin, 1986; D. Burn, *Nuclear Power and the Energy Crisis*, London, Macmillan, 1978.
2 One nuclear programme alone has cost £3.5 billion. Each reactor has taken 10–15 years to build.
3 For the pre-privatisation arrangements, see Open University, *Nuclear Power*, (Control of Technology, Unit 5), pp. 12–13; also Williams, op. cit., ch. 1; and L. Pearson, *The Organisation of the Energy Industry*, London, Macmillan, 1981, pp. 103–17.
4 Before the Department of Energy took responsibility, nuclear power was the province, at various times, of the Ministry of Supply, of the Ministry of Fuel and Power, the Ministry of Technology, and the Department of Trade and Industry.
5 I. Breach, *Windscale Fallout*, Harmondsworth, Penguin, 1978.
6 Williams, op. cit., pp. 25–7.
7 Ibid., p. 28; also Counter Information Service, *The Nuclear Disaster*, London, CIS, n.d., pp. 38–40; and D. Elliott, *The Politics of Nuclear Power*, London, Pluto, 1978.
8 Pearson, *The Organisation of the Energy Industry*, pp. 83–90.
9 Ibid., chs 8–10; Open University, op. cit., pp. 7–15.
10 See J.C. Chicken, *Nuclear Power and Hazard Control Policy*, Oxford, Pergamon, 1982, pp. 15, 47.
11 See, for example, the reports of the Select Committee on Science and Technology: *United Kingdom Nuclear Power Programme*, HC 381, XVII (1966–7), *United Kingdom Nuclear Power Industry*, 4th Report, HC 401 (1968–9), *Nuclear Power Policy*, 2nd Report, HC 350 (1972–3), *The Choice of a Reactor System*, 1st Report, HC 145 (1973–4).
12 W.C. Patterson, *Nuclear Power*, Harmondsworth, Penguin, 1976, chs 1, 2.
13 For safety, see A. Cottrell, *How Safe is Nuclear Energy?* London, Heinemann, 1981; for reactor efficiency, see Burn, op. cit., chs 4, 5, 9, 13.
14 M. Gowing, *Britain and Atomic Energy 1939–45*, London, Macmillan, 1964; and M. Gowing, *Independence and Deterrence: Britain and Nuclear Energy, 1945–1952*, (2 volumes), London, Macmillan, 1974.
15 K. Morgan, *Labour in Power 1945–51*, Oxford, Oxford University Press, 1984, pp. 281–2.
16 See Patterson, op. cit., pp. 23–41; and N. Moss, *The Politics of Uranium*, London, André Deutsch, 1981, pp. 1–37.
17 Gowing, op. cit., vol. 2, pp. 186–93, 251–3, 285–97.

18 Quoted in P. Bunyard, *Nuclear Britain*, London, New English Library, 1981, pp. 29–30.
19 Williams, op. cit., p. 209.
20 Gowing, op. cit., vol. 2, ch. 19.
21 Williams, op. cit., p. 56.
22 Ibid., ch. 2.
23 P.D. Henderson, 'Two British errors: their probable size and some possible lessons', *Oxford Economic Papers*, 1977, pp. 159–205; Williams, op. cit., pp. 80–7.
24 Quoted in The *Sunday Times*, 16 December 1979.
25 Williams, op. cit., pp. 93–9.
26 Ibid., ch. 6.
27 The *Sunday Times*, 16 December 1979.
28 C. Ponting, *Breach of Promise*, London, Hamish Hamilton, 1989, p. 278.
29 Williams, op. cit., pp. 141–2, 144–6.
30 Henderson, op. cit., pp. 163–5.
31 Ibid., pp. 180–5; Burn, op. cit., pp. 133–41.
32 Quoted in H. Bacon and J. Valentine, *Power Corrupts*, London, Pluto, 1981, p. 65.
33 Quoted in Williams, op. cit., p. 201.
34 Select Committee on Science and Technology, *United Kingdom Power Industry*, 4th Report, HC 401 (1968–9).
35 Williams, op. cit., p. 216; Pearson, op. cit., p. 113.
36 The *Financial Times*, 13 November 1979.
37 According to Brian Sedgemore, Benn's Parliamentary Private Secretary, Marshall's advice was compromised by his other work as adviser to the Shah of Iran; see B. Sedgemore, *The Secret Constitution*, London, Hodder & Stoughton, 1980, p. 107.
38 Burn, op. cit., pp. 224–6.
39 Williams, op. cit., pp. 219–27.
40 Bunyard, op. cit., p. 52.
41 Williams, op. cit., pp. 215–17.
42 Sedgemore, op. cit., p. 114.
43 Ibid., ch. 4; Williams, op. cit., pp. 242–59.
44 Sedgemore, op. cit., pp. 107–9.
45 Ibid., p. 116.
46 The *Guardian*, 2 February 1982; Williams, op. cit., pp. 242–3.
47 Sedgemore, op. cit., pp. 122–4; The *Guardian*, 4 February 1980.
48 The *Financial Times*, 19 December 1979; The *Guardian*, 2 July 1981; T. O'Riordan, R. Kemp, and M. Purdue, *Sizewell 'B': An Anatomy of the Inquiry*, London, Macmillan, 1988.
49 Bunyard, op. cit., p. 55.
50 *The Times*, 2 February 1982.
51 See W. Rudig, 'Public participation and nuclear power politics', *Politics*, 1981, vol. 1, no. 2, pp. 35–42.
52 The *Guardian*, 2 February 1982.
53 H. Young, *One of Us*, London, Pan, 1990, p. 563.
54 Ibid., p. 529.
55 R. Peston, 'Tangle of crossed wires in the corridors of power', *The Independent on Sunday*, 19 August 1990, p. 12.

56 Department of Energy, *Privatising Electricity*, Cmnd 322, London, HMSO, 198
57 Peston, op. cit., p. 14.
58 R.E. Goodin, 'No moral nukes', *Ethics*, 1980, vol. 90, April, pp. 417–49.
59 D. Collingridge, *The Social Control of Technology*, Milton Keynes, Open University Press, 1981, pp. 23–43.
60 J. Street, 'Controlling interests: technology, state control and democracy', in G. Duncan, (ed.), *Democracy and the Capitalist State*, Cambridge, Cambridge University Press, 1989, pp. 215–32.
61 See chapter two of this volume.
62 The *New Statesman*, 28 March 1980.
63 O'Riordan *et al.*, op. cit.

7 THE RISE AND FALL OF THE CIVIL SERVICE DEPARTMENT

1   C. Pollitt, *Manipulating the Machine: Changing the Pattern of Ministerial Departments 1963–80*, London, Allen & Unwin, 1984; G.K. Fry, *The Administrative 'Revolution' in Whitehall*, London, Croom Helm, 1981.
2   P. Hennessy, *Whitehall*, London, Secker & Warburg, 1989, p. 262.
3   H. Roseveare, *The Treasury: The Evolution of a British Institution*, London, Allen Lane, 1969; Lord Bridges, *The Treasury*, London, Allen & Unwin, 1964; R A. Chapman and J.R. Greenaway, *The Dynamics of Administrative Reform*, London, Croom Helm, 1980.
4   R.A. Chapman, 'The rise and fall of the CSD,' *Policy and Politics*, vol. 11, no. 1, pp. 41–61.
5   Especially influential outside criticisms came from Thomas Balogh, 'The apotheosis of a dilettante' in Hugh Thomas (ed.), *The Establishment: a Symposium*, London, Blond, 1959; B. Chapman, *British Government Observed. Some European Reflections*, London, Allen & Unwin, 1963; Fabian Tract 355, *The Administrators, the Reform of the Civil Service*, London, Fabian Society, 1964.
6   P. Kellner and Lord Crowther-Hunt, *The Civil Servants: An Enquiry into Britain's Ruling Class*, London, MacDonald and Jaynes, 1980, esp. chs 1–5; J. Garrett, *Managing the Civil Service*, London, Heinemann, 1980.
7   Sir James Dunnett, 'The Civil Service. Seven years after Fulton', *Public Administration*, 1976, vol. 54, pp. 372–3.
8   Expenditure Committee, Session 1976–7, (535), Eleventh Report, *The Civil Service*, London, HMSO, 1977, (hereafter cited as 'English Committee'), vol. 2, minutes of evidence, q. 1499.
9   R. Crossman, *The Diaries of a Cabinet Minister*, London, Hamish Hamilton and Jonathan Cape, 1975, vol. 1, p. 103.
10 Ibid., p. 98.
11 Ibid., p. 103.
12 B. Castle, *The Castle Diaries 1964–70*, London, Weidenfeld & Nicholson, 1984, pp. 467–8.
13 R. Crossman, op. cit., vol. 3, p. 107. Hennessy, op. cit., pp. 199–203 gives a full account.
14 Lord Crowther-Hunt, Treasury and Civil Service Committee, Session 1980–1, (54), first report, *The Future of the Civil Service Department*, London, HMSO, 1980, evidence, q. 950, (hereafter cited as 'Sheldon

Report'); Kellner and Crowther-Hunt, op. cit., pp. 78–81; Garrett, op. cit., pp. 59–61.

15 Sheldon Report, op. cit., q. 864.
16 See *The Times*, 16, 17, 18, 19 November 1981 for correspondence on this accusation.
17 Sheldon Report, op. cit., q. 950.
18 For a similar point of view, though more critical of 'confusions' of the Fulton Report, see Garrett, op. cit., pp. 16–23.
19 The *Listener*, 18 July 1968; R.A. Chapman, op. cit., p. 49.
20 Sheldon Report, op. cit., q. 1152.
21 Sir Ian Bancroft, ibid., q. 818.
22 English Committee, op. cit., evidence q. 1931.
23 The phrase was invented by Bill Kendall of the National Staff Side of the Whitley Council.
24 *The Times*, 6 October 1977, 15 July 1980.
25 Hennessy, op. cit., p. 274.
26 Sir John Hunt, English Committee, op. cit., q. 1817.
27 *The Times*, 8 July 1980.
28 Sheldon Report, op. cit., q. 770.
29 English Committee, op. cit. qs 1822–24, 1830.
30 Ibid., report.
31 Garrett, op. cit., pp. 62–3.
32 *The Times*, 4 October 1977.
33 Sheldon Report, op. cit., evidence of Sir Ian Bancroft, qs. 860–3.
34 Hennessy, op. cit., pp. 623–35; J.R. Greenaway, 'The higher Civil Service at the crossroads: the impact of the Thatcher Government', in L. Robins (ed.), *Political Institutions in Britain: Development and Change*, London, Longman, 1987; G.K. Fry, 'The British career Civil Service under challenge', *Political Studies*, 1986, vol. 34, pp. 535–55.
35 Hennessy, op. cit., pp. 589–605; G. Drewry and T. Butcher, *The Civil Service Today*, Oxford, Blackwell, 1988, pp. 198–203.
36 The *Guardian*, 12 October 1979.
37 The *Sunday Times*, 24 August 1980.
38 *The Times*, 8 September 1981.
39 Sheldon Report, op. cit., evidence, q. 991.
40 Ibid., qs 770–817.
41 The other members were Michael English (Lab.), Richard Wrainwight (Lib), and three newly-elected Conservative backbenchers, Anthony Beaumont Dark, Timothy Eggar and Richard Shepherd.
42 Sheldon Report, op. cit., p. vii.
43 E.g. ibid., evidence, q. 878.
44 'The integration of HM Treasury and the Civil Service Department', report of the study team, Civil Service Department, October 1980, para. 1.
45 *The Times*, 27 October 1980.
46 Sheldon Report, op. cit., evidence, qs 877–94 *et seq.*; *The Times*, 3 December 1980.
47 *The Times*, 27 October 1980.
48 Sheldon Report, op. cit., pp. vii–xx.
49 *H.C. Debs* (*House of Commons Debates*), 29 January 1981, col. 1070.

50 *The Future of the Civil Service Department*, Cmnd. 8170, February 1981, London, HMSO; *The Times*, 20 March 1981.
51 *H.C. Debs*, 12 November 1981, cols. 658–9.
52 *The Times*, 8 September 1981.
53 Gerry Gillman, General Secretary of the Society of Civil and Public Servants and Ken Thomas, General Secretary of the Civil and Public Services Association, quoted in *The Times*, 13 November 1981.
54 Hennessy, op. cit., pp. 605–22.
55 L. Metcalf and S. Richards, *Improving Public Management*, London, Sage, 1987.
56 Seventh report from the Treasury and Civil Service Committee, 1985–6: *Civil Servants and Ministers: Duties and Responsibilities*, vol. I report, vol. II annexes, minutes of evidence and appendices, HC 92-I-II London, HMSO, 1986.
57 Government response to the seventh report from the Treasury and Civil Service Committee, Cmnd 9841, London, HMSO, 1986.
58 The *Financial Times*, 8 August 1987.
59 A. Seldon, 'The Cabinet Office and Coordination 1979–87', *Public Administration*, 1990, vol. 68, pp. 105–7.
60 Sheldon Report, op. cit., evidence, qs 770–818.
61 Ibid., q. 818.

8 LEGISLATING FOR TRADE UNIONS

1 Quoted in H. Wilson, *The Labour Government 1964–70*, Harmondsworth, Penguin, 1974, p. 808.
2 J. Callaghan, *Time and Chance*, London, Collins, 1987, p. 274.
3 Quoted in R. Taylor, *The Fifth Estate*, London, Pan, 1980, p. 454.
4 *In Place of Strife*, Cmnd 3888, London, HMSO, 1969.
5 C. Ponting, *Breach of Promise*, London, Hamish Hamilton, 1989, p. 351.
6 Royal Commission on Trade Unions and Employers' Associations 1965–8: Chairman, the Rt Hon. Lord Donovan, *Report*, Cmnd 3623, London, HMSO, 1968.
7 R. Hyman, *Strikes*, London, Fontana, 1972, p. 33.
8 Ponting, op.cit., p. 352.
9 Ibid., p. 354.
10 B. Castle, *The Castle Diaries 1964–70*, London, Weidenfeld & Nicholson, 1984, p. 582.
11 R. Crossman, *The Crossman Diaries* (edited by Anthony Howard), London, Methuen, 1979, p. 557.
12 Ibid., p. 558.
13 Ibid., p. 559.
14 Ponting, op.cit., p. 357.
15 Crossman, op.cit., p. 623–8; Castle, op.cit., p. 673.
16 R. Neustadt, *Presidential Power and Modern Presidents: The Politics of Leadership*, Boston, Free Press, 1990.
17 Callaghan, op.cit., p. 277.
18 M. Moran, *The Politics of Industrial Relations*, London, Macmillan, 1977, p. 61.
19 T. Russel, *The Tory Party*, Harmondsworth, Penguin, 1978, ch. 7.

20 Moran, op.cit., chs 4–5.
21 Ibid., p. 75.
22 P. Jenkin, *The Battle of Downing Street*, London, Charles Knight, 1970, p. 49.
23 Symposium on Trade Unions and the Fall of the Heath Government, *Contemporary Record*, vol. 2, Spring 1988, p. 38; see also, D. Marsh and G. Locksley, 'Labour: the dominant force in British politics?', in D. Marsh (ed.), *Pressure Politics: Interest Groups in Britain*, London, Junction Books, 1983, p. 74.
24 Moran, op.cit., p. 79.
25 Ibid., pp. 122–3.
26 Ibid., pp. 153–4;
27 C. Crouch, *The Politics of Industrial Relations*, London, Fontana, 1979, p. 81.
28 Symposium on Trade Unions, *Contemporary Record*, pp. 39–40.
29 Taylor, op.cit., pp. 113–14.
30 P. Riddell, *The Thatcher Government*, Oxford, Martin Robertson, 1983, p. 36.
31 J. Prior, *A Balance of Power*, London, Hamish Hamilton, 1986, p. 159.
32 Ibid., pp. 161–7.
33 A. Gamble, 'Economic policy' in Z. Layton-Henry (ed.), *Conservative Party Politics*, London, Macmillan, 1980, p. 28.
34 A. Gamble, *Britain in Decline*, 3rd edn, London, Macmillan, 1990, chs 2, 3.
35 H. Young, *One of Us*, London, Pan, 1990, p. 232.
36 Riddell, op.cit., p. 181.
37 Ibid., p. 186.
38 N. Wapshott and G. Brock, *Thatcher*, London, Futura, 1983, pp. 206–7.
39 A. King, 'Politics, economics and the trade unions, 1974–79', in H. Penniman, *Britain at the Polls*, Washington, AEI, 1981, p. 70; also Riddell, op.cit., p. 17.
40 C. Tyler, 'Tebbit's Law', *Marxism Today*, April 1982, p. 23.
41 A. Heath, R. Jowell and J. Curtice, *How Britain Votes*, Oxford, Pergamon, 1985, pp. 18–19, 109.
42 D. Kavanagh, *Thatcherism and British Politics*, Oxford, Oxford University Press, 1987, p. 240.

9 TRIDENT

1 Minority draft report in *Fourth Report from the Defence Committee, Session 1980–81, Strategic Nuclear Weapons Policy*, London, HMSO, 20 May 1981, p. xxxviii.
2 The Trident issue is discussed from a variety of angles in Peter Malone, *The British Nuclear Deterrent*, London, Croom Helm, 1984; L. Freedman *Britain and Nuclear Weapons*, London, Macmillan, 1980; and in P. Hennessy, *Cabinet*, Oxford, Blackwell, 1986, ch. 4. Much of the historical material in this chapter is based on these. For the Government's view of the strategic, political and economic aspects see Ministry of Defence, *The Future United Kingdom Strategic Nuclear Deterrent Force*, London, HMSO, Defence Open Government Document 80/23, 1980; and in Ministry of Defence, *The United Kingdom Trident Programme*, London, HMSO, Defence Open Government Document

82/1, 1982. See also Cmnd 8529-I, *Statement on the Defence Estimates, 1982*, London, HMSO, 1982; Cmnd 8212-I, *Statement on the Defence Estimates, 1981*, London, HMSO, 1981; Cmnd 8288, *The United Kingdom Defence Programme: The Way Forward*, London, HMSO, 1981; Cmnd 8517, *The British Strategic Nuclear Force*, London, HMSO, 1982; Cmnd 7979, *The British Strategic Nuclear Force*, London, HMSO, 1980. For economic effects see D. Greenwood, 'Economic constraints and political preferences', in J. Baylis (ed.) *Alternative Approaches to British Defence Policy*, London, Macmillan, 1983, pp. 31–61; M. Chalmers, *Paying for Defence*, London, Pluto Press, 1985, chs 7, 8; M. Chalmers, *The Cost of Britain's Defence*, Bradford, University of Bradford, School of Peace Studies, 1983; and D. Smith and R.Smith, 'British military expenditure in the 1980s', in E.P. Thompson and B. Smith (eds), *Protest and Survive*, Harmondsworth, Penguin, 1980, pp. 186–202. For the moral and strategic dimensions see, as examples, J. McMahon, *British Nuclear Weapons: For and Against*, London, Junction Books, 1981; G. Prins *et al.*, *Defended to Death*, Harmondsworth, Penguin, 1983, pp. 171–94, and K. Booth and J. Baylis, *Britain, NATO and Nuclear Weapons*, London, Macmillan, 1989.

3 M. Gowing, *Independence and Deterrence: Britain and Atomic Energy 1945–1952, vol. I. Policy Making*, London, Macmillan, 1974, p. 406.

4 For an historical overview of the development of the British nuclear force see Freedman, op. cit., and Malone, op. cit. See also A. Pierre, *Nuclear Politics*, London, Oxford University Press, 1972; A.J.R. Groom, *British Thinking about Nuclear Weapons*, London, Frances Pinter, 1974; P. Hennessy, *Whitehall*, London, Secker & Warburg, 1989, pp. 707–17; C.J. Bartlett, *The Long Retreat: A Short History of British Defence Policy*, London, Macmillan, 1972; R.N. Rosecrance, *Defence of the Realm: British Strategy in the Nuclear Epoch*, New York, Columbia University Press, 1968; W.P. Snyder, *The Politics of British Defence Policy, 1945–62*, London, Benn, 1964; J. Baylis, *Anglo-American Defence Relations 1939–84*, 2nd ed, London, Macmillan, 1984; J. Baylis, *British Defence Policy*, London, Macmillan, 1989; D. Sanders, *Losing an Empire, Finding a Role*, London, Macmillan, 1990.

5 The history of the Skybolt incident is discussed in R. Neustadt, *Alliance Politics*, New York, Columbia University Press, 1970.

6 Freedman, op. cit., pp. 52–68.

7 Ibid., p. 52.

8 Ibid., p. 55.

9 J. Simpson, 'Britain's nuclear deterrent: The impending decisions', *ADIU Report*, 1979, vol. 1, no. 1, p. 1.

10 I. Smart, *The Future of the British Nuclear Deterrent: Technical, Economic and Strategic Issues*, London, Royal Institute of International Affairs, 1977a; a summary appears in I. Smart, 'Beyond Polaris', *International Affairs*, 1977b, vol. 53, no. 4, pp. 557–71.

11 See Cmnd 7819, *Sixth Report from the Expenditure Committee Session 1978–9 – The Future of the United Kingdom's Nuclear Weapons Policy*, London, HMSO, 1979, p. xiv.

12 Smart, 1977b, op. cit., p. 560.

13 Smart, 1977a, op. cit., pp. 2–3.

14 Cited in P. Hennessy, 'Planning for a future nuclear deterrent', *The Times*, 4 December 1979, p. 4.
15 *Statement on the Defence Estimates: 1975*, Cmnd 5976, London, HMSO, 1975, para. I, 25d.
16 *HC Debs. (House of Commons Debates)*, 21 March 1978, cols 1314–15.
17 Cited in Cmnd 7819, op. cit., p. xiv.
18 *HC Debs.*, 16 January 1979, col. 1500.
19 Hennessy, 4 December 1979, op. cit., p. 4.
20 Ibid.
21 Ibid.
22 Cited in Freedman, op. cit., p. 63.
23 See *Fourth Report from the Defence Committee, Session 1980–81 Strategic Nuclear Weapons Policy*, op. cit., p. 228.
24 These are discussed in Malone, op. cit., pp. 107–25 and Freedman, op. cit., pp. 63–78.
25 Freedman, op. cit., p. 71.
26 Malone, op. cit., p. 113.
27 See *Fourth Report from the Defence Committee, Session 1980–81, Strategic Nuclear Weapons Policy*, op. cit., pp. 76–9.
28 Cmnd 8529–1, op. cit., p. 5.
29 Ibid., p. 4.
30 See *Fourth Report from the Defence Committee, Session 1980–81, Strategic Nuclear Weapons Policy*, op. cit., pp. xxxvii–xxxviii.
31 Cmnd 7819, op. cit., p. 2.
32 Ibid., p. 6.
33 Ibid., p. 7.
34 Ibid., p. 8.
35 *HC Debs.*, 18 December 1979, cols 501–24.
36 *HC Debs.*, 28 April 1980, cols 1005–6.
37 *HC Debs.*, 15 July 1980, col. 1237.
38 Ibid., col. 1239.
39 *HC Debs.*, 4 August 1980, col. 352.
40 Ibid., col. 323.
41 *HC Debs.*, 3 March 1981, cols 144–51; cols 182–5.
42 *Fourth Report from the Defence Committee, Session 1980–81, Strategic Nuclear Weapons Policy*, op. cit., p. vi.
43 Ibid., p. xviii.
44 Ibid., p. xv.
45 Ibid., p. xxxviii.
46 Ibid., p. xxxix.
47 Ibid., p. lxii.
48 Ibid., pp. lxi–lxii.
49 S. McLean (ed.) *How Nuclear Weapons Decisions are Made*, London, Macmillan, 1986, ch. 3.
50 Hennessy, 1986, op. cit., p. 155.
51 Baylis, 1989, op. cit., p. 55.
52 A. Cox and S. Kirby, *Congress, Parliament and Defence*, London, Macmillan, 1986, see especially ch. 6.
53 McLean, op. cit., ch. 3.
54 Hennessy, 4 December 1979, op. cit., p. 4.
55 Quoted in McLean, op. cit., p. 149.

Index

Advanced Gas-cooled Reactor
(AGR) 120, 121, 123, 136, 221,
223; second nuclear programme
125–6; third nuclear programme
127; fourth nuclear programme
128–9
adversarial politics model 52–4,
59, 231–2, 238
advocacy coalitions 40–5 *passim*,
229–30, 238
agenda setting 30–1, 202–3
Aggleton, P. 246
AIDS (Acquired Immune
Deficiency Syndrome) 13, 69–91;
deaths from 71, 72, 83, 245;
decision-making theories:
(belief-systems 226; bounded
rationality 219–20; bureaucratic
politics 224; disjointed incrementalism 221; groupthink 227;
implementation 228; organisational
process 223; rational actor 216;
Sabatier model 229, 230);
education campaigns 70–1,
73–7; form of policy 72–81;
(prevention 79–81, 226;
research 77–8; treatment
78–9, 224); heterosexual
transmission as focus 86–7;
policy making 87–91; political
system models and 230–5
passim; timing of policy 81–7
Alcorn, K. 245
All Party Group on AIDS
89

Allen, Sir D. (later Lord Croham)
146, 147, 153, 154
Allison, G. 29, 32, 222, 242
Altman, D. 84, 90, 246
Amalgamated Engineering Union
(AEU) 174, 179
Amery, L.S. 55, 243
Anaya, Admiral 109
Anderson, Sir J. 121
Anti-Ballistic Missile (ABM) system
186, 187
anti-nuclear movement 130
appreciative judgement 23
Argentine Government 93–4,
96, 107; *see also* Falklands War
Armstrong, Sir R. (later Lord) 156,
158, 159, 160; CSD 145, 153; and
Treasury 149, 223
Armstrong, Sir W. (later Lord) 160;
CSD 143, 144; 'Deputy Prime
Minister' 147; Fulton Report 143;
Treasury 30; (and Civil Service
work 149)
Arrow, K. 16
Ashford, D. 59, 244
Attlee, C. 50, 121
Automobile Association 58

Bachrach, P. 38, 242
Bacon, H. 249
Bagehot, W. 2–3, 17, 241
ballistic missiles 192; *see also*
Polaris; Trident
Balogh, T. 250
Bancroft, Sir I. 162–3, 251;

CSD 145, 153, 154, 157; implementation and efficiency 160–1; Thatcher and 147, 160
Baratz, M.S. 38, 242
Barnett, A. 112, 247
Bartlett, C.J. 254
Baylis, J. 254, 255
Beer, S.H. 8–9, 241, 243, 244; pluralistic stagnation 53, 59
Beith, A. 199
belief-systems 225–6, 238; departments and 30–1; nuclear weapons 209, 225–6; *see also* ideology
Benn, T. 128, 129
Berridge, V. 246
biographies 4
bipartisanship 205–6
Birch, A.H. 48, 243
blood donations 79
Blue Streak missile 185, 206, 229
bomb, nuclear 121, 122; *see also* nuclear weapons
Bonsor, N. 87
Booth, K. 254
Bottomley, V. 73
Boulding, K. 34–5, 242
bounded rationality 21–3, 219–20
Bradbury Committee 141
Braine, Sir B. 92
Brandt, A. 87, 91, 246
Braybrooke, D. 24–5, 241
Breach, I. 248
Bridges, Lord 30, 242, 250
British Aerospace 206
British Antarctic Survey 98
British Medical Association (BMA) 80
British Nationality Act 104, 107
British Nuclear Associates 118, 127
British Nuclear Fuels Ltd 118
Brittan, S. 53, 243
Brock, G. 253
Buchanan Report 23
Bucuvalas, M.J. 42, 242
Bunyard, P. 249
Burch, M. 243
bureaucracies, interests of 62–3

bureaucratic dispersion 56–7, 232–3
bureaucratic politics model 29, 32–4, 215, 222, 223–5; CSD 161–2, 224; nuclear weapons 208–9, 225; policy communities and 238, 239
Burn, D. 248, 249
Butcher, T. 251

Cabinet 223, 230; bureaucratic dispersion 56–7; Falklands War 105, 110, 232; (War Cabinet 110–11); *In Place of Strife* 169–70; nuclear power 117, 119; nuclear weapons 184–5, 202, 232; role of 17, 55; *see also* Cabinet government model
Cabinet Committees 55; AIDS 87–8; Defence and Oversea Policy 96, 99, 100, 104–5, 110; nuclear weapons: (Callaghan's *ad hoc* Committee 190–1, 198, 202; MISC 7 191); trade unions (MISC 230) 168
Cabinet government model 54–6, 232
Cabinet Office 141, 151, 157, 158–9, 228
Cabinet Secretariat 55
Cabinet Secretary 156, 159
Calder Hall nuclear power station 122
Callaghan, J. 252; Civil Service 150; Falkland Islands 97, 100; *In Place of Strife* 165, 170; nuclear power 129; nuclear weapons 189–90, 198, 207; (*ad hoc* committee 190)
Callaghan Government 9; nuclear weapons 190–1, 202, 207; 'Winter of Discontent' 178, 182
Campbell, D. 83, 245
Campbell, J.E. 245
capital 65–6, 67
Carr, R. (later Sir) 171, 173–4
Carrington, Lord 191, 247; Falkland Islands 95, 104, 105, 108; (public education 102, 103, 105, 107; Ridley initiative 100–1);

resignation 99; Rhodesia and back-benchers 103, 222

Carter, E. 245

Carter, J. 191, 198–9

case-study approach 1, 11–14, 211–13

Cassels, J. 156–7

Castle, B. 56, 242, 250, 252; 'departmental enemies' 33; Fulton Report 144; *In Place of Strife* 165–6, 168–70, 224–5

Cawson, A. 66, 244

CBI (Confederation of British Industry) 168–9, 173, 174

Central Electricity Generating Board (CEGB) 119; nuclear power 131–2, 138; (first programme 122–3, 124; second programme 125, 126; third programme 127, 128; funds for public education 131)

Central Policy Review Staff 140

Chalfont, Lord 97, 100, 102

Chalmers, M. 254

Chandler, J.A. 62, 244

Chapelcross nuclear power station 122

Chapman, B. 250

Chapman, R.A. 250, 251

Charlton, M. 247

Chevaline missile 187–8, 205, 206, 209, 220, 229; Callaghan Government 187–8, 207; costs 187, 213; (overruns 188, 193); Healey and 227

Chicken, J.C. 248

Churchill, W.S. 185

Civil Service 58; control of 140–2, 157–9; role in Trident 205; unrest 157, 160; *see also* Civil Service Department

Civil Service Department (CSD) 13, 69, 139–63; creation of 140–6; decision-making theories: (belief-systems 226; bounded rationality 219; bureaucratic politics 161–2, 224; disjointed incrementalism 221–2; implementation 228; organisational process 223; rational actor 217;

Sabatier model 229); demarcation disputes 148–50; dismantled 139–40, 156–7; functioning after 1968 146–8; Image Unit 147; Permanent Secretary's position 147; political system models and 231–4 *passim*; Thatcher and 151–7, 161, 221–2

Coates, D. 244

Collingridge, D. 250

Commission on Industrial Relations 166, 169, 174

community power structures 37–8

condoms 71, 80–1, 82

conflicting objectives 17, 20–1

Connor, S. 245

Conservative Party 7–8, 10; trade unions 171, 178, 234; ('Fair Deal at Work' 171–2, 173); *see also* Heath government; New Right; Thatcher Governments

constitution 2, 48

consultation 58–9

continuity, nuclear weapons policy and 187–8, 199, 205–6, 207

Cosgrave, P. 247

Cost Benefit Analysis (CBA) 18–19

Cottrell, Sir A. 129, 248

council house sales 64, 67

counselling, AIDS 78–9

Counter Information Service 248

Cox, A. 204, 255

Cox Report 245

Croham, Lord (formerly Sir D. Allen) 146, 147, 153, 154

Crosland, A. 100

Crossman, R. 242, 243, 250, 252; departmental preoccupation 33, 56; *In Place of Strife* 169, 170; Land Commission 31; Wilson 143; (Fulton Report 143–4)

Crouch, C. 175, 253

Crowther-Hunt, Lord (formerly N. Hunt) 142, 143, 250–1; CSD 144, 146, 153

cruise missiles 192

Cuban Missile Crisis 29

Currie, E. 6, 73

Curtice, J. 253

Dahl, R. 37, 242
Dalyell, T. 92, 246
Davidoff, Sr. 98, 109
Davies, P. 246
Day Report 245
decision-making theories 15–46,
    213–30; *see also under
    individual names*
Defence Committee; inquiry on
    future of nuclear deterrent 197,
    199–200, 225; (Government
    pre-emption 203; secrecy 201);
    role in Trident decision 204–5,
    208, 210
Defence and External Affairs
    Subcommittee (of Expenditure
    Committee) 189, 196, 197–8
defence policy community 58
democracy 2, 211, 238–40
democratic sovereignty model
    47–50, 54, 230–1, 238
Department of Economic Affairs
    31, 148
Department of Education and
    Science (DES) 75, 224
Department of Employment 81
Department of Energy 117–18,
    119, 125, 132, 223, 230
Department of the Environment 150
Department of Health 6, 7,
    9, 87, 245
Department of Health and Social
    Security (DHSS) 140, 245; AIDS
    87, 88, 89, 224, 230, 233;
    (education campaigns 71, 74, 76,
    90; Expert Advisory Committee
    88; heterosexual transmission 86;
    report 'On the State of Public
    Health' 82; research 77, 78;
    transmission mechanisms 82)
Department of Trade and Industry
    140
Department of Transport 19,
    30–1, 58
departments: belief-systems 30–1;
    conflicting 148–50, 232–3;
    see also bureaucratic politics
Diamond, Lord 150

Dicey, A.V. 48, 243
Dillon, G.M. 108, 246, 247, 248
disjointed incrementalism 24–9,
    220–2
Donovan Commission 167, 168, 252
Downs, A. 16, 241
Drewry, G. 251
Dror, Y. 27–8, 242
drug use, AIDS and 80, 84, 85
Duff, A. 190, 198, 205
Duffy, T. 179
Duncan, G. 250
Dunleavy, P. 67–8, 235, 243, 244
Dunnett, Sir J. 143, 250

East London River Crossing Public
    Inquiry 19
economic decline 8
economic interests 65–6, 66–7
Economic and Social Research
    Council (ESRC) 78
education: campaigns (AIDS
    70–1, 73–7; Falkland Islands
    102; nuclear power 130–1);
    policy community 58; reforms 64
efficiency, Civil Service 151–3,
    160–1, 217
electricity, privatisation of 131–2;
    see also nuclear power
electricity generating boards 118,
    119, 132
Elliott, D. 248
Employment Acts 177–8
Employment Protection Act (1975)
    176
Endurance, HMS 98, 104, 107, 225
Energy Select Committee 130
English Committee 150, 154, 251
European Community (EC) 80,
    236–8
Evans, M. 179
expenditure, control of public
    148–50
Expenditure Committee, Defence
    and External Affairs Subcommittee
    189–90, 196, 197–8

Falkland Islanders 94–5, 97,
    106, 107
Falkland Islands Company 94, 95

Falklands lobby 101–2, 233
Falklands War 13, 92–115;
    chief actors 93–6; chronology
    96–9; decision-making after
    invasion 110–15; decision-
    making theories: (belief-systems
    225; bounded rationality 219;
    bureaucratic politics 224; disjointed
    incrementalism 222; groupthink
    227; implementation 229;
    organisational process 223;
    rational actor 217; Sabatier model
    229); foreclosing of policy options
    104–7; inter-departmental
    pressures 101–4; ministerial
    control over policy options
    99–101; perception 107–10;
    political system models and
    230–3 *passim*, 235
Family Planning Association 80
Financial Management Initiative 157
Finer, S.E. 52–3, 243
Fishlock, D. 127
fission, nuclear 121–2
Foot, M. 112
Foreign and Commonwealth Office
    (FCO): AIDS screening 80;
    Falklands War 98, 223, 224, 233;
    (belief-system 217, 225; clash
    with MOD 103–4; lack of
    information 105, 217; negotiations
    with Argentina 97, 99; policy
    options 100; priority of Falkland
    Islands 95); future policy-making
    236; Rhodesia 103
Forman, F.N. 51–2, 243
Fowler, N. 73, 78–9, 89
Franks Report 13, 93, 102,
    246, 247; Falkland Islands 99,
    105–6
free market economy 63
Freedman, L. 187–8, 246,
    247, 253
Friedman, M. 9
Friends of the Earth 241
Frow, B. 102
Fry, G.K. 250, 251
Fulton Committee 142–3,
    145–6

Fulton Report 142–4, 145,
    217, 224, 228

Galosh ABM system 186, 187
Galtieri, General 98, 108, 109, 219
Gamba-Stonehouse, V. 246, 247
Gamble, A. 53, 67, 179, 243,
    244, 253
'garbage can' model 61
Garland, R. 246
Garrett, J. 150, 250, 251
GCHQ 178
General Belgrano 99, 115, 227
General Electric Company (GEC)
    118, 127, 128, 129
George, B. 198
Gilbert, J. 199
Gillman, G. 252
Goodin, R.E. 250
government 2; autonomy and
    defence 207–8, 210; control
    of nuclear power 135–6;
    machinery of 139–40; (*see also*
    Civil Service Department);
    performance of 19; *see also*
    Cabinet; Parliament
Gowing, M. 248, 249, 254
Gray, A. 34, 242
Greenaway, J.R. 250, 251
Greenwood, D. 254
Groom, A.J.R. 254
groupthink 36, 227
Gulf War 35–6

haemophiliacs 72, 245
Haig, A. 99, 111
Haldane Committee 140, 141
Hall, T. 248
Hart, G. 246
Hastings, M. 246, 247, 248;
    Falkland Islands 100, 104, 112,
    113, 114
Havers, Sir M. 111
Hawtin-Moore study 154
Hayek, F.A. 9
Hayhoe, B. 73, 78
Healey, D. 190, 207, 227
health authorities 73, 89
Health Education Authority (HEA)
    71, 74, 75, 77, 245

Heath, A. 253
Heath, E. 10, 147, 181, 231
Heath Government; CSD 151, 160;
nuclear power 127–8; trade
unions 164, 171–6
Heclo, H. 41, 242
Helsby, Lord 146
Henderson, Sir N. 114, 247, 248
Henderson, P.D. 126, 249
Hennessy, P. 246, 250, 251, 252,
253, 254, 255; Civil Service 140,
147; successor to Polaris 190, 191,
207
Hill, J. 138
Hinkley Point nuclear power
station 131
Hinton, Sir C. 124, 125
historical approach 3–4
HIV (Human Immunodeficiency
Virus) 71, 77, 78, 81; testing for
79–80
Hogwood, B. 54, 61, 243, 244
Home Office 224, 233; Advisory
Council on the Misuse of Drugs
80
homosexuality, AIDS and 72,
83, 90, 226, 246; exclusion from
policy-making 89, 90; group
specificity 84–5; sexual behaviour
changes 76
Hoskyns, Sir John 10
hospital services 79
Howe, Sir G. 105, 155, 177, 191
Howell, D. 130
Hughes, C. 241
Hunt, Sir J. 145, 149, 190, 251
Hunt, N. *see* Crowther-Hunt, Lord
Hussein, Saddam 36
Hyman, R. 167, 252
hypodermic needles 80

Ibbs, R. 158
ideas 239–40; influence of
6, 239–40
ideology 5–6; CSD 160–1;
incrementalism and 28; perception
and 34–6; trade unions and 179;
see also belief-systems
ignorance: AIDS and 69–70,
82; nuclear power 134–5, 138

implementation 37–9, 227–9,
238, 239; gap between initiation
and 137; internationalisation and
237; organisational process model
31–2
In Place of Strife 165–71, 220, 252
incrementalism 59, 209; disjointed
24–9, 220–2
Independent, The 116, 248
Independent Broadcasting
Authority 71
Industrial Relations Act (1971)
171–6, 228
Industrial Relations Court 172
industrial relations legislation *see*
trade unions
information 219, 221; AIDS and
importance of 91, 216;
belief-systems 34–5, 225, 226;
perception and Falklands 107–10;
rational actor model 21, 216–18
passim
institutional momentum 136,
137–8
institutions 2–3, 4, 8, 212–13;
see also organisational process
model
intelligence data, misreadings of
107–10
interest groups 8, 53–4, 62,
89–90; *see also* policy
communities; policy networks
interests, power and ideas and
239–40
Iran 22
Iraq 22, 66

Janis, I. 36, 242
Jay, P. 145
Jenkin, P. 253
Jenkins, B. 34, 242
Jenkins, R. 143, 170
Jenkins, S. 246, 247, 248; Falkland
Islands 100, 104, 112, 113, 114
Jervis, R. 35, 242
John, B. 199
Johnson, P. 84
Joint Intelligence Organisation
(JIO) 96, 108
Jones, G.W. 243

Jones, J. 173–4, 179
Jordan, A.G. 57–9, 244
Joseph, Sir K. 151, 180
Jowell, R. 253
judgement, appreciative 23

Kapila, M. 88, 246
Kavanagh, D. 182, 253
Kellner, P. 250, 251
Kemp, R. 249
Kendall, B. 251
Kennedy, J.F. 185
Keynesian economic management 7
King, A. 53, 181, 243, 253
Kingman, S. 245
Kinnock, N. 50
Kirby, S. 204, 255
Kirchheimer, O. 7
Klein, R. 85, 246

labour 67
Labour Party 7–8, 9, 166,
    231–2; 'intra-party democracy'
    50; nuclear weapons 189, 205,
    213, 231; trade unions 165,
    168, 170, 234; *see also* Callaghan
    Government; Wilson Government
Land Commission 31
Layton-Henry, Z. 253
Leach, Sir H. 110, 113, 227
learning, policy 41, 42–4
Lee, F. 126
Lewin, Sir T. 110–11
Lewis, J. 245, 246
Light Water Reactor (LWR)
    120, 124, 125
Lindblom, C. 24–5, 26–7,
    241–2
Locksley, G. 253
Lothian region 79
Lukes, S. 38, 242

Mackay, J. 84
Macmillan, H. 141, 185
macropolitics 63–4
Magnox nuclear reactor 120,
    123, 125, 127, 132, 136
Malone, P. 253
manpower, control of 148–50
March, J.G. 61, 244

Marsh, D. 253
Marshall, W. 127–8, 131–2,
    132, 249
Marxism 9, 65–8, 234–5
Mason, R. 190, 192, 198, 205
McLean, S. 201, 204, 255
McMahon, J. 254
McNeill, W.H. 85, 86, 246
Management and Personnel Office
    (MPO) 156, 157, 158
media *see* press; television
medical profession 89, 224
Medical Research Council (MRC)
    72, 73, 77
Mellish, B. 170
Mellor, D. 69, 89
Mendez, Costa 109
Metcalf, L. 252
micropolitics 62–5
Middlemas, K. 66, 244
Ministry of Agriculture 6
Ministry of Defence (MOD)
    253; Falklands War 95–6, 98,
    103–4, 224; Trident 199–200,
    201, 205, 208, 209
Ministry of Housing and Local
    Government 31
Moore, J. 88
moral majority groups 90
Moran, M. 171, 172, 175, 252,
    253
Morgan, K. 248
Moss, N. 248
Mulley, F. 189, 190, 198

National Health Service (NHS)
    32, 72, 79
National Liberal Federation 50
National Nuclear Corporation
    (NNC) 118, 127, 128, 130
National Power 132
national sovereignty 237
NATO 8
needles, hypodermic 80
Neustadt, R. 170, 252, 254
New Right 9, 19–20, 62–5,
    234–5
Newton, T. 73
Niskanen, W.A. 9
non-decisions 37–9, 208

North West Thames Health
Authority 73
Northcote-Trevelyan Report 140,
142
Northern Ireland 7, 30, 61, 166
Norton, P. 243
Nott, J. 111, 112, 113, 195, 201
nuclear bomb 121, 122; *see
also* nuclear weapons
Nuclear Electric 132
nuclear fission 121–2
Nuclear Installations Inspectorate
(NII) 119, 128
nuclear power 13, 116–38;
decision-making theories:
(belief-systems 225; bounded
rationality 219; bureaucratic politics
223; disjointed incrementalism
221; groupthink 227;
implementation 137–8, 228;
organisational process 223;
rational actor 217–18; Sabatier
model 229–30); institutions
117–19; policies 119–21;
political system models and
230–4 *passim*; programmes:
(first 122–4; second 124–6;
third 126–8; fourth 128–31)
Nuclear Power Advisory Board
127, 128
Nuclear Power Company (NPC)
118, 130
nuclear power lobby 123–4
nuclear weapons 121–2, 184–5,
213, 227, 229; *see also* Trident

Oakeshott, M. 21–2, 241
objectives, conflicting 17, 20–1
Official Committee on Atomic
Energy 121
O'Leary, B. 243
Olsen, J.P. 61, 244
Olson, M. 53, 243
Open University 248
Organisation for Economic
Cooperation and Development
(OECD) 236–8
organisational process model
29–32, 33–4, 222–3
O'Riordan, T. 249, 250

Overseas Development Agency
103, 224
Owen, D. 100, 190, 207

Parkinson, C. 111, 131, 132
Parliament 2, 8, 239; democratic
sovereignty model 48–9;
Falklands War 101–3, 112;
nuclear power 119; role and
Trident 196–201, 204, 210
Part, A. 175
parties, political 5–6; adversarial
politics model 52–4; *see also*
Conservative Party; Labour Party
party government model 50–2,
54, 231–2, 238
Patterson, W.C. 248
Pay Research Unit 157
Pearson, L. 248
Peele, G. 243
perception 35–6, 107–10
Peston, R. 249, 250
Peters, B.G. 54, 243
Pierre, A. 254
Pirie, M. 62–5, 234, 244
Plowden, W. 153–4
Plowden Committee 141
plutonium 121–2, 123
Polaris missile 185–6, 206;
modified *see* Chevaline missile
submarines 188–9
policy brokers 40, 42, 44, 229–30
policy communities 57–60,
61–2, 233–4, 236–7, 238,
239
policy engineers 63
policy learning 41, 42–4
policy networks 60–2, 70,
233–4, 238
policy subsystems 40–5 *passim*
policy succession 54
political interests 66–7
political process 4–5
political system models 47–68,
230–6, 238–40; *see also under
individual names*
Pollitt, C. 250
Ponting, C. 158, 168, 248, 249, 252
Poor Law 32
popularity, political 181

Poseidon missile 186, 187, 193
power 6, 37–9, 179–80, 239–40
PowerGen 132
prediction 22
press 74–5, 77, 87
Pressman, J. 37, 242
pressure groups *see* interest groups; policy communities
Pressurised Water Reactor (PWR) 120, 121, 125, 126, 131; third nuclear programme 127–8; fourth nuclear programme 128–30
Prime Minister, role of 55–6, 57
Prins, G. 254
Prior, J. 176–7, 180, 253
privatisation 64; electricity 131–2
public control 207–8, 231
public debate 206
public expenditure 148–50
Public Health Laboratory Service 80
public opinion 111–12, 231
public participation 130–1, 138
Public Record Office 13
Purdue, M. 249
Pym, F. 111, 191; Chevaline 188, 207; Trident 194, 198, 199, 206

RAF (Royal Air Force) 186, 209
Rampton, J. 129
rational actor model 15–21, 215–19
Rayner, Sir D. 152, 162; scrutinies 152–3, 158, 224, 229, 234
Reagan, R. 76, 98, 110, 194
Rees Mogg, W. 84
research 41–2, 77–8
Rhodes, R.A.W. 60–1, 243, 244
Rhodesia 103
Richards, S. 252
Richardson, J.J. 57–9, 60, 244
Riddell, P. 180, 253
Ridley, N. 98, 100–1, 102, 104
Robins, L. 251
Rodgers, W. 199
Rosecrance, R.N. 254
Roseveare, H. 250
Roskill Commission 18–19
Rowlands, T. 100, 102

Royal College of Obstetricians and Gynaecologists 80
Royal Commission on Trade Unions and Employers' Associations 167, 168, 252
Royal Navy: Falklands War 112–13, 224; nuclear weapons 186, 209, 225
Rudig, W. 249
Russel, T. 252

Sabatier, P. 39–46, 229–30, 242
Sanders, D. 254
satisficing 23, 219–20
Scanlon, H. 179
Schumpeter, J.A. 51, 243
Science and Technology Select Committee 119, 127, 248, 249
Scotland 8, 30, 61, 85
secrecy 3, 210–12
Sedgemore, B. 129, 150, 249
Seldon, A. 252
Self, P. 18–19, 241
sexual behaviour 76, 77–8, 82, 90–1
Seymour-Ure, C. 247
Shackleton, Lord 97
Sheldon, R. 153, 155
Sheldon Committee 153–5, 250–1, 252
Sherman, Sir A. 10
Silkin, J. 170
Simon, H. 21, 22–3, 219, 241
Simpson, J. 188, 254
Sizewell nuclear power station 130, 131, 132, 138
Skybolt missile 185, 186, 206, 209, 229
Smart, I. 188–9, 206, 234, 254
Smith, B. 254
Smith, D. 254
Smith, R. 254
Smith, S. 242
Snyder, W.P. 254
Soames, Lord 147
Social Democratic Party 9
social security 32
Social Services Select Committee (SSSC) 71, 88, 89, 90, 245, 246
South Georgia 98, 99, 109, 225

sovereignty; democratic 47–50, 54, 230–1, 238; national 237
state 2–3; Marxism and 66, 67; New Right and 9
Steam Generating Heavy Water Reactor (SGHWR) 120, 121, 127, 128
Steel, D. 199
Stewart, M. 96, 97, 101–2
Stowe, K. 158
Street, J. 250
strikes 167, 168, 173, 220
Strong, P. 246
submarine-launched ballistic missiles (SLBMs) 185–6, 192–3; *see also* Polaris; Trident
Sunday Times 116, 125–6, 181, 248, 249
Sunday Times Insight Team 246, 247
systems approach 4–5

Task Force, Falklands 99, 112–15, 224
Taylor, R. 176, 252, 253
Tebbit, N. 180–1
television 71, 75–6, 77, 87
Terrence Higgins Trust (THT) 70, 72, 88, 89
Thatcher, M. 10; AIDS 81–2, 88; Cabinet Committees 55, 88; Civil Service 158, 162, 228, 233; (Bancroft 147, 160; CSD 151–7, 161, 221–2); European Community 237; Falklands War 100–1, 103, 111, 112; nuclear weapons: (MISC 7 191; Trident 194, 199); trade unions 177, 179, 180, 226, 231
Thatcher Governments: Civil Service 139–40; Falkland Islands 97–8, 111–12; ideology 28; (AIDS 83–4); interest groups 59–60; micropolitics 64; nuclear power 130; nuclear weapons 191, 202; radical change 10–11; trade unions 164, 176–82, 226, 228
think tanks 64–5
Thomas, H. 250

Thomas, K. 252
Thompson, E.P. 254
Three Mile Island 221
Times, The 145, 202, 224, 251
Tombs, Sir F. 128
Trade Union Act (1984) 178
Trade Union and Labour Relations Acts 176
trade unions 13, 164–82; decision-making theories: (belief-systems 226; bounded rationality 220; bureaucratic politics 224–5; disjointed incrementalism 220; groupthink 227; implementation 228; rational actor 218; Sabatier model 229); Heath Government 171–5; political system models 231–5 *passim*; Thatcher Government 176–81; (ideology 179; legislation since 1979 176–8; political context 178; political popularity 181; political tactics 180–1; rival power sources 179–80); Wilson Government 165–71
transport 30–1, 58
Transport 2000 58
Transport and General Workers' Union (TGWU) 174, 179
Treasury 67, 151; Civil Service and 141, 158–9; (CSD 148–50, 153–6, 161, 162, 223, 224); economic framework 30, 31; Falklands War 95–6, 224
Treasury and Civil Service Committee 158, 252; *see also* English Committee; Sheldon Committee
Trend, Sir B. 56, 243
Trident 13, 183–210; British politics and 201–8; (agenda-setting 202–3; bipartisanship and continuity 205–6; civil servants' role 205; Defence Committee's role 204–5, 208, 210; opposition-government behaviour 207; public control 207–8; public debate 206; secrecy 201–2; size of decision-making group 202);

decision 188–96; decision-making theories 208–9, 213; (belief-systems 225–6; bounded rationality 220; bureaucratic politics 225; disjointed incrementalism 220; groupthink 227; implementation 229; rational actor 218; Sabatier model 230); historical background 184–8; Parliament's role 196–201, 204; political system models 230–5 *passim*
TUC (Trades Union Congress) 169, 170, 173–5, 179–80
Tyler, C. 253

uncertainty, AIDS and 69–70, 82
United Kingdom Atomic Energy Authority (UKAEA) 118–19, 120, 131, 135; Magnox reactor 123; nuclear power programmes: (first 124; second 125, 126; third 127, 128; fourth 129); plutonium 122; role in policy 129, 136–7, 138, 223, 233
United Nations (UN) 99
United States (US) 202; AIDS 76, 77, 89, 90; Falklands War 115; nuclear weapons 121, 185–6, 191, 193, 197, 209; (Trident 194–5, 198–9); Sabatier model 230
uranium 120, 121–2, 123
Ure, J. 101
utility 18, 23

V Bombers 185
vaccines, AIDS 77

Valentine, J. 249
Varley, E. 128
Vickers, Sir G. 12, 23, 241
Vinter Committee 127

Wakeman, J. 132
Walkland, S.A. 53, 243
Wapshott, N. 253
War Cabinet 110–11
Wass, Sir D. 56–7, 243–4
Waters, W.E. 245
Watney, S. 245
Weinstock, Sir A. 129
Weiss, C.H. 41–2, 242
Westland affair 158, 160
Whitelaw, W. (later Lord) 88, 111, 191
Wildavsky, A. 37, 242
Williams, R. 123, 248, 249
Wilson, H. 166; Civil Service 140, 146–7, 162; (Fulton Report 142, 143–4); trade unions 168, 170, 226, 231
Wilson Government 181; Fulton Report 143–4, 160; nuclear power 126; trade unions 164, 165–71
Windscale (Sellafield) Reprocessing Plant 118
Windscale Inquiry 138
'Winter of Discontent' 178, 182
Woodcock, G. 169

Yorkshire 79
Young, Lady 156
Young, H. 131, 179, 245, 249, 253